Also by Anne Orde

Great Britain and International Security, 1920–1926
British Policy and European Reconstruction after the
First World War

The Eclipse of Great Britain

The United States and British Imperial Decline, 1895–1956

Anne Orde

Formerly Senior Lecturer in History, University of Durham

First published 1996 by
MACMILLAN PRESS LTD
Houndmills, Basingstoke, Hampshire RG21 6XS
and London
Companies and representatives
throughout the world

ISBN 0–333–66283–0 hardcover
ISBN 0–333–66284–9 paperback

A catalogue record for this book is available from the British Library.

10   9   8   7   6   5   4   3   2   1
05   04   03   02   01   00   99   98   97   96

Printed in Hong Kong

Published in the United States of America 1996 by
ST. MARTIN'S PRESS, INC.,
Scholarly and Reference Division
175 Fifth Avenue, New York, N.Y. 10010

ISBN 0–312–16140–9 hardcover
ISBN 0–312–16141–7 paperback

Contents

Preface

This book is a study, not of Anglo-American relations as such, but of the relationship between Great Britain's imperial decline and the ascent of the United States to the position of a super-power, and the ways in which people in both countries – politicians, officials, publicists, and as far as possible public opinion – perceived the process of the replacement of the one power by the other while it was happening.

For these perceptions, I have made extensive use of contemporary books and journalism. In writing a book of this nature, covering a long period and a wide range of affairs, an author incurs debts to many other historians, whose research it would be futile to try to duplicate. The extent of my obligations will be apparent from the references: these authors, however, are in no way responsible for inferences that I have drawn from their work. For facilitating my own research I am grateful to the staff of the Public Record Office, Kew, to a number of librarians, and to custodians of all the other archives listed in the bibliography. Staff at the Franklin D. Roosevelt Library and Yale University Library were especially hospitable. The British Academy gave me a grant to visit the United States. Friends and former colleagues at the University of Durham helped by asking as well as answering questions and discussing problems. Dr Brian Ward elucidated a piece of musical history.

Crown Copyright material is quoted by permission of the Controller of HM Stationery Office. For other permissions I am indebted to the Bodleian Library and Dr Alexander Murray (Gilbert Murray Papers); the British Library, Lord Hankey and Professor A.K.S. Lambton (Balfour Papers, Cecil of Chelwood Papers, Curzon Papers); Curtis Brown Ltd on behalf of the Estate of Sir Winston S. Churchill and C & T Publications Ltd (Martin Gilbert, *Winston S. Churchill,* copyright the Estate of

Sir Winston S. Churchill); *The Economist*; HarperCollins Publishers Inc. and Random Century, London (Henry L. Stimson and McGeorge Bundy, *On Active Service in Peace and War*, copyright 1948 by Henry L. Stimson and McGeorge Bundy, copyright renewed 1976 by McGeorge Bundy); Harvard University Press (*The Letters of Theodore Roosevelt*, ed. Elting E. Morison *et al.*, copyright 1979 by Elting E. Morison); The Keeper of the Records of Scotland (Lothian Muniments); Princeton University Press (*Churchill and Roosevelt. The Complete Correspondence*, ed. Warren F. Kimball; *The Papers of Woodrow Wilson*, ed. Arthur Link and others); The Royal Economic Society and Macmillan, London and Basingstoke (J.M. Keynes, *Collected Writings*); Bureau of Public Affairs, Department of State (*Foreign Relations of the United States*); Yale University (Walter Lippmann Papers, Henry L. Stimson Papers). Every effort has been made to trace all copyright-holders, but if any have been inadvertently overlooked the publishers will be pleased to make the necessary arrangements at the first opportunity.

ANNE ORDE

Introduction

Power may be defined as the capacity to use resources for the attainment of desired ends. It always involves relations with others, as objects, rivals or allies. It is never static, and always relative. Resources can be quantified; ends and ability to achieve them involve factors such as policy and will, which can not.

The decline of Great Britain from the position of a world power during the first half of the twentieth century, and the ascent of the United States to the position of a super-power are linked in time and geographically. The relationship between the two processes is not one of simple cause and effect; but neither were they wholly independent. They have to be seen, moreover, in the general context of the distribution of international power. Within this context the two countries have been both rivals and allies; and, throughout, their relations have had a peculiar flavour derived from cultural connections and historical experience, real and imagined.[1] All these factors and the relationship between them form part of our discussion.

In terms of economic resources, Britain's relative decline can be noted from the very beginning of the century. In 1880 the United Kingdom produced 22.9 per cent of world manufacturing output, in 1900 18.5 per cent; it has been overtaken by the United States which had grown from 14.7 per cent in 1880 to 23.6 per cent, and was being approached by Germany which had grown from 8.5 per cent to 13.2 per cent (and which overtook Britain in 1913).[2] This was mainly the catching up of later comers, who also had advantages of size. In particular once the great area of the United States, its wealth of physical resources and rapidly growing population, began to be fully developed, Britain's early lead was bound to be reduced and then eliminated. The trend continued. It was not continuous: wars and depression altered circumstances and performance; other

1

countries industrialized. And the decline was relative, not absolute: the British economy grew throughout; in 1958 British industry produced two and a half times as much as in 1913; in per capita output Britain was still in 1953 second only to the United States. Nevertheless relative economic decline meant relatively reduced capacity to maintain a world position.

At the beginning of the century Britain's interests were spread all round the world, informally by trade and investment, formally in territorial empire. The formal Empire reached its greatest extent at the end of the First World War, covering nearly a quarter of the world's land surface and about the same proportion of its population. It was a cause of pride, of complacency, and of anxiety. In 1907 the recently retired Permanent Under-Secretary of State in the Foreign Office, Lord Sanderson, likened it to 'some huge giant sprawling all over the globe, with gouty fingers and toes stretching in every direction, which cannot be approached without eliciting a scream'.[3] The value of the Empire to Britain is a matter of continuing debate, too complicated to be summarized here.[4] It is, however, worth making three points.

In the first place, Britain did not closely govern or control the economies of most of the Empire. The Dominions were virtually independent in domestic affairs by 1914 and increasingly so in external affairs by 1939. India had fiscal autonomy from 1919 and British rule was exercised by an astonishingly small number of Europeans. The colonies, of varying sizes and resources, were governed partly directly, partly indirectly through local élites. In the Middle East, Egypt was at first a protectorate, then a treaty partner; Iraq (until 1930) and Palestine were held between the wars under mandate from the League of Nations. The Empire and Commonwealth were important to British trade and investment, but that is not to say that trade and investment depended on political control.

Secondly, the military balance sheet shows both assets and liabilities. Before 1914 and in the 1920s the Empire and Commonwealth could be defended for fairly modest cost; while Britain was secure in Europe, rivals were not too numerous or strong, and local opposition to British rule was weak. India was a very important source of military manpower for Britain's world-wide commitments in peace and for war. Ties of personal and family loyalty brought massive support from the Dominions in both world wars, and in the second Canada in particular gave large financial aid. On the other hand parts of the Empire, and its communications, were vulnerable, and it never paid for the whole of its defence. The cost, especially of naval defence, fell mainly on Britain. In 1926 the Australian prime minister calculated that Britain spent on defence nearly twice as much per capita as his country, four times as much as New Zealand, ten times as much as Canada, and twenty times as much as South Africa.[5] Britain was of course richer than any of the Dominions, and suggestions for spreading the burden more evenly met little response. During the 1930s, as the world situation darkened and widely separated threats developed, planners in London concluded that Britain could not defend the whole Empire and Commonwealth simultaneously against external enemies, and the point was proved in 1942. After 1945 as the tide of Arab and then Caribbean and African nationalism mounted, the costs of maintaining internal security began to seem too great: it was evident to Ernest Bevin, for example, that the British people would not fight simply to maintain hegemony in the Middle East.

But thirdly, whilst the economic and military value of the Empire are debatable, there is no doubt that in the intangibles of power – prestige and influence – it was what made Britain great. In retrospect it may seem indeed that prestige was the most vital ingredient in its survival. Change did occur. Between the wars growing Dominion sense of nationhood was accommodated. After 1945 this model of Commonwealth was expected to serve first for India and in the long run for viable colonial territories. By 1957 the number of members of the Commonwealth had risen from six to ten; by 1970 it was 29, and the institution had become much more diffuse. Meanwhile in southeast Asia Britain's prestige never fully recovered from the disasters of 1942, and in the Pacific exclusion from the ANZUS pact in 1951 was symbolic of Australasian independence in foreign policy and reduced British power. In the Middle East, postwar British governments had a vision of transforming the old paramountcy into a new relationship of equals in an area seen as strategically vital, but all efforts failed in the face of Arab nationalism. Finally in the 1960s rapid decolonization in the Caribbean and Africa, defence cuts and withdrawal from east of Suez, and the end of the sterling area, compelled recognition that Britain was a power of only the second rank.

In the same period American economic power continued to grow, relatively and absolutely. The 23.6 per cent share of world manufacturing output in 1900 reached 39.3 per cent in 1928 and 44.7 per cent in 1953. Gross national product doubled between 1900 and 1920 and nearly quintupled between 1920 and 1960.[6] These resources gave the United States enormous weight in the world economy, a weight used to promote American national interests. In the western hemisphere, economic power produced a substantial degree of political influence already by 1914. In Europe less was aimed at, except briefly at the end of the First World War. Faithful to Washington's farewell warning against entangling alliances, the United States avoided before 1942, so far as Europe was concerned, all forms of continuing organized political cooperation, and so reduced the opportunities for exerting influence. The Second World War brought a radical change. Economic resources were used to induce Britain to fall in with American aims; economic aid became an important component of foreign policy.

Apart from a brief excursion in the First World War the United States before 1940 chose not to translate its economic resources into military power. This was a further, and largely unrecognized, handicap to political influence in the 1920s and 1930s. In 1938 expenditure on military purposes was about 1.5 per cent of net available national product, compared with 7.9 per cent by Britain, 16.6 per cent by Germany, and 25.4 per cent by Japan. The armed forces totalled some 200 000 men, not much more than half Britain's total and not much more than a quarter of Germany's, which had half the population.[7] The United States had no need of large land forces; but she had set out before 1914 to be a major naval power, and her potential was recognized very early in Britain. By 1907 she came third in the world in numbers of battleships built and being built. In the 1920s naval policy was explicitly directed against Britain's maritime supremacy – at the least possible cost, by mutual limitation rather than competition, although the threat of a race was visible in the background. The policy was highly symbolic: throughout the nineteenth century, American external security and the Monroe doctrine had rested on British naval power; now that power was challenged directly. But it was not only a symbol: whilst the United States navy's most probable opponent was Japan, possession of a fleet equal to Britain's would enable the United States to conduct her overseas trade at will and 'wage neutrality', defying, if she wished, not only Britain's exercise of belligerent rights but international sanctions mounted against a peace-breaker by the League of Nations. All other naval powers had to take the United States into account between the wars: her land and air potential were largely discounted, because of her political detachment and supposed lack of ambition. The decision to raise great forces was taken of necessity in 1940. The decision to maintain great forces after the Second World War was a mark of the will to behave as a very great power.

As regards imperial power the American record has been mixed. During the nineteenth century the acquisition of new territory on the North American continent, by conquest or purchase, was reckoned not as empire-building but as natural growth. Beyond continental territory, informal empire in the Caribbean and the Pacific largely sufficed, but in the 1890s Hawaii, the Philippines and Puerto Rico were annexed amid public controversy. The American ethos remained anti-imperialist, the British Empire its chief bugbear. The future of the British Empire was an issue in relations between the two countries during the Second World War, at the same time as American authorities were recognizing the need for strategic bases in the Pacific. After the war the contribution of a (reformed) British Empire to world stability was more widely acknowledged: its dissolution was not actively promoted. But anti-colonial forces were given patronage, and in the Middle East and Asia American policy undermined the British position. Very soon the United States expanded the number of client states supported by aid, advice and military protection, and became known in much of the world as the arch-imperialist power. Yet an imperial philosophy was not developed. This 'failure' fully to take Britain's place did not, it has been argued, help world stability;[8] but it must be doubted whether an avowedly imperial policy could have been accepted by the American people or by client peoples in postwar world conditions.

The causes of Britain's decline and the United States' ascent were many. Europe's dominance in the world was coming to an end; economic change had its momentum; imperial relations would have evolved in any event; and Americans would probably have discovered the wider uses of political power. But chief place among the immediate causes must go to the two world wars. In the first, Britain spent accumulated capital, and lack of full recovery detracted from the increase in imperial territory and the weakening of rivals. The war hastened the growth of American economic power, although not the development of ideas on its political use. In the second war British victory was even more dearly bought, while the United States not only developed its own power but subsidized its allies with massive aid. The Second World War also brought on to the stage another very great power, the Soviet Union, whose share in the costs and the victory was at least as great and whose policies determined much of British and American actions for years thereafter.

Analysis of all this process must include perceptions, on both sides of the Atlantic, about each country's position and their relations with each other. This last raises the question of the so-called 'special relationship'. So far as the term has any meaning and is not simply uttered as a kind of shibboleth, it is mostly used in the sense of a particularly close alliance based on an affinity between the two peoples. This sense was popularized by Winston Churchill, and indeed it may have been he who first publicly used the term, in November 1945.[9] The *Oxford English Dictionary* records from the early 1960s use, on both sides of the Atlantic, of the term in quotation marks, which suggests that by then the notion had become a myth.

The alliance that existed between 1940 and 1945 became very close. Before 1940 at the level of inter-state relations there was no closeness, not even in the 'association' of the First World War. At the end of the Second World War the United States showed many signs of reverting to unilateralism, maintaining an equal distance from Britain and the Soviet Union. That course was ended by renewed crisis in Europe, in which Britain was the only possible ally. This state of affairs then continued for ten years or so, changing gradually as British power diminished and other allies revived. Whether and for how long Britain retained a position greater than her measurable strength warranted, when she became 'just another star'[10] in the American system, is not easy to determine. Later attempts to display a special kind of closeness, as in the 1980s, may prove on examination to have been no more than rhetoric.

Some of the closeness developed during the Second World War survived and continued. Politicians and officials went on being able to converse with an openness and a degree of understanding of the other's position markedly different from the prewar and early war years. In certain branches of defence close collaboration continued beneath a surface of official distance.[11] But how much practical difference it made is another matter. The basis of relations has always been interest, not sentiment, and it is doubtful whether the friendly intercourse ever caused the American government to act otherwise than it would have done anyway. There are plenty of instances during and after the war of cold disregard of British needs; it is clear that Britain has had no influence on American strategic decisions. It is not possible to document examples of a contrary kind, although there may have been instances of a special consideration not shown to other allies of the same stature. On the British side, on a number of occasions consciousness of dependence caused wartime and postwar governments to sacrifice positions for the sake of speculative future American good will.

Ease of intercourse is greatly facilitated by easy communication in a common language. This is an important advantage in many spheres, but those with good enough English can share it, and increasing numbers of Europeans have done so. All allies may (or may not) share a sense of common purpose and interest. The notion of a special affinity between the British and American peoples, however, is much older than the alliance. Manifestations may be seen in the 1890s, having little effect on inter-state relations and, typically, felt more in Britain than in the United States. Americans who, at that time and later, valued the common high culture and certain traditions (for example in the common law) were also more aware than Britons of the differences wrought by history and geography. Britons continued to believe in the existence of 'racial' affinity long after such partial basis as there once was in shared ancestry had gone. In the United States, to be anglicized was not a

domestic political asset even when crude Anglophobia had almost disappeared. Over the twentieth century the culture has
changed, and whilst American history has become much more
widely taught in Britain, American children, it appears, are taught
less British history than their great-grandparents. It has been
suggested that despite easier travel and many personal and
business links, the two countries have become less responsive
to one another than they once were.[12] On the British side anti-
Americanism has always been present alongside a generally
favourable attitude; only the grounds for dislike have changed,
and therefore the groups holding them. Before the Second
World War American resentment of British condescension was
widespread. With British decline resentment has grown on the
other side, but it has been softened by a feeling that the sup-
planter is a lawful heir. It is not unreasonable to believe that
resentment of any other successor apart from a member of
the Commonwealth would have been greater. Nor is it surprising that the notion of a 'special relationship' has had a greater
resonance in Britain than in the United States. In so far as the
notion has acted as a consolatory myth, soothing British feelings about the transition, it has probably been mildly beneficent;
but in so far as it has encouraged delusions it has done harm.
Yet in another more general sense it seems clear that thanks
to a variety of factors the relations between Britain and the
United States have been different from those that either has
had with any other country. In that sense the relationship can
truly be said to have been special.

All these aspects are explored in the chapters that follow.
The year 1956 has been chosen as the terminal date as marking, not a turning point but a milestone on a longer road, a
point when conclusions could be drawn about what had been
happening over a number of years. The Suez crisis revealed as
with a sudden bright light the fact that Britain could no longer
act militarily without American consent in an area thought to
be of great importance, and could be brought to heel without
mercy by economic means. What subsequently happened to
British policy and to American power is another story.

1
Britain and the Assertion of American Hegemony in the Western Hemisphere, 1895–1914

The last years of the nineteenth century and the first of the twentieth saw important changes in international politics. European rivalries reflected and were reflected in imperial activities in Africa and Asia. Japan emerged as a regional power in east Asia; the United States increasingly asserted power in the western hemisphere and began activity in the Pacific. Britain, as a power with literally world-wide interests, was affected by all the developments and had to make adjustments. Expansion in Africa was maintained at the cost of a difficult war. European affairs increasingly demanded involvement. An understanding on imperial matters, with European implications, was reached with France; relations with Russia were stabilized in Asia. In the Pacific, Britain formed an understanding with Japan and welcomed the arrival of American imperialism. And in North and Central America and the Caribbean, Britain, without abandoning any material interests, accepted the assertion of United States hegemony. From the British point of view this was one adjustment among others, but it had a distinctive flavour. Britain was not the only European country affected by American assertiveness, but from the American end, too, the British aspect had a flavour of its own. The changes, and the perception of them on both sides of the Atlantic, are the subject of this chapter.[1]

*　　*　　*

The first dramatic American intervention took place in the relations between Britain and a Latin American country. The boundary between British Guiana and Venezuela had been a matter of dispute for many years and had aroused little public attention anywhere. Early in 1895 the United States government decided to take a hand, and to claim the right to adjudicate. In a note to the British government Richard Olney, Secretary of State in Cleveland's administration, invoked the Monroe doctrine and claimed that the safety and welfare of the United States were so bound up with the independence of every American state that it had a right to intervene in this dispute. In reply Lord Salisbury, the Prime Minister and Foreign Secretary, contested Olney's interpretation of the Monroe doctrine and denied the United States' right to intervene.[2] President Cleveland then, in a special message to Congress on 17 December, announced his intention of himself having the correct boundary determined, and of resisting any British encroachment beyond it.[3] This appeared to imply the use of force, and for some weeks there seemed to be a real danger of war between Britain and the United States. But in February 1896 the British government agreed to Anglo-American negotiations on the form and scope of arbitration, and the crisis passed. In the end the arbitral award largely confirmed the British position, but by the time it was made in 1899 few people noticed.

What was it all about? The United States government was certainly not actuated by a desire to champion Venezuelan interests. The Venezuelan government had been asking for American help for years without success, and it was not consulted during the crisis. Cleveland seems to have been much influenced by domestic considerations, but was also impressed by the lobbying of William Lindsay Scruggs, former American Minister in Caracas.[4] Olney, newly appointed to his post, was determined to secure the settlement of a troublesome long-running dispute. In trying to gain the attention of an apparently standoffish British government, Olney seems to have got carried away by his own advocacy. His assertion 'That distance and 3,000 miles of ocean make any permanent political union between an European and an American State unnatural and inexpedient will hardly be denied', positively invited the emphatic denial it received from Salisbury 'on behalf of the British and American people who are subject to [Her Majesty's] Crown'. The assertion that 'Today the United States is practically Sovereign on this continent, and its fiat is law upon the subjects to which it confines its interposition', was a novel international doctrine. But neither Cleveland nor Olney wanted war. Olney sought to initiate diplomatic negotiations rather than a public confrontation; and Cleveland's special message, despite the belligerent language, was actually temporizing. Nevertheless Olney did intend a far-reaching extension of the Monroe doctrine, and to a large extent his challenge was successful.

On the British side, in 1895 Salisbury's attention was much occupied with relations between the European powers and Turkey. In addition Salisbury was always temperamentally averse to hasty action. The four-month interval between Olney's note and the British reply was not evidence of contempt or deliberate stalling, but largely due to the summer holidays of that more leisurely age. Yet Cleveland's message to Congress and the attendant agitation alarmed the Cabinet, and so the process began, first of unofficial soundings and then of official negotiations. In the Cabinet, Joseph Chamberlain, an imperialist of a new school, was Colonial Secretary and so responsible for British Guiana. He had a better knowledge and greater sympathy than Salisbury for America and Americans. He had been in the United States: his second wife was American – from that East Coast social class that knew Britain well and unintentionally gave their British friends the illusion that they in turn understood the United States. At any rate Chamberlain, while deprecating anything like 'showing the white feather' to the Americans, whom he regarded as 'great people for bluffing, and bad to run away from', took more seriously than Salisbury appeared to do the consideration that 'probably a majority of Americans would look forward without horror to a war with this country', a contingency that he himself would regard as 'the very worst thing that could possibly happen to us'.[5]

The crisis gave some impetus to studies of the defence of Canada, but the Admiralty was more concerned with other areas. It had been advising that the fleet could not force the Straits for the purpose of putting pressure on Turkey, and was asking for increased expenditure to meet a Franco-Russian combination. Another consideration for the Cabinet was South Africa.

Hard on the heels of Cleveland's special message came the news that Cecil Rhodes's partner Jameson had launched a rash and unsuccessful raid against the government of the Transvaal; and the Boer leader, Kruger, received a congratulatory telegram from the German Emperor Wilhelm II. The Jameson raid caused a political storm in London; the Kruger telegram enraged the Tory press and British nationalists; and the government created a 'flying squadron' of ships ready to sail to any threatened part of the empire. The coincidence in time of the two crises emphasized Britain's isolation, especially since they were clashes with powers not hitherto regarded as the country's main rivals. Significant for this study is the difference in the public reaction. It was not just that southern Africa was regarded as a major interest and British Guiana was not, important though that fact is. The tone of British public discussion reveals a peculiar perception of Anglo-American relations.

Throughout the crisis and the subsequent negotiations Parliament hardly discussed the matter at all, and when it did so the debate was muted, all speakers being anxious to say nothing that would cause difficulty. But there was plenty of comment elsewhere. In a speech at Manchester on 15 January 1896 A.J. Balfour, First Lord of the Treasury and Salisbury's nephew, described the idea of war with the United States as carrying with it 'some of the unnatural horror of a civil war'. He looked forward to the time when 'some statesman of authority, more fortunate even than President Monroe, will lay down the doctrine that between English-speaking peoples war is impossible'.[6] The metaphor of civil war was used also by *The Economist*. William Watson used that of kinship, exclaiming:

> O towering Daughter, Titan of the West . . .
> Thou to whom our inmost heart is pure
> Of ill intent; although thou threatenest
> With most unfilial hand thy mother's breast,
> Not for one breathing space may earth endure
> The thought of war's intolerable cure
> For such vague pains as vex today thy rest![7]

More soberly the author and journalist Edward Dicey remarked that the question 'Do we English wish for war?' hardly required an answer. 'I do not suppose there is one Englishman in a thousand who would not denounce a war with the United States as a calamity if not a crime.'[8] At the height of the excitement after Cleveland's message there were demands that the peace all desired must be based on respect;[9] but the most widespread initial reaction in Britain was undoubtedly astonishment. Astonishment in the first place at the existence of the dispute: as James Bryce, the historian and Liberal politician, wrote to American friends, 'not one man in ten in the House of Commons even knew there was such a thing as a Venezuelan question pending'.[10] Astonishment in the second place at the violence of American popular hostility to Britain, for which the British were quite unprepared. The trouble here was mostly ignorance. Not many of those who crossed the Atlantic in increasing numbers after the introduction of a regular steam passenger service in 1840 travelled extensively within the United States or met people other than their own kind. Even Bryce, whose *American Commonwealth*, first published in 1888, became enormously influential in conveying to British readers a sense of the greatness of the United States, drew his friends mostly from the intellectual patrician class of the eastern seaboard. In 1895 *The Times* was the only newspaper to have a permanent correspondent, George Smalley, in the United States, and he too seldom moved beyond the east coast and Washington. Now the crisis inspired a number of correspondents, British and American, to examine American feeling. Writers of letters to *The Times* disagreed as to the existence and extent of anti-British sentiment. Lord Playfair, for example, who had an American wife, refused to believe that Americans were not as fond of the British as the latter were of them, whereas 'L.W.' said bluntly that the mass of Americans detested Britain as a nation. Several correspondents pointed out that few Americans were moved by sentiments of kinship, and that the proportion of 'Anglo-Saxon blood' in the American population was shrinking, There was much emphasis on American quasi-religious attachment to the Monroe doctrine coupled with haziness as to what it really said. Leo Maxse, editor of the *National Review*, commented that if, as it appeared, what British organs of opinion had been saying for years about American feeling had no broad foundation of fact, it was better that 'a misleading though cherished illusion' should be dispelled.[11]

On the American side, attitudes were compounded of several elements, of which dislike of Britain and new nationalism were the most important. American commentators, like the writers of letters to *The Times*, were not unanimous as to the extent of hostility to Britain but agreed on its existence and for the most part on its causes – the way history was taught in the schools and the Fourth of July celebrated, British governmental unfriendliness to the North in the Civil War, resentment at cases of British condescension; and in some quarters Irishism, resentment at British opposition to the monetization of silver, or fear that Britain was somehow standing in the way of the United States. A year earlier Franklin Eastman had explained in the *Atlantic Monthly* that:

> whole States . . . would enjoy a war with you next week, because they believe the influence of our connection with England is wholly pernicious . . . If you really want to maintain peace between the nations, you must . . . recognize the United States once for all, not as a daughter, a pupil, or a forest guide, but your full-equal sister in all that constitutes an enlightened, historic, imperial nation.[12]

During the crisis E.L. Godkin, the editor of the New York *Nation* and the *Evening Post*, wrote privately to Bryce that the great mass of Americans:

> are fanatically for war . . . They do not know why they should fight England except that she is 'grabbing' and insolent. They resent English contempt for American manners and customs, and envy her greatness, and think that America ought to make as big a figure in the world as she does.[13]

George Burton Adams, professor of history at Yale, pointed out the widespread belief that:

> England is thoroughly selfish . . . She is trying to secure everything for which she can advance a plausible pretext, or, in a

somewhat literal sense of the slang phrase, she 'wants the earth', and she will stick at nothing in her efforts to get it . . . There is on the part of many a positive dislike of England, a readiness to accept the worst interpretation of any act of hers, a belief that she is particularly our enemy and would do anything that she can to embarrass or injure us . . . On the part of many more, probably a much larger number, who do not feel the positive dislike or actual hostility, there is still a feeling of suspicion, a conviction that England is capable of much evil, that she is not kindly disposed towards us, and that she must be carefully watched.[14]

To a large extent the general dislike resembled the anti-British sentiment prevalent in most other countries at the time. Among particular fears was the notion that Latin America was about to fall, like Africa, prey to an imperialist 'scramble'. Henry Cabot Lodge, Republican senator from Massachusetts, had British friends, but nevertheless asserted, in a debate in Congress in 1891, that Britain was 'drawing about this country a cordon of forts and bases of supply for a navy manifestly for use in case of war'. For a speech in March 1895 in favour of the annexation of Hawaii, Lodge caused to be brought into the Senate chamber a map marked with red crosses showing British bases, with a gap in the Pacific. Already, he said, America's Atlantic coast was ringed with British bastions: it would be madness to allow Britain to take Hawaii too. In articles of 1895 he wrote of Britain having 'studded the West Indies with strong places which are a standing menace to our Atlantic seaboard', and he envisaged the whole of South America falling into the hands of Britain and other European powers unless the United States 'enforced' the Monroe doctrine. Lodge did not favour a 'general acquisition of distant possessions' by the United States, not even in Central America; but 'outworks' essential for defence must not be abandoned, and Canada was a proper objective.[15]

The novelty of Olney's interpretation of the Monroe doctrine was increasingly noted during the Venezuela crisis, and not everyone was convinced, either that it was sound or that the United States had the power to maintain it. Theodore Woolsey, a publicist specializing in foreign affairs, claimed that the doctrine did not give the United States a title to interfere in the Anglo-Venezuelan dispute. Even if it were applicable:

> Proof must still be furnished that a failure to enforce it would endanger our peace and safety. If they are not so endangered, we have no ground for interference ... Does British control over the wild frontier region in dispute between Venezuela and Guiana really threaten the safety of the United States? If so, why and how? We are entitled to specifications.[16]

Godkin castigated a Senate resolution as virtually constituting an invitation to any Latin American country adjacent to a European colony to claim any boundary it pleased and to be guaranteed American armed support. 'This notice, too ... is addressed to one of the strongest powers in the world ... and it is addressed by a nation which is borrowing money quarterly to keep its demand notes at par, has no army at all and only a very small navy.'[17]

Alfred Mahan, the great expositor of doctrines of sea power and advocate of a strong United States navy, wrote to British friends that he could conceive of no greater evil than war between their two countries; but he hoped that Englishmen might welcome the awakening of the American people to the necessity of emerging from isolation.[18] Mahan doubtless agreed with the journalist Sidney Low, who wrote that with Olney's interpretation the United States had taken on 'a vast addition to its burdens and its duties'. If a scramble for South America began:

> Neither the latent resources nor the moral influence of the United States will avail to protect its clients without the display of effective material strength ... The New Monroe Doctrine (which in some respects is rather the antithesis than the legitimate development of its predecessor) cannot assuredly be maintained unless the citizens of the Republic are prepared to endure burdens and incur obligations from which hitherto they have been enviably free.[19]

Within a few more years Britain acknowledged sole American control over the isthmian canal that, after very long discussion, was nearing practical realization. This question caused no crisis, although it was more important to both parties than the boundaries of Venezuela. There was no doubting the American interest: the British interest was not territorial and rested on a treaty that many acknowledged had been overtaken by changed circumstances. There was, however, one point of similarity with the Venezuela crisis: the adverse international situation in which Britain found herself.

In 1850, at a time when the British had acquired concessions in Honduras and the Mosquito Coast and the United States was not interested in Central America, the British and United States governments concluded the Clayton–Bulwer treaty agreeing that neither would ever fortify, nor obtain exclusive control over, the proposed isthmian canal. Both would protect its construction and guarantee its neutrality, and would invite other governments to join in the guarantee.[20] For years American capitalists showed no interest in actually building a canal, but after the completion of the Suez canal in 1869 interest was stimulated. The Spanish–American war of 1898 gave the United States a base in Cuba and made plain to Americans the importance of being able to pass ships from one ocean to the other. Informal Anglo-American negotiations on modifying the Clayton–Bulwer treaty led to agreement on a new convention in January 1899. The general principle of neutralization was reaffirmed; but the United States was to have the sole construction and management of the canal.

British official opinion was uncertain. The Board of Trade thought that the guarantee of equal treatment was sufficient and that British shipping would be the largest users of the canal for many years; but the Director of Military Intelligence, Sir John Ardagh, advised that a canal would impair Britain's naval supremacy and increase her responsibilities, so that Britain should not agree to sole United States control without compensation.[21] An attempt was made to link the canal question with a settlement of Canadian–American differences over fishing, sealing and the boundary of Alaska; but the United States government refused and after a short delay the new convention was signed. President McKinley was under domestic pressure and there was a risk that Congress would declare the Clayton–Bulwer treaty abrogated. Even more important was the fact that British resources were stretched to the utmost in the Boer war, and continental powers were discussing intervention and the involvement of the United States. Despite the moral obligation created by Canadian support in South Africa, the British government decided to appeal to Canada not to oppose signature.

British opinion was so preoccupied with the situation in South Africa that the Hay–Pauncefote treaty seems to have attracted little notice. It was not debated in Parliament; press comment was sparse. In the *Nineteenth Century* Benjamin Taylor acknowledged that Britain was giving up a good deal in relinquishing the right to joint possession and control of the canal, but believed that:

> we can concede this cheerfully in sympathy with the legitimate aspirations of our kin beyond sea, confident also that what is for their good will ultimately be for ours, and convinced that every sacrifice made by either nation for the other will help to draw closer the Anglo-Saxon bond.[22]

American opinion was much less satisfied. Most criticism fastened on two points. The invitation to other powers to adhere to the treaty seemed to be inconsistent with the Monroe doctrine. More important, a neutralized canal would strengthen the position in relation to the United States of any power with a larger navy (at that time not only Britain but France and Russia as well). Opposition outside Congress was led by Theodore Roosevelt, at that time Governor of New York, who sent a protest to the press and wrote privately to Hay, the Secretary of State, to explain his views:

> If that canal is open to the war ships of an enemy it is a menace to us in time of war; it is an added burden, an additional strategic point to be guarded by our fleet. If fortified by us, it becomes one of the most potent sources of our possible sea strength. Unless so fortified it strengthens against us every nation whose fleet is larger than ours.[23]

Senators claimed a right not merely to reject a treaty negotiated by the Executive, but to amend it. Lodge could see no reason why Britain should not agree. 'The American people', he wrote:

mean to have the canal and they mean to control it. Now England does not care enough about it to go to war to prevent our building it, and it would be ruinous if she did make war on us. As she is not prepared to go to war, why is it not better that the canal should be built under the Hay–Pauncefote treaty with her assent to the amendments than to have her refuse the amendments and force the United States to abrogate the treaty and build the canal?[24]

In December 1900 the Senate voted to ratify the Hay–Pauncefote treaty with three amendments. The most important added, to the sections laying down rules for the neutralization of the canal, a further clause giving the United States the right to take any measures to secure its own defence. The President accepted the Senate amendments, fearful that if he vetoed them Congress would unilaterally abrogate the Clayton–Bulwer treaty, and Hay attempted to persuade the British that the amendments were harmless. Lansdowne, Salisbury's successor as Foreign Secretary, was disposed to accept them in the last resort. The Admiralty thought it was not in Britain's strategic interest that the canal should be constructed at all. Britain could not expect to maintain, unaided, 'in the West Indies, the Pacific, and in the North American Stations, squadrons sufficiently powerful to dominate those of the United States and at the same time hold the command of the sea in home waters, the Mediterranean, and the Eastern seas, where it is essential that she should remain predominant'. In case of a war with the United States the latter would derive the preponderance of advantage from the canal.[25]

The government's object, however, was not to obstruct construction of the canal, nor even to contest United States control of it. It was to ensure that if the Clayton–Bulwer treaty were abrogated it should be by consent, and that Britain was not left bound by restrictions that did not apply to other countries not parties to a new treaty. The Senate amendments were rejected, and Hay set to work to produce a new text. After further negotiations the second Hay–Pauncefote treaty was signed on 18 November 1901. The Clayton–Bulwer treaty was formally superseded; the canal was to be free to the shipping of all nations without interference, but the United States might maintain military police to protect it; there was no mention of fortifications; the United States adopted the rules governing the Suez canal. After the treaty was signed there was little disposition in the United States to treat it as a triumph. In Britain the treaty was greeted with unalloyed satisfaction. Some commentators noted that the joint ownership and control provided for in the Clayton–Bulwer treaty could not have been exercised, so that Britain had not really sacrificed much. Others assumed that there was not – could not be – any conflict of interest between Britain and the United States, and that American fortification of the canal would even be to Britain's advantage.[26] In Parliament peers and MPs were fulsome in their expressions of pleasure. Colonel McCalmont contrasted the present state of mutual regard with conditions only six years earlier. 'I am sure', he said,

> the country is to be congratulated on . . . our present cordial relations with the United States of America, when one thinks that the clouds have disappeared entirely from that part of the political horizon which loomed so darkly there not so long ago when differences of opinion . . . threatened to plunge us into a struggle with those we look on as kinsfolk across the Atlantic; a struggle which would have been more disastrous than one with any other country to which we are not so bound by blood, language, and tradition.[27]

The press took care to play down the significance of anti-British utterances in America and claimed credit for the absence of public controversy over the Hay–Pauncefote treaty. 'The flame which blazed up so briskly on the other side of the Atlantic was not fanned on this side, and in the absence of this artificial encouragement it rapidly died down', The *Economist* wrote.[28]

There was still a tendency to assume that anti-British sentiment was somehow 'artificial', the product of domestic politics or pressure groups, and that 'real' American feeling reciprocated the British regard. No evidence was ever adduced to support this assumption. That the friendliness professed – and indeed felt – by such statesmen as Hay and Roosevelt depended on Britain making all the concessions was explained by Samuel E. Moffat, chief editorial writer of the *New York Journal*. The two countries, Moffat wrote, could be friends if, but only if, British policy could be consistent with that of the United States. The latter was simple:

> It is based upon the fact that the United States is, and intends to remain, the paramount Power of the Western Hemisphere ... For other Powers the only question is whether they will accept it or collide with it. If this fundamental principle be once accepted, no country will have any trouble in maintaining harmonious relations with the United States.[29]

When Arthur Lee complained privately to Roosevelt that 'it can not be "all give and no take"', the latter was quite untroubled. He maintained that the United States had a perfect right to abrogate a treaty; and he warned Lee that America had always been jealous about the canal, and there would be trouble if concessions were made to Canada over the Alaska boundary.[30] Roosevelt became President of the United States on the assassination of McKinley on 6 September 1901, and his influence was decisive in the final settlement of that frontier.

The fact that the boundary had never been fully demarcated had been of little importance until the Klondike gold rush of 1897 brought numbers of American miners to the Canadian north west and raised problems of access and jurisdiction. Canada now demanded arbitration of her claim to a line that gave her an outlet to the coast: the Americans claimed uninterrupted possession and refused. The parallel with the Venezuela boundary dispute was close, with the roles reversed. Negotiations continued sporadically, with the Canadians slow and sticky, and the government in London obliged to urge arbitration but conscious that the Canadian case was weak.[31] Roosevelt was not willing to have the United States case tested impartially. Eventually he agreed to a tribunal of six, three jurists from each side. This, it was obvious, would lead to deadlock unless at least one jurist voted against his own side. In case of deadlock there would be no award and the United States would remain in possession. Roosevelt agreed to this solution, it seems, with the object of enabling the British government to retreat with dignity. But in order to make assurance doubly sure he appointed as the American members not 'impartial jurists of repute', as

provided for in the agreement, but three legally-trained politicians, at least two of whom had already pronounced publicly
on the merits of the case. One of the three was Lodge, who
had never practised law and made no pretence of impartiality.
When the tribunal was finally agreed, and met in London in
September 1903, Roosevelt made sure that the British government was left in no doubt that he would not accept an unfavourable decision. In the event the one British member of the
tribunal (the other two on the British side were Canadian),
Lord Alverstone, the Lord Chief Justice, gave his opinion in
favour of the United States. Alverstone maintained afterwards
that he had acted solely on the legal merits, but he had been
subjected to great pressure and the Canadians at any rate did
not credit his impartiality.

American opinion came to feel strongly about Alaska. British
opinion did not. A few newspaper articles pointed out the determination of the United States, but only a handful of questions about Alaska were asked in Parliament between 1898 and
1903, none of them showing real concern. The setting up of
the tribunal was hardly debated, and its composition received
no adverse comment from British (as opposed to Canadian)
papers. When the result was announced there was some sympathy for Canada, but *The Times*, among others, offered the
consolation, already, it thought, felt by Englishmen, that 'the
inestimable gain of settling definitely a question which offered
perennial opportunities for exciting discord between the two
great kindred nations is one that far outweighs any disappointment aroused by a decision which, after all, practically leaves
things as in fact it found them'.[32] Canadian opinion was naturally less complacent, and blamed the British government for
sacrificing Canadian interests for the sake of American good
will. At this period, unlike later, Canada's voice in Anglo-American relations was weak.

Thus by the end of 1903, by a series of concessions for which
the United States made no return, Britain had acquiesced in
American supremacy in the western hemisphere from Venezuela to Alaska. The reasons seem to have been a mixture of
calculation and sentiment. The element of calculation is not
very well documented. British cabinets have not been addicted
to long-range planning or philosophical discussion, and those

of the period covered by this chapter were no exception. Salisbury indeed was particularly averse to looking ahead, and did not readily explain his thoughts. But a consistent thread from the middle of the nineteenth century, well before public sentiment was much engaged with the question, was the running down of the defences of British possessions in North America and the Caribbean. In the early 1860s none of them was adequately garrisoned, and further retrenchment followed. The end of the civil war confirmed the United States' achievement of its manifest destiny, and thereafter British policy was based on an assumption that the preponderance of power in North America lay with the republic. To some liberals this even implied the loss of Canada. But the next thirty years saw a growth in Canadian feelings of nationhood and a decline in sentiment favouring union with the United States. Although waves of American annexationism continued, those who, like the publicist Goldwin Smith, looked forward to the dissolution of the British Empire and a rearrangement of its component parts, were always a small minority.[33]

Little was done to defend Canada directly: little, it was assumed, could be done. Her British connection would depend, if it ever came to a conflict with the United States, on the preponderance of British sea power. The Venezuela crisis caused Salisbury to write to the Chancellor of the Exchequer that 'recent events have introduced a new element into the calculation' of naval spending. 'A war with America – not this year but in the not distant future – has become more than a possibility.'[34] Lord Dufferin, a former governor-general of Canada, wrote to Queen Victoria:

> President Cleveland's action will have ... taught us what we may expect, and what we must be prepared for. Fortunately, in the event of an immediate war, we should be complete masters at sea, and Canada appears to be perfectly loyal, provided of course she can be certain of our support, which Lord Dufferin presumes would be promised.

Dufferin recommended, not increasing Canada's defences, but increasing Britain's naval strength to confront not the two next largest powers as at present, but three.[35] In the following year the government considered the question of colonial defence. Lansdowne started by asking the larger strategic and political question: 'Is war with the United States a probability for which it is our duty to provide in the same way as we might provide for war with any of the Continental Powers of Europe?', and replied: 'I cannot believe that this question is to be answered in the affirmative.' The American potential for naval expansion was recognized, and Lansdowne argued:

> We have already committed ourselves in regard to our Navy to the doctrine that for every ship of war constructed by certain foreign Powers we should construct another. It is hard to say where this doctrine may lead us. If we include the United States among the Powers, whose progress in naval matters is to be met by a similar rejoinder on our part, our Naval Estimates are likely to be a curiosity before we are much older.[36]

The situation on land was worse. The Director of Military Intelligence pointed out in another report that the resources of Canada could not stand comparison with those of the United States. The Canadian militia was very small, and the people showed no disposition to improve it. The United States had raised $2\frac{1}{2}$ million men in the civil war and might well make the same effort again for a popular cause – 'and I fear it must be admitted that a war with this country would be popular'. Any early British successes would prove temporary: 'We should eventually be swept out of the country by mere superiority of numbers, and Canada would be overrun and occupied.' Moreover, such a war would offer a tempting opportunity to continental powers:

> with whom we may have, or they may create, questions of dispute in other parts of the world. Such a prospect is one which our military forces are inadequate to exercise a serious influence upon; and which even the most sanguine optimist in regard to our naval predominance, must regard with anxiety. The apparently simple question of the Defence of Canada, thus drags in its train greater and more momentous issues, and conducts us to the inference that a land war

on the American Continent would be perhaps the most un-
profitable and most hazardous military enterprise that we could
possibly be driven to engage in.[37]

Conclusions for British policy were soon drawn. Towards the
end of 1899 the Permanent Under-Secretary at the India Office wrote to Lord Curzon (at that time Viceroy of India, Foreign
Secretary after the First World War):

> I will confess that there are two Powers, and two only, of
> whom I am afraid, viz. the United States and Russia, for the
> simple reason that they have or (in the case of Russia) must
> soon have better military access to an important part of our
> dominions, than we have ourselves. It is to be regretted that
> Canada and India are not islands, but we must recognize
> the fact, and must modify our diplomacy accordingly.[38]

Officials and politicians had no intention of not defending India,
but decided not to try to defend Canada. In 1901 the First
Lord of the Admiralty, Lord Selborne, foreshadowed a decision
of the Committee of Imperial Defence in modifying the two-
power standard. Within the last five years, he wrote, three new
navies had emerged – those of the United States, Germany
and Japan:

> It is certain that it would be a hopeless task to attempt to
> achieve an equality with the three largest navies; but I go
> further and say that, if the United States continue their present
> naval policy and develop their navy as they are easily capable
> of developing it if they choose, it will be scarcely possible
> for us to raise our navy equal to that both of France and the
> United States combined. I propose therefore to consider our
> position almost exclusively from its relative strength to that
> of France and Russia combined.

Three months later Selborne wrote to Curzon:

> I would never quarrel with the U.S. if I could possibly avoid
> it. It has not dawned on our countrymen yet . . . that, if the
> Americans choose to pay for what they can easily afford, they

can gradually build up a navy, fully as large and then larger than ours and I am not sure they will not do it.[39]

The vulnerability of Canada was of course perfectly well known to Americans, and was emphasized on appropriate occasions by Roosevelt and Lodge. In considering naval power Americans were less sanguine about their prospects in war with Britain. Lodge was nervous about British Atlantic bases. Mahan was nervous about the vulnerability of an isthmian canal, and even suggested that it should be an 'inviolable resolution' of American policy that no European power should acquire a coaling station within 3000 miles of San Francisco – a distance, as a British reviewer noted, greater than that from New York to Brest.[40] But it was all curiously abstract. Britain's overall strategic position was never considered, nor was the actual American situation.

The Spanish–American war of 1898 is often said to have been a turning point in Anglo-American relations, especially for converting American public opinion to a pro-British disposition. Public friendliness was certainly marked during the war, finding expression in resolutions, Anglo-American associations, and representations such as that of Britannia seated beside Columbia on a float symbolizing 'Blood is thicker than water' in the Lord Mayor's Show in November. British warmth was reciprocated in the United States. The British Ambassador was 'overwhelmed with addresses in prose and verse in the form of music or drawings or illustrated buttons with flags intertwined'.[41] That kind of enthusiasm was of course fleeting. But a belief persisted in high quarters that British refusal to join European powers in pressing mediation on the United States had saved her from serious risk. In so far as Britain was now no longer regarded as a threat, it does seem possible to date a real improvement in feeling on the American side from 1898. What would probably have been an instinctive pro-Boer response to the South African war was modified. Roosevelt explained it to the hunter and explorer Frederick Selous. 'I used', he wrote,

to be rather anti-British in feeling . . . but England's attitude towards us in our war with Spain impressed me deeply and I have since kept it in grateful remembrance. In consequence,

when the South African war broke out, I felt that... from
the standpoint of the advance of civilization, which to my
mind is wrapped up in the advance of the English-speaking
race, it was best that the English should triumph.

And Lodge: 'There is a very general and solid sense of the
fact that however much we sympathize with the Boers the downfall of the British Empire is something which no rational American would regard as anything but a misfortune to the United
States.' And Samuel E. Moffat: 'Two years ago America's attitude would have been one of sympathy for the Boers, intensified by hostility towards England. Now it is one of sympathy
for the Boers, checked by friendship for England.'[42]
Another factor was the entry of the United States into the
ranks of imperial powers. Neither in the Caribbean nor in the
Pacific was American imperialism regarded as a threat to British interests, by any except a small body of British opinion.
Mahan, advocating the acquisition of Hawaii, had supposed in
1893 that Britain must necessarily want the islands as a link in
a line from British Columbia to Australia and New Zealand.[43]
Mahan was mistaken. Britain's communications with Australia
and New Zealand had never gone via Canada, and did not
begin to do so when the Canadian Pacific Railway was completed in 1885. The American argument over the annexation
of Hawaii remained almost entirely a domestic one, finally settled
in 1898 with little British comment. The Philippines were another matter. They played no part in the causes of the Spanish–American war; even after the occupation of Manila,
annexation was not the only option. American opinion was
divided, with an immediate public clamour for annexation followed by an anti-imperialist wave. The British government let
it be known that so long as the islands remained Spanish or
became American, it would not express any opinion; but it
might object if the islands were transferred to any European
Power.[44] Unofficial commentators such as Edward Dicey found
the new American imperialism both inevitable and welcome:

it is bound to bring together more closely two kindred nations, whose ideas, ambitions, and institutions are almost as
identical as their language. Thus in the Imperialist movement,

which has led the United States to embark on a career of annexation, I see the promise of gain rather than loss to our own country. Even if this were not so, I should still find cause for congratulation in the fact that the American Republic has now reverted to the hereditary policy of the Anglo-Saxon race.

And Rudyard Kipling invited the United States to 'Take up the White Man's Burden – and reap his old reward' of blame and ingratitude.[45]

Dicey's reasons for approving of the emergence of the United States as an imperial power were typical, a mixture of a rational acceptance of historical inevitability with an emotional belief in racial affinity as qualifying the United States to share in the civilizing mission of the Anglo-Saxon peoples. It was at this time, around the turn of the century, that talk of race, racial affinity and Anglo-Saxonism reached its peak. In Britain Anglo-Saxonism was stimulated in the middle of the nineteenth century by Oxford historians emphasizing the Teutonic origins of the English nation. Some of these historians also saw the New England town meeting reproducing or restoring the original Germanic folk gathering. Bryce's *American Commonwealth*, although showing a much greater understanding of the complexities of the United States, nevertheless implied a history of racial unity and continuity, and helped to reinforce the British perception of Americans as, in Gladstone's words, 'Kin beyond Sea'.[46] No one attempted to define the 'Anglo-Saxon race'; the term 'race' was habitually used in a cultural rather than a biological sense; 'Anglo-Saxon' was used interchangeably with 'English-speaking'. Thus the fact that the American population manifestly did not all originate from Great Britain was largely glossed over.[47] It was at the height of this wave that Cecil Rhodes, in 1899, provided in his final will for the scholarships which he hoped would encourage appreciation of the advantages of a union of the English-speaking peoples, the scholars to be drawn from 15 British colonies and all the states of the United States.[48]

In the United States, Anglo-Saxonism was rather different. In the first place, it was more explicitly cultural – of necessity. The proportion of the British element in the population was known to be shrinking. Whereas, according to estimates, at the

time of the first census in 1790 two-thirds of the white population were of English and Scottish stock, by 1850 among the
foreign-born population Great Britain was only the third most
important source, after Ireland and Germany, and its share
dwindled thereafter.[49] But American culture was predominantly
Anglo-American, and there was no suggestion that the inherit-
ance was weakened by migration. On the contrary, awareness
of English origins was easily compatible with a conviction of
American superiority. As early as the 1850s Emerson believed
that the future of English culture lay in the United States. Josiah
Strong, a social reformer, believed by the 1890s that the two
great ideas of which 'the Anglo-Saxon race' was the exponent
– namely pure spiritual Christianity and civil liberty – were being
developed more fully and more energetically in the United States
than in Britain. George Burton Adams saw only one possible
answer to the question of which of the two greatest Anglo-
Saxon nations was more fit for the leadership of 'the race'.
Brooks Adams wrote of the historical westward movement of
the social centre of civilization. Others talked the language of
breeding. Francis A. Walker, Director of the Bureau of the
Census, claimed that:

> The climate of the United States has been benign enough
> to take the English short-horn and greatly to improve it . . .
> to take the English race-horse and to improve him . . . to
> take the English man and improve him too . . . so that in
> rowing, in riding, in shooting, and in boxing, the American
> of pure English stock is today the better animal.[50]

Devotion to English origins was compatible, especially in New
England, with dislike of Britain. Lodge the Boston Brahmin
wrote a PhD thesis on Anglo-Saxon land law and praised the
Teutonic virtues of the English people. In an analysis of the
entries in a biographical encyclopedia he demonstrated that
three-quarters of those of foreign birth who had gained distinction in the United States came from Great Britain.[51] Lodge
the nationalist, and representative of a state with a large Irish
population, denounced the British threat to the United States.
  A further aspect of American Anglo-Saxonism was not par-
alleled in Britain at this time. Until the 1880s Germans,

Scandinavians and Dutch on the whole passed the test of assimilation; Highland Scots and even the Irish, although clearly not Teutonic, shared some of the culture and language. But the new immigration of the 1890s, the mass arrival for the first time of Italians, Slavs and east European Jews, raised many doubts. Popular nativism grew, and members of the still predominantly New England intellectual elite began to advocate restricting immigration. However, not everyone joined in the nativist rhetoric, and a note of irony could be struck for non-Anglo-Saxon Americans, as when 'Mr Dooley' told his friend Hennessy:

> I tell ye, whin th' Clan an' th' Sons iv Sweden an' th' Banana Club an' th' Circle Francaize an' th' Polacky Benivolent Society an' th' Rooshian Sons of Dinnymite an' th' Benny Brith an' th' Coffee Clutch that Schwartzmeister r-runs an' th' Turnd'yemind an' th' Holland Society an' th'Afro-Americans an' th' other Anglo-Saxons begin f'r to raise their Anglo-Saxon battle-cry, it'll be all day with th' eight or nine people in th' wurruld that has th' misfortune iv not bein' brought up Anglo-Saxons.[52]

While the supposed racial or linguistic community was much invoked in Britain there were different views on what it ought to produce on the political level. Would the tie of more or less common language and culture ensure friendship, or closer links still? At a time when the general desirability of alliances and understandings was being debated in Britain, it was natural that the United States should be considered as one possible partner. In 1894 the author Arthur Silva White suggested an alliance by which Britain would guarantee the United States against attack by any European power and the United States would undertake to remain neutral if Britain were at war.[53] Alfred Austin, the Poet Laureate, appeared to envisage something more active, writing in March 1898:

> Now, fling them out to the breeze,
> Shamrock, Thistle, and Rose!
> And the Star-Spangled Banner unfurl with these
> A message to friend and foes.

> Wherever the sails of Peace are seen
> and wherever the War-wind blows!
> A message to bond and thrall to wake,
> For, wherever we come, we twain,
> The throne of the Tyrant shall rock and quake,
> And his menace be void and vain;
> For you are lords of a strong young land,
> And we are lords of the main.[54]

A.V. Dicey, professor of English Law at Oxford, suggested common citizenship.[55] Andrew Carnegie advocated the 'coming together' of the English-speaking 'race', though not a formal alliance.[56] W.T. Stead foresaw the British Empire merging into a United States of the English-speaking world under American leadership.[57] The most prominent advocate of an Anglo-American alliance was Joseph Chamberlain. In a famous speech at Birmingham on 13 May 1898, during the Spanish–American war, he said that the first duty of statesmen, after drawing the British Empire closer together, was:

> to establish and maintain bonds of amity with our kinsmen across the Atlantic ... I do not know what the future has in store for us, I do not know what arrangements may be possible with the United States, but this I know and feel – that the closer, more cordial, the fuller and the more definite, these arrangements are with the consent of both people, the better it will be for the world. And I even go so far as to say that, terrible as war may be, even war itself would be cheaply purchased if in a great and noble cause the Stars and Stripes and the Union Jack should wave together over an Anglo-Saxon alliance.[58]

The speech caused a sensation, and Chamberlain had to qualify the alliance concept in the House of Commons a month later, saying:

> Nothing in the nature of a cut-and-dried alliance is at this moment proposed. The Americans do not want our alliance at this moment. They do not ask for our assistance, and we do not want theirs, at this moment. But will anyone say that

the occasion may not arise, foreseen as it has been by some American statesmen, who have said that there is a possibility in the future that Anglo-Saxon liberty and Anglo-Saxon interests may hereafter be menaced by a great combination of other Powers . . . I think that such a thing is possible, and in that case, whether it be America or whether it be England that is menaced, I hope that blood will be found thicker than water.[59]

In the following year, with Britain subjected to a torrent of European abuse over the South African war, Chamberlain reverted to talk of an alliance, this time an Anglo-German-American one, 'a new Triple Alliance between the Teutonic race and the two great branches of the Anglo-Saxon race', as 'a potent influence in the future of the world'.[60] But Chamberlain spoke mainly for himself: and most British talk was more cautious. A good many commentators hoped to cultivate a 'moral alliance' or a 'perfect entente'; some warned that sentiment was not a sufficient foundation. Edward Dicey could foresee contingencies under which the imperial interests of the two countries might conflict.

If such contingencies should arise I have no great confidence in war being rendered an impossibility on the strength of platitudes, uttered on either side of the Atlantic, as to our common brotherhood, and as to blood being thicker than water. The real bond of union between our two countries lies in the fact that the interests we have in common are more numerous and more powerful than the interests which are – or may be – antagonistic.

Dicey's brother warned against the supposition that far-reaching policies could be grounded on emotions which were proper to individuals, not states, and against 'the delusion that the interests of England and America will always obviously coincide'.[61]

On the American side statesmen like Hay and Olney could now express confidence in Anglo-American friendship, but no one advocated an alliance with any country: Washington's farewell address was unquestioned gospel. In September 1899 Hay was obliged by the exigencies of political campaigning publicly to denounce Democratic attempts to accuse the Administration of having concluded an alliance with Britain.[62] When in the dark days of the Boer war Carnegie forecast that if the European powers combined against Britain, the United States would come to the rescue, Godkin poured scorn on the idea: 'English statesmen must have grinned when they read this. As it is their business to know the facts, they are fully aware that a European alliance for the purpose of crushing England would be bidden God-speed by a powerful, and very likely a predominant part of our population.'[63]

Talk of alliance or understanding on the British side lacked substance. Lansdowne laid it down in 1901 as a principle of British policy that nothing should be done that might be hostile to the United States,[64] but there were few areas in which there was occasion even for collaboration between the two governments. In China, Hay's Open Door note of September 1899 might have owed something to British inspiration but neither forecast nor led to any American action or cooperation with other countries. Over the Boxer Rising in 1900 the United States did collaborate with others, but the idea that Britain and the United States had common interests in the Far East was not well founded. Had either intended to pursue an active policy, the hollowness would have been revealed. In Central America and Panama the Americans proceeded entirely on their own; and on the whole Britain welcomed Roosevelt's corollary to the Monroe doctrine, enunciated in 1904. British commentators had been saying, and American commentators were coming increasingly to recognize, that if the United States were to refuse to allow any European power to trespass on the rights of an American state it should not 'countenance any shirking' of their obligations by such states, and should if necessary see that breaches were remedied.[65] Balfour made the point in a speech in 1903, in connection with trouble over claims against Venezuela. 'The Monroe doctrine', he said,

has no enemies in this country that I know of. We welcome any increase of the influence of the United States of America upon the great Western hemisphere ... I go further, and say that, as far as I am concerned, I believe it would be a great gain to civilization if the United States were more actively to interest themselves in making arrangements by which these constantly recurring difficulties between European Powers and certain States in South America could be avoided.[66]

Balfour would have liked 'some arrangement'. It was suggested to the Cabinet a year later that there should be 'some cooperation between the two governments' that would put an end to the possibility of controversy over the punishment of a wrong done to a British subject by a Central or South American republic.[67] But Roosevelt acted entirely on his own in enunciating his corollary to the Monroe doctrine:

> All that we desire is to see all neighbouring countries stable, orderly and prosperous. Any country whose people conduct themselves well can count upon our hearty friendliness . . . [But] Brutal wrongdoing, or an impotence which results in a general loosening of the ties of civilized society, may finally require intervention by some civilized nation, and in the Western Hemisphere the United States cannot ignore this duty.[68]

The omission of the United States from calculations of the British naval standard was hardly ever questioned. Archibald Hurd, a naval writer, expressed a doubt in 1907, but Fisher, First Sea Lord from 1904 to 1910, pursued a policy of concentrating the Royal Navy and never accepted that war with the United States was possible.[69] Strategic withdrawal from the western hemisphere continued. The growth of the United States navy from fifth to third place in world battleship and cruiser strength was accepted with equanimity – in striking contrast to the growing alarm about the development of the German navy.[70] Some British commentators contemplated naval cooperation. Sidney Low, for example, pointed out in December 1904 that the United States would soon possess a navy not far behind Britain's, and had greater resources to sustain one. He went on:

> We may, and must, keep the first place. But we shall not sweep the seas as if no other flag existed . . . The Anglo-Saxon navies could enforce the law of the sea against all the world, if they chose . . . Supposing that Great Britain and the United

States entered into an agreement to employ their splendid navies, their immense moral and material force, for certain common beneficial objects?[71]

On the American side, however, there was little such talk. Mahan never advocated challenging British naval mastery, but only envisaged division of areas of interest. In 1898 he officially advised against trying to acquire coaling stations in the Mediterranean or on any route via the Cape of Good Hope to the east. In 1909 Mahan admitted that 'the British Navy is far superior to ours, indeed, to a degree that no one proposes to overtake'. But he now saw no danger in this position; and again in 1911 he wrote that to rival the British navy was 'inexpedient, because for many reasons unnecessary'.[72] Captain P.R. Hobson, USN, was more ambitious, asserting in 1902 that all considerations of material interest indicated that the United States should maintain 'the greatest navy in the world; indeed, the size being proportioned to her needs, the Navy of the United States should be almost equal to the combined navies of the world'. The United States 'will be the controlling World Power, holding the sceptre of the sea, reigning with mighty beneficence with the guiding principle of a maximum of world service.'[73] But Hobson's dreams seemed excessive to many. Imperialism was attended with vulnerability: Britain's 'unparalleled navy' might be needed to help 'make us invincible on the ocean'. Gradually opinion in the US Navy, which up to 1898 had been largely anti-British, became more wary of Germany and then of Japan, and able to contemplate cooperation with Britain for some definite purpose.[74]

In the late nineteenth and early twentieth century the United States economy was transformed. Between 1875 and 1900 manufacturing production more than trebled, and it rose again by nearly half between 1900 and 1910. The value of external trade more than doubled between 1875 and 1900, and rose again by nearly half between 1900 and 1910: in the total, manufacturing exports – iron and steel, and machinery – became increasingly significant. These developments were important for the world economy, for American power, and for British power. Meanwhile Anglo-American trade grew by leaps and bounds: in 1875 it was worth £94.7 million; in 1900 £176.1 million.

The two countries had long been, and remained, each other's single most important trading partner; but the nature of the trade began to change. British capital exports to the United States remained important; but now American capital began to enter Britain; and in January 1900 the British government, for the first time since the Seven Years War, borrowed abroad – and did so in the United States. The growing volume of imports of American manufactured goods into Britain, and American competition in world trade, did not arouse the same public anxiety in Britain as did German competition. Some papers saw the United States as a more powerful rival than Germany, but given her size and resources this was accepted as inevitable. A few books and pamphlets described the 'American invasion', explained American superiority in resources, and urged Britons to compete in education and willingness to work and innovate. Sir Christopher Furness, a shipowner and MP for Hartlepool, was much impressed by American achievements and exhorted his countrymen to 'high thinking, strenuous mental and physical toil'. The *Review of Reviews* reproduced cartoons from the American press, such as one from the New York *Journal* showing Uncle Sam and John Bull playing cards and the former saying: 'Come, John, let's play for your durned little island; I might as well win that too.' Frederick Mackenzie, a journalist and author, drew a humorous, and exaggerated, picture of the penetration of British markets by American goods:

In the domestic life we have almost got to this. The average citizen wakes in the morning at the sound of an American alarm clock; rises from his New England sheets, and shaves with his New York soap, and Yankee safety razor. He pulls on a pair of Boston boots over his socks from West Carolina, fastens his Connecticut braces, slips his Waterbury watch into his pocket and sits down to breakfast. There he congratulates his wife on the way her Illinois straight-front corset sets off her Massachusetts blouse, and begins to tackle his breakfast... Concurrently he reads his morning paper, set up by American machines, printed with American ink, by American presses, on American paper... Rising from his breakfast table the citizen rushes out, catches an electric tram made in New York, to Shepherd's Bush, where he gets into a Yankee elevator, which takes him on to the American-fitted railway to the City. At his office of course everything is American. He sits on a Nebraskan swivel-chair, before a Michigan roll-top desk, writes his letters on a Syracuse typewriter, signing them with a New York fountain pen, and drying them with blotting sheet from New England. The letter copies are put away in a file manufactured in Grand Rapids . . . When evening comes . . . he drinks a cocktail or some Californian wine, and finishes up with a couple of 'little liver pills', made in America.[75]

Yet although American aspirations to special commercial advantages in Latin America aroused the wrath of the British Minister in Mexico, British trade was not yet endangered.[76] Discussion of the American economic threat was part of the wider discussion of Britain's apparent economic decline at the turn of the century, but did not occupy a predominant position in it. Writers were as divided on the remedies for it as on the wider problem, some advocating protection, some improved competitiveness; and the idea of a European commercial union directed against the United States was dismissed.[77]

Only in one case – that of North Atlantic passenger shipping – did American encroachment cause serious alarm and government action. The purchase in 1902 of certain shipping companies by the International Mercantile Marine company formed by J.P. Morgan and Co., and the prospect that the White Star Line might also come under American ownership, caused a great deal of public disquiet. There was a naval aspect to this case. The Admiralty expected to rely on requisitioning fast merchant ships in wartime and therefore paid the shipping companies concerned a regular subvention. The government stepped in to secure British ownership of the ships in question and provided a subsidy for the building for Cunard of two new liners, the *Mauretania* and *Lusitania*.[78]

After 1898 an increasing number of Americans saw their country moving into the position of 'what is commonly called a world power'.[79] For many this was simply a matter of status, but others anticipated responsibility. Herbert Croly, the influential Progressive writer, thought that 'the American nation must assume a more definite and a more responsible place in the international system'. At some future time, he suggested, American power might be able to tip the scales in favour of a comparatively peaceful settlement of international complications. Lewis Einstein advocated making understandings with other countries, and warned that 'a world position inevitably entails world responsibilities'.[80] Theodore Roosevelt told a German acquaintance in 1911 that he saw the United States becoming 'more and more the balance of power of the whole globe'. Roosevelt in office aimed to further the process, acting as mediator in ending the Russo-Japanese war in 1905, and acting as a go-between in bringing about the Algeciras conference to settle the first Moroccan crisis. Roosevelt was pleased with his role, but the Senate attached to the Algeciras agreement a reservation that there was 'no purpose to depart from the traditional American foreign policy which forbids participation by the United States in the settlement of political questions which are entirely European in their scope'.[81]

After about 1904 the general perception on both sides of the Atlantic was that Anglo-American relations were good and that war between the two countries was virtually impossible. That did not mean that Roosevelt was disposed to rely on British friendship; nor did it prevent Congressional disregard for treaty obligations over tolls for the Panama canal, or accusations of sinister British involvement in the Mexican revolution.[82] Mahan, however, thought that there was 'certainty of a very high order that the British Empire will stand substantially on the same lines of world policy as ourselves', and that weakening of the Empire would not be to the advantage of the United States. The United States army and navy generally assumed that war between the two countries was extremely improbable.[83] Signature in 1911 of a general arbitration treaty provided the British government with the means of excluding the possibility of war with the United States from the latest version of the Anglo-Japanese alliance.[84]

On the British side the acceleration of the German naval programme and the consequent naval scare in 1909 led a number of papers to speculate optimistically on the prospect of American support if Britain should be at war with Germany; but such speculations were firmly quashed by the American press and by better informed British observers.[85] There was now little doubt that American friendship might be very important. Balfour, contemplating early in 1909 the actual and expected challenges to Britain's imperial position from Germany, Russia and Japan, thought it essential to prevent an American one. A challenge was possible, since American expansion could only take place at Britain's expense; but: 'Have England and America anything to gain by refusing to pursue their destinies together and electing to be in opposition? Nothing that anybody judging from a broad standpoint – that of posterity, can see.' Balfour's long-term solution was a loose federation in which 'a common Anglo-Saxon patriotism' would be 'superimposed on English, American, Canadian, South African, and Australian national sentiment'.[86]

Imperially minded Americans might see things otherwise. As Maurice Low pointed out, they might not 'assist destiny' by actively bringing about the 'inevitable' decay of the British Empire, but they would not resist it. A writer in the *National Review* in 1913 recognized that the United States had an interest in the maintenance of the general balance, but would not be concerned by a limited German victory over Britain.[87]

This view was almost certainly more representative of American opinion than that expressed by a naval officer on the occasion of a visit to Britain (and not to Germany) by the American Atlantic Fleet at the end of 1910. At a lunch at the Guildhall for the American officers the Lord Mayor, Sir Thomas Strong, said in his speech of welcome:

We in these islands cannot think of America as a foreign Power. It is an integral part of the English-speaking family, and we always regard America as lying outside the number of our possible enemies . . . Should the time ever arrive when a hostile land threatened us with dishonour and destruction, then I believe there would at once be heard from the English-speaking world beyond the seas a voice saying in tones of thunder:

Woodman, spare that tree,
Touch not a single bough.
In youth it sheltered me,
And I'll protect it now.

The American admiral and the ambassador replied in conventional terms; but at another lunch the following day Commander W.S. Sims, USN (who was to command American naval forces in Britain in 1918) said: 'If the time ever comes when the British Empire is seriously menaced by an external enemy, it is my personal opinion that you may count upon every man, every dollar, every ship, and every drop of blood of your kindred across the sea.' This opinion earned Sims a rebuke from his superiors but, noted one observer, 'his words, spoken from the heart, went to the heart, and will never be forgotten'.[88]

The conclusion to be drawn from the experience of these two decades seems to be that the rise of American power was not seen as presenting a serious challenge to British power. It was limited, so far, to areas where British interests were not thought vital; it was not detrimental to British trade. There was no readiness to hand over actual British possessions; but the development of Dominion self-government implied, even for imperial federationists, that Canada would decide its own future. The British reaction was also coloured by the belief in kinship. During these years the notion of Teutonic kinship, never very solid, fell victim to Anglo-German antagonism. That of Anglo-Saxon kinship survived.

2
Resources and Responsibility: The First World War and the Peace Settlement

The First World War marked an important stage in the rise of American power, absolutely and in relation to that of Britain. By the end of the war the United States was acknowledged to be not merely a potential but an actual great power of the first rank. Whereas the European belligerents had expended lives and capital with a prodigality never seen before, United States resources grew and her losses were insignificant. She was able and willing to use her power. But it was not unlimited. Economic and financial resources, important though they were in relations with the belligerents, were not enough to give a neutral United States the position of arbiter in the conflict that President Wilson desired. Military intervention was eventually forced on a reluctant country, and was decisive in the Allied victory. Wilson then aimed to apply American ideals and principles to the peace, and thus to serve American interests as well as those of humanity. He articulated the aspirations of many European as well as American liberals. But the peace, like the war, was that of a coalition, and already before the treaties were signed it was uncertain whether the American people would endorse the role that the President wished to give their country.

Britain's position in the summer of 1919 seemed very powerful. She had borne a great share of the burdens and costs of the war, and the outcome fostered pride in national and imperial greatness. Her main European challenger was for the time being eclipsed; the settlement brought accretions of imperial

41

possessions. Her territory was not physically devastated; and she was less visibly drained than was France. She played a leading role in the peace settlement. In retrospect it is evident that the war brought losses that could not be made good, and hastened a process of relative decline; but at the time the extent and the intractable nature of the problems were not obvious even to well-informed observers, still less to public opinion. Britain's financial dependence on the United States in the latter part of the war was not expected to be permanent. Some aspects of developments in the next decade could be foreseen; others hardly could. A balance sheet drawn up in 1919 would have contained items of very uncertain value.[1]

In the first two years of the war public attitudes on both sides of the Atlantic fluctuated with events, and particularly with the state of disputes over British measures to strangle Germany's overseas trade. American neutrality caused some initial perplexity among people in Britain who had really believed the rhetoric about kinship of blood and ideals. Such people expected, at the least, expressions of sympathy for the Allied cause, protests against the German violation of Belgian neutrality, and also ready acquiescence in British economic measures.[2] Some of them comforted themselves with the belief that American public opinion was more sympathetic than the Administration, a belief based either on anecdotal evidence or on wishful thinking, and contradicted by the poll of newspaper editors conducted in the autumn of 1914 by the New York *Literary Digest*.[3] There was, however, from the start an undercurrent of disappointment or resentment that the United States was not actively involved on the Allied side. Anger at American lack of understanding or apparently anti-British actions broke through from time to time. Observers then became troubled at British press rudeness, and journalists were prompted to point out the benefits the Allies were receiving and to explain the American position.[4] Nevertheless, after the sinking of the *Lusitania* on 6 May 1915, expressions of sympathy for the loss of American lives were soon soured by resentment at President Wilson's phrase about a man being 'too proud to fight', and reminders that modern war could not leave non-combatants immune. Ups and downs of this kind recurred throughout the period of American neutrality, the downs prompted by each American protest against British measures and each of Wilson's utterances betraying, as it appeared, moral superiority or indifference as between the contending sides.[5]

On the other side of the Atlantic press and public opinion was initially inchoate. The sufferings of Belgium evoked great private generosity; the sufferings of American cotton growers evoked public anger; the issues could not seem, to Americans, as clear cut as they did to each belligerent. And whilst probably, by 1916, a majority would have preferred an Allied victory, there was no particular sympathy for Britain, and all but a very few Americans were determined to remain out of the war. After the *Lusitania* sinking some talk of belligerency began, but as late as the winter of 1916 the mass of American opinion remained opposed to intervention.[6]

Official opinion in Britain did not expect United States involvement in the war in its early stages, but did to some extent share the expectation of American sympathy. Grey, however, who set great store by American friendship, was not complacent and laboured to minimize causes of dispute. But not all British official opinion was tender of American susceptibilities. The Admiralty naturally favoured a hard line on the blockade; and some senior officials in the Foreign Office agreed. The ambassador in Washington, Sir Cecil Spring Rice, was at first confident of the support of American public opinion; but as the war settled to a long haul and causes of American grievance multiplied, he became disappointed, cynical about the practical value of American benevolence, and inclined to see German spies and influence everywhere. Spring Rice, a career diplomat, was not a success as a wartime ambassador. He knew the United States, having served there in the 1880s and 1890s, and his observation of American politics was acute. But he suffered from a kidney disorder which took a heavy toll of his energy and temper; and he did not have access to the President. This did not matter so much – since Wilson saw no other foreign ambassadors either – as the fact that gradually Colonel House, Wilson's alter ego in foreign affairs, lost confidence in Spring Rice's judgment and did not conceal his low opinion. But Spring Rice was not withdrawn until January 1918, when he was abruptly recalled and died in Canada on his way home.[7] Instead the British developed a series of parallel organizations and *ad hoc* special representatives in the United States.

On the American side official opinion was on the whole, to start with, either genuinely neutral and pacific (as in the case of William Jennings Bryan, the Secretary of State, who resigned after the *Lusitania* sinking rather than face being sucked into belligerency by insisting on Americans' right to expose themselves to danger), or instinctively pro-Allied but detached. As time passed, some members of the Administration became more convinced that American interests were bound up in an Allied victory, but none thirsted for belligerency. Bryan's successor Robert Lansing sympathized with Britain, and believed by 1917 that the United States ought to enter the war on the Allied side, but he had little influence with Wilson. Walter Page, the ambassador in London, became personally more and more bound up with mainstream British feeling, and steadily lost influence with Wilson and House. He too was never replaced. Since he was popular in London, withdrawing him might have been taken as a sign of coolness that was better avoided; but there is little evidence that this was the consideration in Washington. The reason seems rather to have been the low status accorded to the State Department and Wilson's inability to trust anyone but House.[8]

In addition to the general desire in Britain for American sympathy and supplies, liberal groups hoped for an American contribution to the peace. Grey sympathized personally with the idea of a league to preserve peace and made it an ingredient of his policy towards the United States, seeking to impress on House the importance of American participation in future guarantees.[9] From early 1915 the question became involved with American efforts at mediation in the war. One element in Wilson's and House's conception of a negotiated peace was an agreement to eliminate 'militarism and navalism'. From the American point of view navalism was the most important: their neutrality and their trade were chiefly threatened by British efforts to enforce naval mastery and a doctrine of belligerent rights at sea which they did not accept, and by German efforts to destroy British supremacy. From the British point of view 'freedom of the seas' came to seem a German policy to cripple British sea power, and American espousal of it seemed to be at best purely self-interested and at worst acceptance of German aims not balanced by an equal concern for the rights of peoples subjected to land warfare. In correspondence and talks with House, Grey emphasized that 'To me, the great object of securing the elimination of militarism and navalism is to get security for the future against aggressive war. How much are the United States prepared to do in this direction?'[10] The answer was not clear.

By the end of 1915, House personally was prepared to commit United States influence in support of a plan by which international obligations should be kept and the peace of the world maintained. Wilson was prepared, if one group of belligerents was willing to discuss peace on the basis of military and naval disarmament and 'a league of nations to secure each nation against aggression and maintain the absolute freedom of the seas', to use 'our utmost moral force' to oblige the other side to 'parley'. He was also ready to cooperate in a policy 'seeking to bring about and maintain permanent peace between civilized nations', although not, House was sure, to join an agreement securing European affairs.[11]

House came to Europe in January 1916 to sound the possibility of mediation. He found that the German war aims were so extensive as to make a compromise with the Allies virtually impossible. In order to keep up the process, therefore, a greater prospect of American support was held out to the Allies. The so-called House–Grey memorandum of 22 February 1916 stated that Wilson, on hearing from the Allies that the moment was opportune, would call for a peace conference. If the Allies accepted and Germany refused, 'the United States would probably enter the war against Germany'. If the conference met, and failed to secure peace terms not unfavourable to the Allies, 'the United States would probably leave the Conference as a belligerent on the side of the Allies'.[12]

This was an ambiguous undertaking. The prospects of American belligerency were left very vague; American 'intervention' in the form of calling for a conference would only have been of value to the Allies if the tide of war went against them. House believed, apparently, that he had convinced the British and French that it would be better for them if the United States did not enter the war; but this is not confirmed by British or French evidence. The moment for the Allies to call Wilson to action never came – the course of the war was not conducive – and House was left disappointed.[13] A further cause of grievance was the tepid British response to Wilson's speech of 27 May 1916, in which he endorsed the idea of a League of Nations and promised American participation.[14] The speech was welcomed by pro-League opinion in Britain and America, but the official response was cool. Wilson's renewed expressions of indifference to the cause of the war caused offence, and so did his references to freedom of the seas without mention of observance of the laws of war on land. Reports that American opinion was as strongly opposed to war as ever and the United States was not ready to accept any military obligations in non-American affairs did not encourage faith in American participation or dependability.[15]

Failure to take up the offer of American mediation was not the only, or even the main, cause of deteriorating Anglo-American relations in 1916. The executions after the Easter Rising in Ireland upset much American opinion. British blockade measures caused increasing strain. Even pro-British Americans, while admitting that at present it would be idle to ask for a relaxation of British efforts to maintain naval preponderance, warned that after the war the United States would not continue to accept British supremacy.[16] Early in 1916 the Administration began, reluctantly, a campaign for 'preparedness'. The most popular feature was a proposal for a large increase in the navy. In a moment of enthusiasm at St Louis on 3 February, Wilson called for a navy 'incomparably the greatest in the world'. Questioned, he rapidly denied that he had meant this literally; some admirals denied that there was any need for friction with Britain; others were 'not sure that we are not going to fight England'. Sixty per cent of newspaper editors polled by the *Literary Digest* favoured a navy as large as any in the world, and one even favoured a two-power standard.[17]

It was not just a question of wartime measures, bad though these were. Alarming for the future were the resolutions of an Allied conference in Paris in June 1916, promising continuing economic discrimination against the Central Powers after the end of the war, and mutual help in reconstruction. These resolutions seemed to presage trade war and discrimination against American interests.[18] A belief that Britain was trying to build up her trade at the United States' expense grew in Washington and was shared by Wilson who, it seems, never again lost his suspicions of British trade policy and his determination to counter it. At the instance of the Administration, Congress at the beginning of September 1916 added to the Revenue bill an amendment authorizing the President to take retaliatory action against countries that discriminated against American citizens. Also on 8 September, Congress passed the naval appropriations. When House suggested that the growth of the American navy and trade were causing British irritation, Wilson replied: 'Let us build a navy bigger than hers and do what we please.'[19] Despite his anger, however, Wilson moved only slowly both before and after the election that returned him to the White House with a larger popular vote than he had received in 1912, from Americans who trusted him to keep them out of war and accepted his references to a League of Nations. In any case it was not clear that commercial retaliation against Britain was feasible.[20]

In London the American legislation prompted an official examination of the extent of Britain's dependence on the United States. This showed that the United States was the sole source of cotton, some foodstuffs and industrial raw materials, oil and petroleum products, and a major supplier of certain munitions and metals, for some of which there was no substitute. No less alarmingly J.M. Keynes, head of the division of the Treasury dealing with external finance, wrote: 'Of the £5,000,000 which the Treasury have to find daily for the prosecution of the war, about £2,000,000 has to be found in North America.' Britain would soon need to raise large unsecured loans, and if the United States government deprecated such loans their flotation would be made practically impossible. Even without government action:

Any feeling of irritation or lack of sympathy with this country . . . in the minds of the American public . . . would render it exceedingly difficult, if not impossible, to carry through financial operations on a scale adequate to our needs . . . It is hardly an exaggeration to say that in a few months' time the American executive and the American public will be in a position to dictate to this country on matters that affect us more nearly than them.[21]

Keynes's advice was confirmed by the Chancellor of the Exchequer, Reginald McKenna, who pointed out to the Cabinet that liquid resources in the form of gold and securities were running down. 'If things go on as at present, I venture to say with certainty that by next June or earlier, the President of the American Republic will be in a position, if he wishes, to dictate his own terms to us.'[22] Britain's credit was still good, and given time she could probably borrow all she wanted: American financial and industrial interests were already so deeply involved that they could hardly afford to leave her without resources. But it was recognized that American opinion was 'really frightened of the probable magnitude of British power after the war and the tremendous weapons we could use if we adopt a selfish and aggressive economic policy'. If they were not reassured about the Paris Resolutions, Britain would lay herself open to an aggressive American trade policy and a large naval and merchant shipbuilding programme.[23]

Financial vulnerability was demonstrated soon after the November elections when, with Wilson's approval the Federal Reserve Board issued a public warning to banks that they should not invest in foreign Treasury bills, and to private investors that they would be wise to seek full information, particularly in the case of unsecured loans. The reaction was immediate: British credit was seriously damaged. Wilson's motive, it was assumed in London, was to put pressure on the British government to accept his forthcoming mediation initiative.

Wilson began to prepare a new initiative as soon as the elections were over. He wished House to urge on Grey that the American people were growing more and more impatient with the 'intolerable conditions of neutrality' and 'might look upon the continuation of the war through another winter with the utmost distaste and misgiving'.[24] But his plans were soon crossed by quite different German intentions. While Wilson was still considering how to make his offer the German Chancellor, Bethmann Hollweg, himself issued a proposal that the Allies should send representatives to a conference on peace terms. This move was largely due to the situation in Austria, but also to domestic German factors and the Supreme Command's determination to demand unrestricted submarine warfare before long. Wilson for his part did not wish to appear to be cooper-

ating with the Germans, but his note inevitably seemed to be
an endorsement of theirs. The Allies did not find it difficult to
dismiss the German proposal as a manoeuvre, but the American note presented a more delicate problem. The government
in London had just changed, to one expected to prosecute
the war more vigorously. Lloyd George had replaced Asquith,
and Balfour had replaced Grey. The Cabinet had to take into
account the possible effect of strong American pressure to stop
the war, and also public opinion in the Allied countries and
America. The decision to state the Allies' terms publicly was
taken partly out of fear of incurring Wilson's displeasure by
an evasive reply, partly out of a desire to show allied and neutral opinion that their professed anxiety for justice and peace
meant something definite and moderate.[25] The joint reply to
Wilson dealt with territory and restitution. In a separate note
Balfour argued that only an Allied victory would secure a dur-
able peace and international reforms.[26]

In one sense, therefore, Wilson's 'Peace without Victory' address to the Senate on 22 January 1917 was a plain rejection
of Balfour's argument. As a statement of the doctrine that international peace is the concern of all countries, that victory may
cost too much, that an imposed settlement may be unstable, it
was and remains a noble utterance. The public response in
the United States was favourable to the lofty sentiments. In
the Allied countries liberals and the Left applauded; but once
again Wilson's key phrase jarred, and a claim to a share in the
peace-making without participation in winning the war was found
impertinent.[27]

On 4 February 1917 the United States broke off relations
with Germany. Wilson was driven by the announcement of unrestricted submarine warfare to fulfil his threat uttered in April
1916. He was deeply reluctant to do so, still believing that it
was the United States' duty to stay out of the war so that it
could rescue Europe afterwards, and still seeing no merit in
an Allied victory. Even after breaking off relations Wilson wished
to avoid going to war: he was determined not to take the first
step, and still hoped to be able to mediate. On the Allied side
the breach of relations was of course welcomed, but as dis-
creetly as possible. Expressions of enthusiasm in the press were
discouraged, as were expressions of impatience as the weeks

passed. Lloyd George, however, spoke to Page about supplies, offered information, and held out to Wilson the prospect of a seat at the peace table.[28] The government should hardly have needed, but the British public probably did need, the warning conveyed by House, that:

> it would be wrong to assume that there is any pronounced pro-Ally feeling on the part of the great mass of the American people. It would certainly be wrong to assume any pro-British sentiment . . . Of all the great Allied powers Great Britain is probably the least popular because all the war measures which have irritated the American people have been carried out by Great Britain.[29]

Finally, compelled by German overt acts, Wilson on 2 April asked Congress for a declaration of war.

Mobilizing the American people and the American economy for war was not a simple task, nor was it accomplished quickly.[30] Intensive domestic propaganda concentrated on the themes of national unity, the wickedness of the enemy, and a crusade for peace and freedom. Despite this, deep differences about the role of the state in American life hampered war organization. The President, as commander-in-chief, had limitless authority over the armed forces, but the Army and Navy Departments were not prepared for modern war. As head of the civil administration the President had virtually no authority over economic affairs, and he did not ask Congress for extensive powers until May 1918. But the American talent for improvisation overcame most obstacles and some remarkable feats were achieved, such as the raising of an army of four million men in 18 months and the despatch of half of them to Europe where, equipped largely with French and British artillery and aircraft, they made a crucial contribution in the summer of 1918.

A large American contribution in manpower was not at first envisaged on either side of the Atlantic; but Russia's withdrawal from the war changed the situation, and after the German spring offensive in 1918 Allied appeals became desperate. General Pershing, the American commander in Europe, was determined to keep his forces independent and intended to lead a decisive offensive in 1919, accepting the risk of French and British defeat before he was ready to commit his army. But Wilson responded to allied appeals; the British found shipping to transport large numbers of troops, and they were thrown effectively into what became the final battles.

Overall, American influence on grand strategy was small. Wilson was committed to winning the war, but did not wish to be closely linked with the Allies: the term 'Associated Power' summed up his idea of the relationship. He supported the creation of the Supreme War Council in November 1917, but was reluctant to send a representative to take part in it. He wished to force his political objectives on his associates rather than persuade them by cooperation. Pragmatic politician though he was behind the mask, he had little idea how to deal with other governments as equals. He was also handicapped by the fact that he trusted no one but House to represent him. The United States' share in making Allied policy in Russia in 1917–19 was important, but no more conclusive than that of others.[31]

The United States' entry into the war was greeted with great enthusiasm in the Allied countries, and with much rhetoric about shared ideals. The British and French governments immediately sent missions headed by eminent persons (Balfour and René Viviani) to, it was hoped, inspire the war effort of the new associate. What the Allied governments most wanted in the immediate term was money and shipping, both naval and merchant. On 3 April the Chancellor of the Exchequer told the Imperial War Cabinet that Britain was effectively at the end of her resources. 'Nothing that day had pleased him more than the news from America and the relief which we might expect to receive from that country.'[32] Financial relief was neither immediate nor straightforward. Balfour's financial mission was only partially successful. Funds were provided for May, and, after a last-minute appeal, for June; but there was no agreement on a longer-term schedule. The problems were various. The United States Treasury had difficulty in understanding the enormous sums Britain said she needed, the complex relationships between British and Allied finances, and the importance of the exchange. McAdoo, the Secretary of the Treasury and Wilson's son-in-law, knew that he would have to convince a suspicious Congress that he was not handing over American money without proper safeguards, and himself wanted to keep a voice in the way the Allies used credits given to them. The Treasury was not sure that it would be able to raise enough money for all its purposes by Liberty Loans. McAdoo complained of lack of information, and was indeed truly ignorant of British war finances and the extent to which Britain was supporting the Allies. He telegraphed to Balfour on 12 July that the United States could not take on the whole burden of financing the war but could only supplement Allied resources. In order that that should be done effectively, the governments seeking loans should disclose their financial resources frankly.[33]

Realizing the danger of allowing the United States Treasury to remain uninformed, Bonar Law, the Chancellor of the Exchequer, replied spelling out the fact that far from the United States assuming the entire burden of financing the war, even since 1 April 'financial assistance afforded to the other Allies by the United Kingdom has been *more than double* the assistance afforded them by the United States, and ... much exceeds the assistance she has herself received from the United States.' Britain was, moreover, supporting Allied expenditure all over the world whereas United States help was limited to expenditure in America. Bonar Law went into considerable detail about how the £5000 million expended on the war so far had been raised and spent, especially the expenditure in the United States, and concluded: 'In short our resources available for payments in America are exhausted. Unless the United States government can meet in full our expenses in the United States, including exchange, the whole financial fabric of the Alliance will collapse. This conclusion will be a matter not of months but of days.'[34] After this things improved. At the end of August Lord Reading was sent out with power to deal with all financial questions. He established a better relationship with McAdoo, who promised agreed monthly advances. Reading returned to the United States as ambassador and high commissioner in the spring of 1918, but he was not there the whole time, and the concessions he thought it necessary to make to secure McAdoo's goodwill were not always appreciated in London. On one occasion a message drafted (but not sent) expressed the Treasury's feelings: 'It almost looks as if they took a satisfaction in reducing us to a position of complete financial helplessness and dependence ... I resent also their habit of refusing all understandings in writing and telling us to accept vague oral assurances.'[35]

Certain negotiations in 1918 showed that the hope of American generosity was not misplaced; but both sides now knew where the financial power lay, and the United States Treasury was quite ready to use it. A long-term strategy was, however, not apparent. The prospect of the dollar replacing the pound as the international means of exchange was canvassed in the press. Wilson told House that he expected to use American financial power after the war to force Britain and France to his way of thinking.[36] When the time came, however, finance did not give Wilson the leverage he hoped for.

Shipbuilding provides illustrations of the mixed feelings generated in Britain by growing American power. In view of the shipping losses in the submarine campaign of 1917, one of the tasks of Balfour's mission to the United States was to encourage American shipbuilding and the direction of American shipping into Allied trade. In this the mission was almost wholly unsuccessful. The American shipbuilding programme did not reach full strength until the middle of 1918. Another of Balfour's objectives was to urge the building of destroyers and auxiliary craft for anti-submarine warfare, rather than the capital ships provided for in the bill of 1916. This led House to suggest that Britain should give the United States an option on some of her capital ships in case of trouble with Japan at the end of the war. Balfour was taken with the idea of a mutual commitment; but in London it immediately raised the question of the Anglo-Japanese alliance and the dilemma that was to persist as long as the alliance lasted: how to increase cooperation with the United States while remaining faithful to Japan? Whilst British and Japanese interests in the Far East had increasingly diverged since 1911, when the alliance had last been renewed, there were many objections to letting Japan go. There was also some doubt whether the United States Senate would ratify a naval alliance, and whether the battleships were needed even against Japan. On the other hand the broad strategic and political advantages of such an alliance with the United States were enormous, and it was important not to rebuff an American suggestion. One suggested solution was a tripartite defensive alliance; another, telegraphed to Balfour, was to suggest to the

Americans that they could safely give up battleship building at present, because British public opinion would certainly insist on going to the help of the United States if she were attacked by Japan.[37]

On his return to London, Balfour told the War Cabinet that, so far as he was aware, the only reason why the United States Navy Department was reluctant to divert all its energies into building destroyers and anti-submarine vessels was its fear of being left at the end of the war with a much smaller fleet of capital ships than it had intended, and faced by a still-powerful German fleet and a Japanese fleet with no potential enemy. Balfour suggested that for four years, the time it took to build a capital ship, 'America should have a right to call other Fleets to her assistance, in case of maritime attack.' A simple treaty of mutual maritime defence between the United States and Britain alone would meet the problem, 'and I confess that, for reasons of high policy, there is nothing I should like more than a defensive alliance with America, even for four years, as would be capable of extension and development, should circumstances prove auspicious.' Balfour did not think that such an agreement would, strictly, be incompatible with the Anglo-Japanese alliance since both would be defensive. But to avoid the danger of 'unpleasant feelings' an attempt should be made to associate Japan and the European allies with the new arrangement. Balfour suggested a formula by which the United States and the Allied governments would undertake to assist each other against maritime attack for a period of four years after the conclusion of the present war.[38]

Sending this proposal to House to be passed to Wilson, Balfour said the Cabinet was 'much attracted by the idea of any defensive arrangement with the United States', and 'clear that with or without a guarantee, popular opinion in this country would undoubtedly force us to go to the assistance of the United States of America if she were attacked by Japan'. Whilst a private assurance of this kind would not be enough to allow the American government to forego the building of capital ships, the main difficulty of an Anglo-American arrangement was that the Japanese would regard it as directed against them, and might throw themselves into German arms. The formula was devised to obviate this danger. If the President liked it, Balfour would do his best to bring it to fruition. If not, he would try to find some acceptable alternative.[39]

But the whole idea of a naval arrangement was a personal one of House's, the product of his fear of Japan and desire for closer Anglo-American relations, and had not been discussed with the President. The latter told Sir William Wiseman, House's British confidant, that he was quite ready to ask Congress for money for building destroyers, and to delay the capital ships about whose value he was in any case doubtful; but he could not alter the 1916 programme without Congressional approval. As for a naval alliance, he thought the Allies had already made to each other undertakings which it would be difficult to carry out after the war, and he did not favour adding to them. Moreover, whilst the United States was now ready to take her place as a world power, the strong feeling in the country was to play a lone hand and not form any alliances.[40] The matter was not pursued farther. In July American capital shipbuilding was in fact postponed for the duration of the war, and a large destroyer programme adopted. This, however, did not come up to expectations, and in the summer of 1918 the Admiralty became worried at the implications of the American merchant shipbuilding programme at a time when British shipyards were heavily engaged in naval building and repairs – including repairs for the US navy.[41]

In the summer of 1917, House held out to Wiseman the prospect that Wilson wished 'to work closely with us when it came to a discussion of terms of peace. Indeed, he contemplated a state of things in which we should consult privately as to what terms of peace we propose to insist upon, and then go into the Council and back one another up.' Lord Robert Cecil, the Minister of Blockade, welcomed the possibility:

> But there seems to me to be more at stake even than cooperation in the terms of peace. The United States are entering upon an entirely fresh chapter of their history. For the first time they are taking a part in international European affairs; they will soon begin to realize what vast power they have; and, unless they are very different from any other nation that has ever existed, they will wish to make use of that power. If they make use of it rightly, it may be of incalculable

benefit to the human race; and by rightly I mean in accordance with our ideas of right and justice. There is undoubtedly a difference between the British and the continental
point of view in international matters . . . If America accepts
our point of view in these matters, it will mean the dominance of that point of view in all international affairs.[42]

What House said about international cooperation, however,
represented much more his personal views than those of Wilson.
The latter told William Howard Taft, the former president and
a leading figure in the League to Enforce Peace, that he doubted
the desirability of drawing the United States and Britain too
closely together. There were 'divergences of purpose and . . .
the United States must not be put in a position of seeming, in
any way, involved in British policy . . . He intimated that the
motives of the United States were unselfish while those of the
British Empire . . . seemed of a less worthy character.'[43] Wilson
resisted all British attempts to discuss the form of a League of
Nations, preferring to keep a free hand until the peace conference.

Among unworthy motives Wilson certainly classed those of
British trade policy. In Britain in the summer of 1918 there
was a recrudescence of talk about an economic alliance against
Germany after the war, and demands for imperial preference.
Speeches by Lloyd George and Bonar Law seemed to endorse
demands for punitive economic peace terms and permanent
Allied control of raw materials. Wilson, to his aides, accused
the British of trying to gain every economic advantage within
reach, and aiming to dominate everything. He got Wiseman to
telegraph to Reading that he had thought the Paris Resolutions had been abandoned and he was convinced it was a great
mistake to threaten Germany now with punitive postwar measures against her trade. 'It is true that the Allies will come to
the Peace Conference practically controlling the supply of the
world's raw materials, but there will be no need to advertise
that fact or threaten anyone. Everyone – especially the Germans – will be quite aware of the fact.' Wiseman went on:

For your own private information, I may tell you that the
President will try to get Congress to give powers to the Executive to control American raw-material exports for a period

of years after peace. While this would not be openly aimed at Germany, it would be a formidable weapon for the United States to bring to peace Conference.

And if that warning was not enough, Wiseman concluded with one from House: if the Allies again advocated a punitive trade policy towards Germany, the President would be obliged to dissociate the United States from it.[44]

Wilson was convinced that the United States did not intend to 'seek any unfair advantage of any kind or to shoulder anybody out, but merely to give the widest possible currency to our own goods', whereas Britain did have such aims; but he suggested to Edward Hurley, chairman of the Shipping Board, that it would be better not to talk too much about the advantage the United States expected to enjoy in the world carrying trade after the war, lest any colour of excuse be given to the British for what they were doing.[45] Hurley had been telling American manufacturers that the United States merchant marine was going to be the largest in the world, and it was up to them to find work for those ships to develop American and world trade. Hurley shared Wilson's belief in the utter purity of American intentions and the selfishness of all others. He had been trying to interest Bernard Baruch, the chairman of the War Industries Board, in investing in overseas sources of raw materials, such as Brazilian manganese, Bolivian tin, or New Caledonian chrome, in order to control supplies. 'The question as to what nation will control the raw materials of the world is uppermost in Europe', he wrote:

> Whatever nation does control them (unless it be America) will make the other nations pay a heavy toll. Great power may be used either for good or for evil. If possessed by the United States we may be sure it will be used for good... America would then be in a position to say to the rest of the world that these commodities would be sold at a fair price... and each nation would receive its share... To my mind, we are the only nation that has taken a completely unselfish position in the war.[46]

Indications of Administration coldness were now sufficiently numerous to prompt Reading to ask Wiseman whether United States policy had changed. Wiseman, after consulting House, replied that it had not, and Wilson was not anti-British. But, Wiseman added:

> I must admit our most practical difficulty is the attitude of the President himself. During his week's holiday at Magnolia, I saw a great deal of him, and, while I do not alter my own affectionate admiration for him, I realize that he is a most difficult person to deal with as head of the government. His attitude lately has tended to become more arbitrary and aloof, and there are times when he seems to treat foreign governments hardly seriously . . . I do not think we are singled out more than any other government.[47]

On 5 October 1918 the German government addressed to Wilson a request for an armistice leading to a peace based on the Fourteen Points. During the ensuing discussions the British became increasingly worried about one of those Points: freedom of the seas. They had feared in 1915 that the concept meant the destruction of British sea power. American belligerency had removed the subject from discussion, but had not clarified its meaning. Now it became alive again. British ministers, discussing on 13 October with their military advisers whether an armistice was desirable, heard the First Sea Lord, Sir Rosslyn Wemyss, assert that freedom of the seas was directed absolutely against the Royal Navy and could not be accepted. Balfour suggested that Wilson was looking at the question entirely in the context of the League of Nations, and had never advocated abolition of blockade; but Wemyss continued to argue that if Britain surrendered to any combination of nations the right to decide questions of such vital interest, 'we should give up by a stroke of the pen the sea power we have for centuries maintained and have never yet misused. On this basis the British Empire has been founded, and on no other can it be upheld.'[48]

Soundings in Washington suggested that Wilson seemed to be thinking along the lines of using British naval power in some way in connection with the League of Nations, so that it would cease to be a cause of international jealousy. He said to Wiseman that the British navy had in the past acted as a sort

of naval police for the world, and that he personally would be
willing to leave the power to the discretion of the British people,
who had never abused it. But other countries might be less
willing. Many nations chafed under the feeling that their maritime trade proceeded only by the permission of the British
navy: he had always thought that the most deeply-rooted cause
of the war had been the German jealousy and fear of the British navy, an unjust feeling but none the less real.[49]

On 23 October Wilson sent to the Allies his correspondence
with the Germans and asked whether they were willing to accept an armistice leading to a peace based on the Fourteen
Points. It was then agreed to hold a conference in Paris, with
American participation, to settle the armistice terms. The War
Cabinet agreed that whilst reservations on some of the Fourteen Points could be postponed until later, freedom of the
seas must be repudiated at once. Therefore when House arrived in London on his way to Paris a considerable tussle began. Lloyd George gave House a memorandum accepting the
Fourteen Points in principle, provided that freedom of the seas
was set aside. House replied that the United States would not
allow Britain to dominate the seas and determine the conditions on which American ships might sail them, and threatened a naval race unless Lloyd George changed his attitude.
He advised Wilson to slow down the transport of American
troops and start cutting down supplies. Wilson then instructed
House to tell the Allies that he would not take part in the
negotiation of a peace that did not include freedom of the
seas – 'because we are pledged to fight not only to do away
with Prussian militarism but with militarism everywhere' – and
to repeat the threat to outbuild the British navy. Finally House
accepted a letter from Lloyd George agreeing to the 'freest
discussion' of freedom of the seas at the peace conference but
refusing to concede the principle.[50]

The approaching end of the war thus raised questions about
future Anglo-American relations. The voices of those who believed in continuing cooperation were joined, and occasionally drowned, by those expressing suspicion and fear. Among
the former was still Wiseman who, shortly after his last inter-
view with Wilson, sent advice on the American attitude to the
coming peace conference. So far as the American people were

concerned, he wrote, it was important that they should not come to believe that the British Empire was the chief obstacle to a peaceful world. A consciousness was growing that after the war the British Empire and the United States would be the only remaining great powers: much of the friction arose from questions as to which would be the greater. Wilson was absolutely committed to the League of Nations. In this he was probably ahead of the general public; but the Allies had to deal with him rather than with his opponents, and would have to go on dealing with him at least until 1920. It was not easy to suggest remedies for the predictable difficulties; but in general British policy should be guided by a spirit of great patience, and co-operation was not impossible, for 'in spite of jealousy and misunderstanding, the British and American peoples believe in the same things and follow the same ideals'.[51]

Which would be the greater power might be affected by the date when the war ended. It seemed clear to General Smuts, the South African Prime Minister, that an early end to the war would be greatly in Britain's interest because she was now at the height of her power whereas with every month that the war continued the power of the United States increased. In another year, Smuts wrote:

the United States will have taken our place as the first military, diplomatic and financial power of the world. She will have the largest armies, as already she has the greatest financial and industrial resources, she will have the largest mercantile marine, and she will be the diplomatic dictator of the world. A new centre of gravity will have been given to the great system of Western civilization with results for the world and the British Empire which no man can foresee.[52]

Wilson and his advisers seem rather to have thought that continued military victory would make the Allies greedier, and that American influence would be greater in an early peace conference.[53] Wilson was determined to keep up the development of American naval power, and approved a new naval appropriation bill, sent to Congress after the armistice, providing for a fresh three-year programme on top of the completion of the 1916 one. He was, however, made aware of British and Allied sensitivities, and on his arrival in Paris gave the British ambassador, Lord Derby, to understand that when he came to England after Christmas he would be reassuring on maritime questions.[54]

This proved to be the case. Wilson, in his talks with Lloyd George and Balfour, concentrated on the League, making it clear that its creation was essential to American cooperation in the peace-making. He was generally more accommodating than British ministers had expected on other matters, including freedom of the seas; and Lloyd George, reporting to the War Cabinet, stressed the areas of agreement. But his report set off an anti-Wilson chorus, led by W.M. Hughes, the Australian Prime Minister, who objected to Wilson's position on the colonial settlement and on indemnities, and who saw no need or reason for the British Empire, with its immense power, to cooperate with the United States. After some time of this, Reading protested that it would be 'lamentable' if the impression were conveyed that Wilson and Lloyd George were sharply divided. Britain would not, indeed, abandon her claims without fighting for them, but he hoped they would also not lightly abandon 'the position that consistently with our rights, our main object was to bring about the closest cooperation hereafter between ourselves and the United States.' Robert Borden, the Canadian Prime Minister, protested that good relations with the United States were the best gain the Empire could make from the war, and he made it clear that Canada would not agree to working 'with some European nation as against the United States'. Cecil stressed that Britain's chief interest was to secure a settled peace, and the best guarantee for that was a good understanding with the United States. At the end of the discussion Lloyd George summed up: he was hopeful that Wilson, provided he could secure the League of Nations, would eventually agree to things that Britain regarded as important. But if he proved obstinate, Britain and France would be entitled by their contributions to winning the war to have a final say.[55]

Neither Britain nor the United States approached the peace conference, which opened in Paris on 18 January 1919, with a detailed programme.[56] The general principles of the settlement and some of the detailed provisions had supposedly been laid down in the American note to Germany of 5 November, incorporating an Allied acceptance of the Fourteen Points with reservations on freedom of the seas and on reparations. But the aspirations of the Americans, the British, the French and the other European Allies were clearly very different. On some aspects the Allies were bound by wartime agreements between themselves; the Fourteen Points were mostly general and ambiguous; the details were highly complex; and the problem of Russia threatened, by introducing social upheaval, to vitiate any settlement that was reached. Despite all attempts at coordination, the structure of the conference was confusing. The individual delegations found it difficult to hold together their own policy on the multitude of territorial and other details. The British delegation was not badly organized, but official thinking and aims had largely been concerned with non-European matters; members of the delegation frequently complained of lack of leadership and decision, and of not knowing what was going on. The American delegation seldom met as a body; three of the five commissioners hardly ever saw Wilson and House; and House himself, while trying to run the delegation, lost influence with Wilson.[57] Wilson was not able to do everything and had not intended to try. He arrived in Paris with the prime aim of getting the League of Nations adopted. Once it was settled, he thought, 'nearly all the very serious difficulties will disappear'; a sufficient sense of security would be created to allow extreme Allied claims to be whittled down, and he would act as arbiter, relying on American disinterestedness, the support of the European peoples, economic power, and in the last resort American military strength.[58] It may be said that in a sense the war ended too soon for the achievement of Wilson's objectives, since American strength was not as fully developed as it would have been a year later. But its implications were already clear, and it is not obvious that Wilson could have used it more effectively later. He succeeded in getting the Covenant of the League of Nations placed first on the peace conference agenda and incorporated as the first part of all the peace treaties. This was not an unmixed advantage. The Allies, and Wilson's domestic opponents, would be committed to the League; but it could not be set up until the rest of the peace terms had been settled. The prospect of the League did not create sufficiently quickly the sense of security that would enable the Allies' claims to be moderated. Here the Americans were obliged to compromise, to subsequent liberal disillusionment. The support of European public opinion was already called into question by the outcome of the general election in Britain in December, and Wilson's one attempt to appeal to an Allied people over the head of its government, in the case of Italy, was a disaster. Economic and financial power were used to stabilize conditions in central Europe and stem the tide of revolution; but they were not used effectively with the Allies. Wilson did, however, use naval power against Britain in one instance.

The first peace conference commission to produce results was that on the League of Nations, presided over by Wilson: its draft covenant was accepted in a plenary conference session and published on 14 February. It was largely an Anglo-American production. As soon as it was completed Wilson left for home, to confront his critics and defend his work. Opposition to the League in the United States was now strong and vocal, and seemed likely to command enough votes in the Senate to make ratification impossible. Wilson reacted by stressing the links between the Covenant and the peace treaty, which would make it impossible to remove the one without destroying the other – and whatever else the Senate had rejected in the past, it had never yet refused to ratify a treaty of peace. But Wilson reluctantly felt obliged to heed advice from Senator Hitchcock, the acting Democratic Senate leader and until recently chairman of the Foreign Relations Committee, and from ex-president Taft, the leading Republican supporter of the League, that some amendments, notably to reserve the Monroe doctrine, would win over moderate opposition. Most of the changes recommended by Hitchcock and Taft were accepted by the League of Nations Commission by 26 March, and the Monroe doctrine was under discussion. But Wilson's vulnerability on the amendments gave Lloyd George the opportunity to attempt a bargain on naval building.

It is not altogether clear why Lloyd George chose this subject for bargaining. The threat of freedom of the seas had receded: Wilson accepted that under the League of Nations as now conceived there would be no neutrals whose freedom to trade must not be curtailed. There was no agitation in Britain. The new American naval programme was a cause of some puzzlement, but there were no cries of alarm and the thought of Anglo-American competition was expressly disclaimed. Even Walter Long, the Conservative First Lord and spokesman for an Admiralty determined to uphold the principle of British supremacy, spoke only of a general anxiety that the navy might be let down.[59] The government had not begun to discuss post-war estimates or fiscal policy. Lloyd George had not hitherto been regarded as a navalist. On the American position there had been suggestions after the armistice, from Americans in London, that a British declaration that the naval standard applied only to European powers would bring about an immediate reduction in the new programme.[60] But all the evidence was that the Americans were determined on naval equality, at least, with Britain. In January 1919, according to the Admiralty's figures, Britain had 42 capital ships in service as against the United States' 16. The Admiralty expected the current United States programme to bring virtual numerical equality by 1923–4, and qualitative American superiority since a number of Britain's ships would be obsolescent and all the American ones would be modern. What Lloyd George attempted was not merely to obviate future expenditure but, in the words of the retiring British commander-in-chief in the West Indies, to ask the United States 'to trust us and sink their national pride, which demands that the naval forces at disposal should be equally divided between us'.[61] This was a tall order, and Lloyd George's tactics were not well suited to fulfilling it.

The American navy, for its part, was not seriously thinking of war with Britain, but believed in a general way that trade rivalry was the root cause of international conflict, that peace would bring Anglo-American trade rivalry, and that just as Britain had in the past defeated by naval power the challenges of Spain, the Netherlands, France and Germany, so she would attempt to meet the challenge of 'a fifth commercial power, the greatest one yet'. To this Mahanist doctrine was added the argument, intended no doubt to appeal to Wilson, that it was not in the interest of humanity that Britain should 'occupy so commanding a naval position that she may regulate the high seas throughout the world in accordance with her will'. The United States could be relied upon to support the League of Nations loyally; but 'if the condition of inequality of naval strength is to continue the League of Nations, instead of being what we are striving for and most earnestly hope for, will be a stronger British Empire.' Britain now had no European naval rival; in future every ship she built or acquired could have in mind only the American fleet.[62]

In the last ten days of March the peace conference reached a crisis, with French aims for the Rhineland and the Saar being strongly opposed by the British and Americans, with the Allies and the Americans sharply divided over reparations, and with chaos looming in central and eastern Europe. Faced with these problems Lloyd George and his chief advisers went off to Fontainebleau for the weekend to rethink British aims and tactics. The outcome was a memorandum addressed to the other members of the Council of Four, with as its main theme a warning, directed at France, that a vindictive treaty might drive Germany into the arms of Russia with dire consequences for the whole of Europe. To prevent this Lloyd George advocated a liberal peace which Germany could accept: all the concessions would be made in Europe. A second theme was addressed to Wilson. Lloyd George stressed the importance of the League of Nations as the effective guardian of international right and liberty. Until Germany had settled down and Russia had shown that she did not intend to embark on a military crusade against her neighbours, the leading members of the League would have to keep up their forces by land and sea; but they must also arrive at such an agreement among themselves as would prevent suspicion arising between them:

> The first condition of success for the League of Nations is . . . a firm understanding between the British Empire and the United States and France and Italy that there will be no competitive building up of fleets or armies between them. Unless this is arrived at before the Covenant is signed the League of Nations will be a sham and a mockery.[63]

To back this Lloyd George summoned Long and Wemyss to Paris to talk to their American opposite numbers, Josephus Daniels and Admiral Benson, telling Cecil that he was objecting to the Monroe doctrine amendment to the Covenant as a bargaining device to induce the Americans to stop their naval programme.[64] Long and Wemyss got nowhere with Daniels and Benson: the two admirals even indulged in a shouting match. Having reached this impasse Lloyd George turned the matter over to Cecil to discuss with House. Cecil began by pointing out the anxiety caused by American talk of a navy equal to or stronger than Britain's. Cecil himself, he said, believed passionately in Anglo-American friendship, but if he were a minister and saw Britain's naval safety being threatened, even by the United States, he would have to recommend increased spending. Would it be possible, he asked, for the Americans to say that when the peace treaty was signed, with the Covenant, they would abandon or modify their new naval programme? If furthermore they could intimate that the two governments would consult in future on their programmes and 'the British sentiment on the matter would not be disregarded', the present anxieties would be completely removed. House replied with a bland assurance that if the kind of peace were made for which they were working and which included the League of Nations, he was sure the British would find the United States ready to abandon the new naval programme (which had not yet been approved by Congress) and to discuss programmes in future. House refused to give an undertaking also on those ships in the 1916 programme that were not yet built. He then agreed with Cecil a memorandum to be given to Lloyd George, assuring him that 'there was no idea in the President's mind of building a fleet in competition with that of Great Britain', that Britain might fully rely on this assurance, and that conversations might begin as soon as the peace treaty was signed.[65] With this Lloyd George had to be content. He withdrew his refusal to countenance a reservation on the Monroe doctrine in the Covenant, and with Cecil's support it was adopted on 11 April.

One important factor in the naval question was the knowledge on both sides that if the United States chose to do so she had the resources to outbuild Britain. Although there might be doubt about future American political will, or the willingness of enough Americans to man a very large navy, the capability was a fact of financial and industrial strength. But this strength was not used to the greatest possible effect at the peace conference. As far as relief was concerned, American officials were ready and anxious to use their country's resources to good effect, relieving hunger, preventing the spread of revolution, and keeping up prices to American farmers. The chief mover in the effort was Herbert Hoover, who had been Director of Relief in Belgium and Food Administrator, and was now appointed Director General of Relief. Hoover was determined to avoid any international control over American supplies: by retaining complete independence of action, he reckoned, the United States would be able to 'confer favours instead of complying with agreements', and would be able to secure 'justice in distribution, proper appreciation . . . of the effort we make . . . and proper return for the service we will perform'.[66]

On longer-term plans for reconstruction, British and Allied ideas conflicted with American conceptions. The French in particular wished to secure preferential treatment for rebuilding their country, and the British agreed that Allied reconstruction should have priority over the return of Germany to international equality. The Americans, on the other hand, pinned their faith to the 'open door', complete equality of access to all markets, as the best way to ensure American prosperity and the leadership of an expanding world economy.[67] They suspected Britain and the continental Allies of trying to continue a policy of economic blocs and discrimination. They were extremely wary of all proposals for cooperation in a comprehensive policy on reconstruction, fearful of European attempts to lock the United States into the problems of the continent, and determined to prevent the formation of a European bloc. Thus they rejected out of hand a scheme, produced by Keynes in the middle of April, for rehabilitating European credit and financing relief and reconstruction, by the issue of bonds – mainly by Germany – guaranteed in the last resort by Allied governments.[68] This rejection did not mean that the Americans were not conscious that their country must have a considerable role in reconstructing Europe. Wilson asked his advisers for suggestions 'on American lines'; but it was difficult to think of comprehensive solutions. The Treasury's authority was strictly limited, and in view of the attitude of public opinion Congress was most unlikely to extend it. It had itself no idea of discussing Allied debts comprehensively. Private credit for reconstruction was forecast, but the prospect of future governmental credits was poor. It was impossible to think of a way of helping Germany that would not also help the Allies to extract reparations. Wilson's advisers in Paris hoped that when he returned home he would launch a campaign to educate public opinion about European reconstruction; but in the event the struggle for the peace treaty drove all other considerations into the background.

The quantity of reparations to be obtained from Germany affected a wide range of problems at Paris. British policy on reparations was directed towards securing the greatest possible share, for the United Kingdom and the Empire which had suffered little physical damage but heavy costs that would weigh upon the national finances for years to come. The concern was mostly about domestic taxation and the national debt. So far as external factors were concerned, Lloyd George and Bonar Law were aware that a large German indemnity would be bad for British trade: since Germany had little gold, she would be able to pay only by greatly expanding her export trade. But the size of the national debt also affected Britain's international standing: it was agreed that drastic reduction of government indebtedness was necessary to allow a return to the gold standard, and that was necessary for Britain's position as an international financial centre and her general commercial status in the eyes of the world. That the burden of the national debt was a handicap to Britain in competition with the United States, now 'the great menace to the trade of the British Empire,' so that 'if there are to be no indemnities it is impossible to say that in course of time British trade may not be completely ruined by American competition,' was emphasized by the committee set up by the Imperial War Cabinet on 26 November to investigate the amount of indemnity which could be extracted from Germany, and how it could be paid.[69]

The tactic adopted by the British at Paris was to widen the claim for war costs in order to secure a larger British share without apparently reducing France's claim for repairing physical damage. This tactic, and the decision to leave the total of reparations to be fixed later, concealed the discrepancies in the British position and allowed concealment of the probability that popular expectations would not be realized. The American position, although more responsible, was not less self-interested. The

United States claimed no reparations, and in consequence claimed moral advantage or at least disinterested objectivity. The United States had suffered no damage on land and had incurred only 3 per cent of total Allied shipping losses. According to an American estimate of May 1919, the per capita war-created public debt plus damages to public wealth amounted to 11.5 per cent of the national wealth in 1919. This was less than the debt of any of the Allies except Japan: France's figure was 94.1 per cent, Britain's 59.4 per cent. There was thus virtually nothing to set against the direct American interest in an early revival of trade with Germany and the indirect interest in a general trade expansion without restrictions. But American methods were not effective. By insisting on complete independence of action, declining to join any cooperative reconstruction efforts, refusing to consider adjusting Allied debts, and abandoning most forms of government action, Wilson and his advisers threw away the means they could have used to induce the Allies to frame far-sighted reparation terms. The peace settlement was bound to reflect compromises between the claims and interests of the major Allies and their conceptions of a just and lasting peace. Wilson had supposed in July 1917 that when the war was over it would be possible to 'force' Britain and France 'to our way of thinking because by that time they will, among other things, be financially in our hands'.[70] But the Allied debts were too big a weapon to be used in this way; and Wilson's inability to offer any rewards for good behaviour ensured that he could not bring American power to bear as effectively as might have been possible.

3
Finding a New Balance: Naval and Other Problems in the 1920s

At the end of the First World War the power of the United States in the world was greatly enhanced, both absolutely and relative to the major European countries. Woodrow Wilson intended to use this power to promote the causes of liberal democracy and an open world trading system, to the good of the the United States and of humanity. His political opponents, and the American people, were less ambitious. To many of them, participation in the war soon seemed to have been a mistake, its results profoundly disappointing. The Republican administration in the early 1920s avoided participation in international political bodies, conducting relations largely on an *ad hoc* and bilateral footing, and finding it hard to adapt to the country's new position as a great creditor. The United States now had enormous weight in the world economy; but financial and commercial policy were governed by domestic considerations and were not well suited to the new position. A consistently favourable balance of trade and payments was compensated for not by increased imports (instead the tariff was raised) but by loans. In both political and economic terms American power was exercised in a hesitant and sometimes contradictory manner.

Britain's position was ambiguous in a different way. Her imperial responsibilities were at their greatest geographical extent. She saw herself, and was seen, as a great world power: the outcome of the war enhanced confidence in national and imperial greatness. But she had lost financial resources and trade, and although at first she expected to make good the losses, the process of relative economic decline continued. It was the empire that made Britain a great world power. In the

70

1920s India was still safe, the disparate colonial empire untouched. For the Dominions, the war hastened the growth of their consciousness of statehood, which was expressed in their individual signatures on the peace treaties and individual membership of the League of Nations. In 1921 Lloyd George could still talk of the Empire as a united power and refer to joint control of and responsibility for policy, which would give Britain 'the shoulders of the young giants to help us along'. That joint control and responsibility were no more than a fiction, and that some of the Dominions wanted neither, was demonstrated only a year later in the Chanak crisis; and in 1926 the Imperial Conference recognized the opposite principle of separate responsibility, combined with a special mutual responsibility symbolized by the Crown. If the new Commonwealth relationship offered any basis for a serious power structure (which is doubtful) the policies followed by several Dominions thereafter ensured that it could not be built.[1] What this would mean in the conduct of international relations and in terms of international power remained to be seen. Some historians have taken 1919, or 1921, as the date when the balance of world power tipped irretrievably against Britain and in favour of the United States. But the course of world affairs in the 1920s left room for doubt, and whilst the decade saw something of a struggle for supremacy between the two countries in particular fields, the outcome was not clear cut.[2]

In the interwar period there were, among the British policy-making élite and educated opinion in general, three broad approaches to the problem of maintaining international peace and Britain's position in the world – the first being the necessary precondition for the second. The approaches have been labelled Atlanticism, imperial isolationism, and world leadership.[3] Atlanticists regarded Anglo-American cooperation as the key to peace and security, and regarded the United States as Britain's natural-born ally. Despite frequent disappointments when the United States demonstrated unwillingness to cooperate in the new world order, and refused to see world problems from a British perspective, Atlanticists remained optimistic about an essential unity of interests. But their influence was more marked outside government than at the centre of policy-making.[4] Imperial isolationists advocated concentration on developing the empire as the basis of Britain's power, and regarded extra-imperial commitments as a distraction or a source of danger. Adherents of this view were to be found in the Colonial and Dominions Offices, the Admiralty, at the centre of government in the person of Maurice Hankey, the Cabinet Secretary, and among certain intellectual groups. The adherents of world leadership regarded active participation in world politics as the best way of preserving Britain's position. They attached greater importance than did the other groups to Europe, and regarded the United States as one power among others, not to be disregarded but not always at the centre of consideration. Men of this outlook were especially numerous in the Foreign Office and among those with European or League of Nations interests. For much of the time the conduct of British policy was in their hands. The groupings were not hard and fast, and the outlooks were not mutually exclusive. 'World leadership' supporters pursued Anglo-American cooperation where it was possible; some imperial isolationists believed in Anglo-Saxonism; Atlanticists became involved in European problems. Nevertheless the categories are useful as indicators of different orders of priority among those who made, executed, and wrote about Britain's external policy.

The first great blow to Atlanticism was the United States' rejection of the League of Nations. After a bitter political struggle the Senate in March 1920 defeated ratification of the Covenant both with and without substantial reservations. The President and his followers made the League the issue of the 1920 presidential election, and were defeated. In the campaign the Republican line was confused and confusing, but afterwards the president-elect, Harding, announced that the issue was closed, and so it remained. Republican suggestions that the United States would take the lead in forming an 'effective' international organization soon ceased. So afraid was the State Department of being accused of trafficking with the League of Nations that it refused at first even to acknowledge letters from Geneva. Not until late 1922 were unofficial observers appointed to League humanitarian organs.[5]

Down to the time of the final Senate votes the British official position had to be cautious. Grey, sent to the United States in the autumn of 1919 as ambassador extraordinary on a special mission, was instructed to do his utmost to convince the American government that Britain was determined to support the League and its ideals, and hoped for United States cooperation.[6] But the prospect of American reservations raised questions of Britain's attitude to the League if the United States did not join, or tried to do so on special terms. Some advisers concluded that the difficulties would be so great that Britain would have to consider giving notice of withdrawal from the League unless the Covenant were revised. But the government was under pressure from pro-League forces at home to proceed with setting up the organization; and Wilson was making it plain that he would not submit the Senate's reservations to the Allies. Lloyd George assured the House of Commons that, serious though the position would be if the United States did not join as an equal member, the government was convinced that the League must go on.[7] Grey, despairing of his mission given the circumstances in Washington and unable to express his own views while he was ambassador, decided to return home. There he continued his efforts to make the American point of view understood, arguing, in a long letter to *The Times*, that United States membership of the League was vital and the reservations would make little difference to its working.[8] But nothing that foreigners said could affect the decisions in Washington. The League was duly set up without changes to the Covenant, and during the 1920s it became accepted as an important part of the international order. British public opinion on the whole favoured the League. British governments did not publicly question the obligations of the Covenant but had private doubts about the feasibility of applying Article 16. They were unwilling to make the obligations more automatic, turning down in 1924 and 1925 proposals in this direction.[9] The absence of the United States from the League was a factor in the British hesitations, but not the only one.

Until the autumn of 1920 Atlanticist writers in Britain were able to assert their faith in Anglo-American unity, their belief in American intentions, and their willingness to accept any amendments to the Covenant that would enable the United States to join.[10] A few voices on the other side of the Atlantic could still be heard expressing a belief that Anglo-Saxon unity was a fact and that Britain positively desired to share the burden of world leadership; but evidence of mutual jealousy increased and became worrying.[11] In 1921 there was even talk of the possibility of war and its causes – Ireland, the Anglo-Japanese alliance, naval competition, trade rivalry. Between April and June 1921 the *Nation* ran a series of articles analysing the causes of Anglo-American differences and concluding that the most important remedy was a solution of the Irish problem, followed by open diplomacy, personal contacts, free trade and economic democracy. Others suggested that Britain should increase American confidence by dismantling her bases in the western hemisphere, or even give up Canada and the West Indies and surrender her fleet.[12]

One of the chief tasks of Grey's mission to Washington in the autumn of 1919 was to secure conversations on the two countries' naval programmes. Colonel House had encouraged Grey to think that if the British government announced that it was not taking the United States into account in framing its naval estimates, the Americans would drop their 1918 programme.[13] But something more than a tacit ignoring of one another's programmes was important to the British. Hankey, recommending in the summer a continuation of the prewar practice of not taking the United States into account, advised one exception to the rule, 'namely, that . . . our fleet should not be allowed to sink below the level of the United States fleet', because of the risk that 'if we fail to maintain this standard, we might be exposed to unbearable pressure, if a truculent, overbearing and anti-British President should secure election'. The solution seemed to be 'to induce the United States to abate their naval armaments in accord with us'.[14]

Even before Grey left England new service estimates for 1920–1 had to be produced, and there was great pressure for economy in government spending. Leaving on one side an Admiralty request for decisions on policy regarding naval supremacy, the Cabinet on 15 August agreed that no new construction should be undertaken in the next year, and no alteration should be made without Cabinet approval to the prewar standard governing the size of the navy.[15] Interpreted strictly, that decision could eventually have led to inferiority to the United States, but it was not intended as a long-term policy. Six months later, the Cabinet accepted the principle that the navy should not be inferior in strength to the navy of any other power – that is, a one-power standard specifically including the United States.[16] No more than the decision of August 1919 did this reflect a thorough analysis of Britain's maritime needs and position. A one-power standard based on American strength might prove beyond Britain's means: equally it could not ensure victory in a naval war against more than one enemy unless the United States was an ally. The Admiralty's critics, among them Lloyd George and a succession of Chancellors of the Exchequer, argued that Britain had never been able to command all the world's seas: she should now simply ignore the United States or give up protecting certain interests and concede to the United States superiority in her 'special seas'. But such a division of the seas would be precarious without a strategic understanding between the two countries of the kind that Britain had had with Japan and France before the war. Although Beatty, the First Sea Lord, would have liked an 'alliance or entente' with the United States,[17] a formal understanding was precluded by the American tradition. Britain had long since conceded the Caribbean and the approaches to the Panama canal, and the chances of a tacit understanding elsewhere were reduced by the American rejection of the League of Nations and by both countries' naval policies. The problem remained unresolved on the British side, while the Americans began to pursue a policy of naval parity.

The first step was an agreement on capital ship tonnage. Battleships and battle cruisers were still the measure of fleet strength, but they were extremely expensive and some naval and civilian opinion now doubted their usefulness.[18] In the circumstances of Wilson's illness and the struggle over the League of Nations, Anglo-American negotiations over naval limitation could not begin until the new administration took over in March 1921. Soon afterwards Senator Borah of Idaho won support with a call for a conference with Britain and Japan. The main motive was economy. There was no disposition to accept a position of permanent inferiority to Britain, and suspicion of Japan was rife; but voices advocating a two-power standard and calling for discussion on how to wage war with Britain and Japan were partly balanced by others asserting that rivalry with Britain would be 'sheer folly', and Harding himself was said to be groping after Anglo-Saxon cooperation.[19] On 11 July 1921, to preempt a British initiative, he announced his intention of calling a conference.

The outcome of the Washington conference[20] was that Britain accepted American equality in capital ships, and both countries conceded Japan's control of her 'special seas', the north-west Pacific. Britain had not for years been strong enough to defend her interests in the Far East single-handed: that had been the motive for the Anglo-Japanese alliance in the first place. Now she dropped the alliance to appease American and Canadian opinion: a four-power consultative treaty took its place. This was the best available answer to a problem with which officials had been wrestling since the end of the war. On the one hand the United States had become more active in the Far East, interested in the rehabilitation of China and suspicious both of Japanese policy and of the alliance. On the other hand, whilst British and Japanese interests in China often conflicted, an estranged Japan might become a dangerous enemy. Friendship with the United States was of great importance to Britain; but American cooperation could not be relied upon, and without it dropping Japan seemed too much of a risk. The Imperial Conference of 1921 brought into the open strong Canadian opposition to the renewal of the alliance, but did not otherwise alter the dimensions of the problem.[21] The four-power agreement on the whole met the case; and whilst Japan was offended, the American navy continued to regard Japan as the most likely enemy, and the interests and activities of the three countries in China remained divergent, politically they did cooperate for some years.

The results of the Washington conference were greeted with almost universal satisfaction in Britain. Naval writers acknowledged that the two-power standard was a thing of the past. The former First Sea Lord, Wemyss, who had stood for the maintenance of British supremacy, did not find many to share his fear that Britain had given up too much.[22] On the American side there was satisfaction at having taken the initiative and at the Secretary of State, Charles Evans Hughes's domination of the conference. Comment on the outcome was more mixed. The popular view of Britain improved strikingly for a short time: the *Dallas News* even talked of Anglo-American unity. But other commentators were less sanguine about lasting Anglo-American friendship; and the Administration had to rebut charges from the other end that it had entered into some kind of hidden alliance with Britain.[23] Navalist complaints at the amount of tonnage the United States had undertaken to scrap, and accusations that Britain was cheating on the armament of capital ships, became regular occurrences. Within five years it was evident that the Washington treaties had not ended the American challenge to British maritime power.

Meanwhile attention was focused on the political and especially the economic consequences of the war. The United States provided the bulk of relief credits to Europe; and in the first few years after the war most of the capital raised abroad by western and northern European countries was American. There was little American cooperation with others, however, governmental or private. Having at the peace conference refused to enter joint reconstruction plans, Wilson held out to Lloyd George a hope of unselfish American cooperation for the benefit of the world. But in practice his officials deprecated the participation of American bankers in calling an international financial conference in 1920, and declined participation. In the winter of 1921–2 some optimists saw a prospect of the United States joining in an economic conference to follow on the work of the Washington conference. The hopes were unfounded, and when the British government pressed ahead with the plan, the Americans declined the invitation to Genoa.[24]

On reparations, that mountain that stood for years in the way of European recovery and reconciliation, American policy was at first extremely hesitant. The need of France, in particular, for reparation for material damage, was not denied, and German attempts to enlist American support received only cool response. But French policy was regarded as unwise and unlikely to be productive, and since the United States claimed no reparation itself it was able to occupy the moral high ground. On the other hand the idea of, and all attempts to create, a connection between the payment of reparations and of Allied war debts were consistently rejected, so that the means of influencing Allied policy were diminished and some moral credibility was lost. The Secretary of Commerce in Harding's administration, Herbert Hoover, who had been in charge of

Belgian relief during the war and Director-General of Relief after it, was determined to avoid any financial commitments until Europe was ready to accept a 'reasonable' reparation settlement; but since the government was unwilling to intervene directly it could do little but hope that time would produce a change in European attitudes.[25] Since, however, any solution was likely to involve Germany raising a loan, American money was bound to be needed. Eventually convinced of the necessity of doing something to facilitate a solution, Hughes offered, in December 1922, American participation in an expert study of Germany's capacity to pay. After the Franco-Belgian occupation of the Ruhr failed to produce tangible results, Hughes's offer was taken up. It then led to American involvement in the Dawes Plan, loans to Germany, and a whole new scene. In framing the provisional reparation settlement of 1924, United States interests, backed by the government, were fully committed and, in conjunction with the British, were able to impose political terms on France.[26] The settlement ushered in a few years of American investment in Europe, with Germany the chief centre of operations, the main recipient of loans and the main base for industrial cooperation. Little attempt was made to influence German policy, political or economic. The United States government encouraged the Germans on the road to the western European security pact of Locarno, but the initiatives and decisions were taken within a purely European context and a new degree of British commitment.[27] In the financial and economic sphere German governments' policy-making was subject primarily to domestic pressures; such opportunities as existed of using American power to achieve desired ends were eschewed.[28]

In these years also some progress was made in organizing payment of the inter-Allied war debts. In this the key position was occupied by the United States: the British role was only slightly less important. Britain had lent to her Allies the equivalent of some $7014 million and had borrowed from the United States some $4074 million. She was thus a net creditor; but the United States, which had lent overall some $9710 million, had no external debts.[29] Having failed with a suggestion immediately after the armistice that all the inter-Allied debts should be cancelled, and having failed at the peace conference to involve the United States in a scheme for European reconstruction, the British at the end of 1919 began talks with the Americans on postponing interest payments on their own debt. They hoped to use their position as a fellow creditor to induce the Americans to help in the reconstruction of Europe, by a general cancellation or at least by offering lenient terms on interest (from which Britain too would benefit). The Americans talked of cooperation but meant by it getting Britain to offer the continental debtors the same terms as they did, and using the British debt as a lever in bringing about the kind of settlement in Europe that they wanted – including moderate reparations and the abolition of preferences.

The Cabinet also considered cancelling the Allied debts to Britain regardless of American action, but were deterred by the thought that it would not influence American policy and would be unpopular at home. In the talks with the Americans neither side could persuade the other; so the British government prepared to pay interest and the question of funding the principal was put on a back burner.[30] In April 1922 the American government invited its debtors to start funding negotiations. The British government continued to hesitate, hoping for a round-table conference on the whole problem of debts and reparations and European reconstruction. But eventually accepting that funding Britain's debt was necessary, the Cabinet, against most expert advice, decided to send the Allied debtors a note saying that Britain would like to cancel their debts and her share of reparations, but was unable to do so without American action. She would, however, ask them only to pay as much as, with receipts from Germany, would cover the payments she had to make to the United States. Ministers do not appear really to have thought that the Balfour Note would persuade the United States to accept debt cancellation. It appears more to have been a gesture, to demonstrate the unfairness of other countries' expectations that Britain could afford to make most of the sacrifices for a moderate reparation settlement, cancel her claims, and still pay the United States. British public opinion was already convinced: elsewhere the note merely caused annoyance.

A debt settlement with the United States was finally reached in January 1923. The terms were the hardest of all the agreements the United States signed with debtors; but Britain was the first to settle and the best able to pay. Most British opinion at the time thought payment was possible, and that, for the sake of Britain's standing in the world and progress towards an overall settlement, almost any settlement was better than none.[31] There was some hope of improved Anglo-American relations and longer-term cooperation. Relations did improve for a short while; but the American government continued to treat each debtor as a separate case and would not extend to Britain concessions that were subsequently made to others. At the same time it continued policies, such as raising the tariff and subsidizing the merchant fleet, that made it harder for foreign countries to earn the dollars with which to pay their debts.

The British debt settlement did facilitate private financial cooperation and stabilization in Europe in the next few years. The reparation settlement in 1924 opened prospects for further Allied debt agreements, and a number were concluded by both Britain and the United States in the next three years. The British ones were designed to secure the principle of the Balfour Note, and it would have been fulfilled eventually if all had continued for two generations; but for the first years there was a substantial shortfall to add to the sums already paid to the United States when nothing was coming in. This fact, and the fact that the American agreements with France and Italy were markedly more lenient than the one with Britain, gave rise to complaints and resentment in Britain in 1926. Misstatements by the American Secretary of the Treasury, Mellon, in reply to American suggestions for debt cancellation or revision did not help injured feelings; but correction of factual errors hardly altered any minds. The British continued to feel aggrieved; the European debtors continued to feel that they should not have to pay anything before they received reparation from Germany. In the United States, despite the calls of some academics, neither the government nor public opinion was prepared to contemplate a change of policy; but the evidence of American unpopularity caused both anger and alarm.[32]

In the second half of the decade, British and American perceptions of the positions, and the relative positions, of the two countries varied quite widely. Some observers, both British and American, saw Britain as decaying and overburdened by debt.

But others disagreed, and the imperial conference of 1926 was treated to an official paean about Britain's influence as 'the moderator and peacemaker of the new Europe created by the Great War'. Some of those who contrasted American wealth and power with American refusal to take world responsibilities and insistence on debt repayment, still hoped for friendship. Americans who acknowledged this hope were inclined to attribute it to a desire for support.[33] But others were convinced that Europe in general feared and resented the United States and that Britain in particular was bound to try to crush her new great rival for world power. Frederick Bausman, in a book published in 1926, proved to his own satisfaction that Britain could destroy American cities from the sea, was a master of Machiavellian diplomacy with a fifth column of sympathetic kinsmen in the United States, possessed 'an iron Roman consistency in the spread and protection of [its] dominions, projecting long spheres of influence around each possession, which spheres [it] annex[es] in turn', and was utterly unmoved by sentiment. Acknowledgment that Britain was not actually preparing war against the United States could not outweigh these fears, for 'a danger that is possible must always be reckoned as probable'. The only basis for a settlement with Britain was that she should yield the principle of the freedom of the seas and consent to 'such an increase of our naval and aerial armaments as would make us perfectly safe in protecting our commerce if we had a war on two fronts and the Panama Canal were blocked'.[34]

Bausman was a harbinger of a wave of acrimony and misunderstandings, official and unofficial, which grew to something like crisis proportions in 1928–9. The Geneva naval conference of 1927 caused much ill feeling. A League of Nations Preparatory Commission, with American participation, was working to prepare for a disarmament conference. At the same time President Coolidge, who believed strongly in economy, was under pressure to undertake a programme of cruiser building. For the United States limitation of land armaments was of no practical importance; and so Coolidge issued an invitation to a new naval conference, to be held at Geneva as an extension of the Preparatory Commission.

The conference broke down over a fundamental difference

between Britain and the United States regarding cruiser strength. The principles from which the two delegations started were incompatible. The British, believing in the power of blockade, having world-wide trade, possessions and interests, and committed by membership of the League to possible action anywhere in the world, were convinced that to fulfil all these requirements they needed a certain number of ships whatever other naval powers had. The Americans wished to extend the Washington principle of limitation by global tonnage, and the Washington ratios, to all classes of ship. They also wished to set the tonnage limits low enough to require only a modest amount of cruiser building on their part in order to reach the desired parity with Britain. The conference was neither well prepared nor well conducted;[35] but the two positions were hard to reconcile. Some compromises were reached, but the Americans were simply unwilling to accept the British claim to decide how many small cruisers they needed. The British said they accepted the American claim to parity; but there were doubts about their sincerity. Some members of the government were opposed to any limitation agreement.

Since becoming Chancellor of the Exchequer in 1925, Churchill had campaigned strongly against the Admiralty's building programmes, which conflicted with his aim of reducing taxation; but he was equally convinced that Britain should not restrict her freedom of action. He thought the existing lead over the United States was so great that the laying down of even ten new American ships would not constitute a danger; but he was not disposed to bow to American pressure:

> We do not wish to put ourselves in the power of the United States. We cannot tell what they might do if at some date they were in a position to give us orders about our policy, say, in India, or Egypt, or Canada . . . Moreover, tonnage parity means that Britain can be starved into obedience to any American decree. I would neither trust America to command, nor England to submit.

Deferring to the United States was unproductive: 'All the concessions that we made at the Washington Conference in giving up the Naval supremacy we had so long enjoyed, in parting with our faithful Japanese ally, and subsequently in paying them these enormous sums, have only resulted in new assertions and demands on their part.'[36] Hankey, similarly, wrote bitterly to Balfour:

Time after time we have been told that, if we made this concession, or that concession, we should secure good will in America. We gave up the Anglo-Japanese Alliance. We agreed to pay our debts and we have again and again made concessions on this ground. I have never seen any permanent results follow from a policy of concession. I believe we are less popular and more abused in America than ever before, because they believe we are weak.[37]

Other ministers took the danger of a quarrel with the United States more seriously, and Cecil, one of the delegates at Geneva, pointed out the strategic inconsistency in the hard-liners' position, writing to his brother:

If we ever did go to war with America, we should have to have an immense number of cruisers to make ourselves safe from American raiders (far more than we are asking for at present) ... As a mere strategical matter, it seems to me that we shall have to exclude the Americans as possible enemies if we are aiming at complete security, and that the doctrine of equality is much more directed to the *amour propre* of the two countries than to any strategic consideration.[38]

On the American side the naval planners were as hesitant as the Admiralty about further limitation, and uncertain about strategic principles. In 1925 the General Board of the Navy had contended that since sea power consisted of warships plus merchant ships plus bases, and since Britain was predominant in the second and third elements, every limitation of warships weakened American sea power in relation to Britain. 'With each further limitation of armament, this relative weakening will increase until, should all combatant ships by [sic] abolished, Great Britain, by reason of overwhelming superiority in merchant marine and bases, would completely dominate the seas.' Rear-Admiral William W. Phelps painted further a picture of a worldwide British-led conspiracy against United States trade:

The American protective tariff and protective coastwise laws impede British expansion of world trade and shipping. British interests for the last seven years, with the powerful backing of the League of Nations, have been slowly consolidating, and may be expected to continue the effort to consolidate a combine in which are to be included continental powers and Japan, for the purpose of breaking down, eventually, the American protective system.[39]

Forced to accept the need for limitation, the General Board assumed as a principle the necessity for parity with Britain, but could not decide on an optimum level. In relation to Britain, the greater the number of cruisers the better, since the British ships were smaller than the American ones. On the other hand in the Pacific each additional Japanese ship increased the danger to American communications and operations, so it would be better to fix a lower number. The position taken at the Geneva conference therefore combined the demand for parity with Britain with a tonnage level that Congress might be expected to pay for and was aimed chiefly against Japan. The Board also admitted that in the Pacific, British and American interests largely coincided, and it did not wish to call British bases in the region into question.[40] British bases in the Caribbean, however, remained a target for press attacks.[41]

After the breakdown of the Coolidge conference, opinion on both sides of the Atlantic was divided about the underlying cause of the difference and the solution. Some British writers saw the answer in a partnership in policy – if only the United States would enter into 'active and continuous and unreserved cooperation with her fellow nations'. Others took the Churchillian line that 'All we need do is to say frankly to the Americans, "Build whatever number of cruisers you deem necessary to safeguard your interests, leaving us the same liberty".' There were warnings that American demands for a big navy, and anti-British agitation, would be stimulated; and Cecil's attack on government disarmament policy helped to do so.[42] During the conference the *New York World* had asserted that it was the second stage in the 'great transition' in Britain's position from one of decisive influence in world affairs and America's ascent to an equal share. Afterwards the 'Big Navy' lobby and its press trumpeted the call for a navy which would make the United States dominant afloat; but others argued that it would be foolish to build ships simply because of the lack of an agreement with Britain. Frank Simonds, the Anglophobic foreign editor of the *American Review of Reviews*, pointed out that, to the British, the American demand for naval equality struck at the very root of their security:

> If we have the ships to 'wage neutrality' . . . then Britain is relatively helpless in the face of a Continental opponent with a large land force . . . On the day on which we actually attain real equality on the blue water, we and not the British will be in a position to determine the course of any new world conflict. Our fleet will not be used against the British, but the fact of our fleet in being will utterly transform the whole character of British action.[43]

The state of American feeling, when even a serving admiral could talk of possible war, began to cause real anxiety in Britain. The ambassador in Washington, Esme Howard, suggested that the public on both sides of the Atlantic should be educated about the harm that each country could inflict on the other without even firing a shot. He discussed the idea with Hoover, who pointed out that in the case of a war Canada would be bound to declare neutrality. But Austen Chamberlain, the Foreign Secretary, was opposed to any public discussion, fearing that it would exacerbate rather than soothe feelings. He was also unwilling to admit that one part of the Empire could remain neutral if the rest were at war.[44] Opinion in Britain, all were agreed, was utterly opposed to any war with anyone. Feeling about the United States was sore, but confused by the continuing habit of regarding the Americans as blood relations. But it was not just a question of how British opinion regarded America. There was considerable doubt as to what United States policy towards Britain really meant, and what were the domestic pressures on that policy. The puzzle was to know whether American policy was deliberately aiming to take away Britain's position, and whether agreements were possible on matters that could cause conflict. The puzzle was made more difficult to solve by the fact that the naval disagreement either could be regarded as largely symbolic or was concerned not directly with Anglo-American relations but rather with what might happen if Britain were involved in war, perhaps through League of Nations action, and the United States remained neutral.[45]

In the autumn of 1927 Chamberlain, among others, became convinced that the root of the difference over naval limitation was this problem of belligerent rights. The subject was technically complex and of great symbolic significance, and the discussion in a committee of ministers revealed differences of view, between ministers and between government departments, on the best way of preserving Britain's position in the world. Almost everyone favoured keeping a high level of belligerent rights as Britain's chief maritime weapon. Almost everyone believed that she would not be able to exercise a high level in a future war in the face of a neutral America's opposition. But one group, that included Chamberlain and the Foreign Office, believed that it was best in general for British interests to reach agreements with other countries, friends and possible antagonists; and in this case they favoured an Anglo-American agreement as the way to forestall what might be a dangerous conflict. The second group included Bridgeman (First Lord) and the Admiralty, Amery (Secretary of State for the Colonies and an ardent imperialist), and Hankey. They were opposed to accepting any treaty restrictions on British freedom of action, even while acknowledging that that freedom might be limited in practice in a future war. Hankey moreover did not believe that the Americans would try to break a British blockade in a future war any more than they had done in the last one; and he saw no advantage in deference.[46]

Long before any conclusions were reached about belligerent rights, the so-called Anglo-French compromise gave a further twist to the downward spiral of Anglo-American relations. This was an attempt in the summer of 1928 to break a deadlock in the Preparatory Commission for the Disarmament Conference, but it gave the impression that the United States was to be limited in the kind of cruisers it wanted while Britain was to be left free.[47] From the point of view of the general limitation of armaments, Anglo-French agreement was very important. Chamberlain set great store by close relations with France as the key to European stability. He also took seriously the need for good relations with the United States; but he was ill that summer and away from work for some months. For the Anglo-French proposal to succeed, it had to be accepted by the other countries on the Preparatory Commission. It failed this test, and was therefore dropped; but damage had been done.

American comment on the Anglo-French compromise was uniformly hostile. Official displeasure was made known. The Secretary of State, Kellogg, avoided a visit to London on his way home from signing at Paris the Pact for the Renunciation of War. This multilateral treaty had been promoted by Kellogg as a counter to a French proposal for a purely Franco-American pact. It imposed no obligation on the signatories to take any action against a peace-breaker, but it had important potential implications for American neutrality policy.[48] The official reply to the British note presenting the disarmament proposals was courteous but uncompromising. The hostility of newspapers such as the Hearst press was to be expected. More worrying was the reaction of traditionally anti-navalist and Democrat papers. Thus for example the *New York World*, edited by Walter Lippmann, gave some credence to the story, of French origin, that Britain and France had discussed the pooling of naval resources.[49]

In Britain too there was much criticism of the Anglo-French compromise. Much of it was directed against the acceptance of the French case on trained reserves, and the suggestion of an Anglo-French entente; but the American aspect featured as well. J.L. Garvin wrote in the *Observer* of 'dull and obstinate mishandling of American psychology', and said that Britain had forfeited American confidence and respect. The *Spectator* denounced the government for 'abominable mismanagement', and for 'providing one of the most perfect examples we can remember of how to defeat your own purpose'. The *Economist* denounced the government's ineptitude and secretiveness. Wickham Steed wrote in the *Review of Reviews* that 'worse bungling is hardly imaginable', and that the cruiser bill currently before Congress 'would not have stood a chance if a large number, probably the majority of Americans were not persuaded that England will never yield a point on the naval issue unless she is coerced into yielding it'. Lloyd George introduced a motion in the House of Commons declaring that the Anglo-French compromise 'endangers the prospect of peace in Europe and good relations with the United States'. In the debate the Labour MP Lt-Commander J.M. Kenworthy said that the government could not have supposed that the Americans would accept the proposal, so the conclusion must be that it was trying to reinsure by an alliance with France against a future American threat.[50]

There now appeared to be, in the words of a Foreign Office official, R.L. Craigie, a danger of 'drifting towards a situation of real gravity. Except as a figure of speech, war is *not* unthinkable between the two countries. On the contrary, there are present all the factors which in the past have made for wars between States.' Britain could not afford one. The United States was 'twenty-five times as large [as Great Britain], five times as wealthy, three times as populous, twice as ambitious, almost invulnerable, and at least our equal in prosperity, vital energy, technical equipment and industrial science.' Estrangement from the United States would put a severe strain on Britain's relations with the Dominions – not just Canada, for whom good Anglo-American relations were literally a matter of life and death, but also Australia, which was beginning to look to the United States as a reinsurance against Japan. Estrangement would also be very unpopular with British public opinion. In the realm of finance, good relations were virtually essential. Their mutual trade was important to both countries, but Britain was the more dependent on it. Good relations strengthened Britain's influence in Europe, and would be needed for a satisfactory final reparation settlement.[51]

Churchill was not convinced that there was a crisis. In private he spoke of an American threat; but he maintained that all that was necessary was 'to sit quite quiet, to be independent and cool and polite ... and the present ill-temper will gradually subside'. Britain with her Empire was a strong force in the world, her day was not over, and she had 'seen the end of many giants in the past'. Amery too emphasized the Empire, pointing out that if Britain was smaller the Empire was four times as large as the United States and had greater resources. The real answer to the American threat was 'the economic upbuilding and consequent closer and more effective political unity of the British Empire'. Britain should disentangle herself from Europe and cease to be involved in the disarmament process at Geneva from which so many difficulties flowed.[52]

Even for those who believed it was necessary to do something to improve relations, it was not clear which cause of difference offered the best point of approach. The Prime Minister, Baldwin, and Chamberlain made soothing speeches about naval parity, but President Coolidge, in an Armistice Day address, gave offence all over Europe by contrasting American idealism with European militarism and claiming that the war had cost the United States more than any other belligerent. In particular he stressed the necessity for the United States to have a larger navy than Britain.[53] American policy-making appeared to be erratic and inconsistent, and Hoover, now president-elect, was thought by some to be anti-British. Some British publicists continued to look for coordination of naval policies and hoped that after the Kellogg pact the United States would tacitly cooperate with League of Nations actions. Others were more anxious, and called for new efforts to put relations on a cordial footing.[54] John Strachey, son of the extremely Americanophile former editor of the *Spectator*, and himself a Marxist budding Labour Party politician, thought after a visit to the United States that the current American attitude was ambivalent and might turn either way. He believed that conflict was possible, because neither country was yet prepared to make the sacrifices that were the inevitable price of peace. Walter Layton, the editor of the *Economist*, likewise saw a danger of war if a situation arose in which 'we could not bear to surrender our "sea-power" into other hands, while the United States would not tolerate "sea-power" continuing to be vested in any hands but hers'. Layton saw the 'position of arbiter' in the European balance of power passing to the United States, and Britain coming to perform 'in the old game on the old chessboard no longer as a queen, but as a pawn'.[55] Few American publicists yet thought cooperation with the League was conceivable, but some deplored the navalist agitation. Others, however, like Simonds, continued to insist that the United States was building in order to 'wage neutrality' the next time that Britain was at war.[56] The real root of the problem, in the opinion of Gilbert Murray, chairman of the League of Nations Union, was that wealth, power and leadership were in the process of being transferred from Britain to America. It would require, Murray wrote to Salmon O. Levinson, a wealthy Chicago lawyer who was founder and chairman of the American Committee for the Outlawry of War:

a very high standard of public duty and intelligence on your part and on ours to conduct that proceeding of the dethrone- ment of Great Britain and the enthronement of the United States without war. If your people are patient enough to allow the process to happen quietly, without rubbing it in too much, and if we continue to have a foreign policy not worse than that of Baldwin and Chamberlain, civilization may get through without a crash. But those are very large ifs.

On the other side Walter Lippmann had written a year earlier of the surrender of Britain's former political supremacy marking a new epoch in human affairs: 'All that statesmen can do is to take measures which will render peaceable Great Britain's descent from supremacy to parity, and America's ascent to an equal share in world affairs.' This, Lippmann recognized, would bring to the United States inescapable obligations:

> It will be impossible for the United States to share with Great Britain the command of the seas and yet maintain a policy of indifference in the politics of the world . . . In asking for a recognition of our power we are committing ourselves to the perplexing obligations which go with it.[57]

Helpful suggestions for lowering the temperature began to come from the American side by the end of 1928. Lippmann propagated the idea that when the new American cruiser bill was passed (as it was in February 1929) the two countries should accept the situation as one of effective parity. Allen Dulles began to float the idea – new to Americans though not to the British – that other factors besides tonnage might be taken into account in determining what parity was. Lippmann agreed with Philip Kerr, an influential liberal imperialist and Atlanticist, that parity was a political idea and a strategic absurdity, meaning different things to the two countries. Britain, wrote Kerr, meant by parity 'equal navies under conditions which would make it possible for Great Britain to protect its own trade and prevent America or anyone else from breaking through the vital communications of the British Commonwealth.' To America, on the other hand, it meant 'equal navies subject to its being able to protect its trade in every ocean in the world from British interference'.

The two meanings were incompatible, but the new American cruiser programme and the reduced British one ought to make possible an agreement that the ratios thus established should be maintained.[58] Even at the height of the public ill-temper, Howard believed that leading Americans really desired a settlement and sound friendship; and he suggested a visit to the United States by a British statesman. Baldwin had been thinking of a visit for a couple of years; Chamberlain was not at all averse. But the process of preparing the ground had not begun before Baldwin and Chamberlain were removed from office by the general election in Britain in May 1929.

In the late 1920s evidence grew of the replacement of British by American financial and commercial power. At the end of the war the British, whilst conscious of their financial losses and of the burden of internal and external debt laid upon them, expected to recover their position. The government accepted the Cunliffe committee's advice that the most important factor in recovery was the restoration of the gold standard and the prewar parities. External trade recovered, but exports did not reach their 1913 volume; and British shares of world exports of manufactured goods and world manufacturing production were smaller in 1919 than they had been in 1913. Return to the gold standard at the prewar parity took place on 28 April 1925. The standard argument in favour, advanced by the City of London and Treasury officials against the doubts and fears of industrialists and some politicians, was that monetary stability was the necessary precondition of price stability, and that parity would mean savings on debt payments to the United States, cheaper imports, maintenance of Empire unity, and above all the restoration of the Bank of England and the City to a world financial leadership from which industry would benefit as well as trade. Some critics argued that Britain would become more rather than less dependent on American financial power, but their voice did not carry weight. It is now generally accepted that the pound was overvalued, by some 10 per cent, with an unfavourable effect on exports.[59] At the Genoa conference in 1922, the British delegation had inspired resolutions calling for a gold exchange standard (which would have helped sterling) and central bank cooperation; but the proposals found no favour with the Governor of the Federal Reserve Bank of New York,

Benjamin Strong, and so came to nothing. In 1924 the Governor of the Bank of England, Montagu Norman, failed to get the new German currency linked to sterling rather than to the dollar.[60] Norman was a friend of Strong's and trusted him, but from now on he found his efforts to restore Britain's financial leadership increasingly thwarted by American policy.

British Treasury officials and the Bank of England took a leading part between 1922 and 1924 in setting up League of Nations financial reconstruction schemes for Austria and Hungary. They were thought to dominate the Financial Committee of the League, which between 1924 and 1927 sponsored a number of loans and schemes for small countries in eastern and south-east Europe. But from 1926 the Federal Reserve Bank of New York took an increasingly important part in the European currency stabilization. Both Strong and J.P. Morgan & Co. rejected the idea of cooperation with the League, as they had earlier rejected attempts by American government departments to influence their lending, and resisted controls over their lending to Germany.[61]

One of the protagonists of loan control in the early 1920s was Hoover, who believed that European governments should not spend borrowed money on armaments and wished to use American finance as part of the drive for commercial leadership. As Secretary for Commerce, Hoover did much to promote American overseas trade, and cooperation between government and business for the purpose. The expansion of trade and the need for a strong navy to protect it were discussed in a frequently aggressive tone, in terms of trade war and of forcing Allied countries to dismantle preferential systems. But the banks on the whole favoured cooperation; some industries mingled cooperation with competition overseas, and various forms of multinational organization developed with American participation.[62] World trade was expanding in any case, but public discussion tended to concentrate on the conflicts.

One early case was oil. By the end of the war it was obvious to all that oil was much more important as a fuel than it had been in 1914. The British government perceived a need to control as much as possible of the sources and supplies of the country's requirements. The chief concern at this stage was oil fuel for the navy, a secure supply at a reasonable price. Control over supplies meant control over oil companies, not by state ownership but by control of voting and some power of veto on the board. The Anglo-Persian Oil Co. was already under British control with a government stake and a contract to supply the navy. At the end of the war the government aimed, not to replicate this model but to bring other companies, especially Royal Dutch Shell, under British control. Control over sources was necessarily limited to the British Empire and areas of informal British empire, but the outcome of the war offered a new opportunity in Iraq, which was to become a British mandate. The oil resources were known although not yet exploited, and were a motive for the government desiring the mandate.[63]

Despite the fact that the United States produced nearly 70 per cent of the world's oil, the American government and people were seized after the war by a fear that British interests were on the point of monopolizing the world's supplies. There was a widespread belief that the resources of the United States were running out: official reports calculated that reserves would last no more than ten to twenty years.[64] Anxiety was heightened by the realization of how little of the world's oil outside the United States and Mexico (the second largest producer) was exploited by American interests. Boastful utterances by British individuals contributed to the alarm. For example Edward Mackay Edgar, a Canadian-born financier with oil interests, was quoted as saying in September 1919 that all the known oil fields and all the likely or probable oil fields outside the United States were in British hands or under British control or financed by British capital, and that in ten years' time the United States would be forced to buy from British companies 500 million barrels of oil a year. Another industrialist boasted to the London Chamber of Commerce in 1921 that whereas America had skimmed the cream of her resources when prices were low, Britain was entering the world market when the value of oil had grown and prices were high.[65]

The obvious answer to the threatened American oil shortage was exploration and exploitation overseas, but Britain appeared to stand in the way. In Iraq the British at first seemed to be using the indeterminate status of the territory before the mandate was formally allotted to prevent prospecting by American companies. Then the San Remo agreement of April 1920 appeared to give preference to Anglo-French interests. The Americans objected that the arrangement was monopolistic and discriminatory, contrary to the principle of equal economic opportunity that mandates were supposed to enshrine. The British denied any discrimination against American companies and complained that the United States was discriminating against British interests in Latin America. They affirmed their intention to provide equal opportunity, but said that they must defend rights already acquired by British companies.[66] The government was determined not to risk loss of control, and so when it became clear that American opposition to the terms of the Iraq mandate would continue until the question of concessions was settled, it decided to offer a minority share in the partly British-owned Turkish Petroleum Co. to the Standard Oil Co. of New Jersey. American companies were more interested in purchasing oil than in exploration or exploitation on their own account, and once the share deal was completed the American government's objection to the monopolistic nature of the concession vanished. Cooperation between the large British and American oil companies in the Middle East and elsewhere grew in the 1920s. At the same time a great expansion of production in the United States, Venezuela and Iran resulted in a world surplus and falling prices. The heat was thus doubly taken out of the oil war. Nevertheless even in 1928 an American writer could entitle a book on Anglo-American world conflict *We Fight for Oil,* and talk of dire consequences when American car owners were told that Britain had cornered most of the world's supply.[67]

Car owners had also recently been alarmed about the price of rubber, where there was a degree of British monopoly control. The two main world producers of raw rubber were the British colonies of Malaya and Ceylon. In 1922 the government introduced a scheme intended to keep up prices to producers and stabilize them, by taxing exports above the 1920 level. Over the six years of its existence the scheme gave profitable prices to the producers but did not give price stability. It was rigid; it failed to take account of rising demand; and it antagonized American opinion.[68] A sharp rise in prices in 1925 led to an outcry from tyre manufacturers, and Hoover was in the forefront of the denunciation. Official representations were made in London; there were threats to restrict exports of cotton or to ban loans; and Hoover in a letter to a senator wrote that the rise in rubber prices was 'mulcting' the United States at the rate of $900 million a year. Hoover seems to have been particularly angry at the governmental element in the Stevenson scheme: price-fixing and price-support policies were common in the United States, and he had no objection to them. He was also unwilling to concede the British argument that import duties were in any way analogous to export duties.[69] But since the Stevenson scheme was proving unpopular in Britain as well, and rubber production in the Netherlands East Indies was expanding to meet the American demand, the restrictions were progressively lifted and the scheme was ended in 1928.

Further problems followed, about resources including copper and nickel, about markets, and about industrial takeovers, until by the spring of 1929 a range of government, business and financial opinion in Britain was thoroughly gloomy about American expansion and the narrow policies of the Federal Reserve Bank of New York. Apprehension about a possible world crisis now gave a spur to efforts to settle reparations finally and bolster international financial stability. In the Young Plan, the United States in effect accepted a link between German payments and Allied debt payments; but the new Bank for International Settlements was not capable of dealing with the coming financial crisis. The British talked of international cooperation but did not practise it much better than the Americans. In its attitude to the proposal by the French Foreign Minister, Briand, in 1930, for a European federal union, the British government was too mindful of overseas connections and still too wedded to free trade to welcome anything that smacked of organizing Europe against the United States. Meanwhile American confidence still seemed unbounded. In 1928 Ludwell Denny, describing what he saw as a struggle for world mastery going on between the two great economic empires, could suggest a compromise that secured American preponderance on the following lines:

> Naval parity and joint control of the seas; a free hand polit-
> ically for Great Britain in her colonies and spheres of influence
> in exchange for a free hand for the United States in Latin
> America with Great Britain ultimately to get out of British

Honduras and Jamaica and immediately stop concession-hunting in Panaman [sic], Colombian and other territory commanding the Panama Canal; Britain to agree not to encourage dismemberment of China and not to seek special commercial advantages there; the United States to hold the Philippines and to that extent prevent Japanese expansion or further nationalistic revolt in the Lower Far East and India; the United States to scale down its high tariff wall to let in British goods, and hasten war debt cancellation; both governments to practise Open Door policy in regard to raw materials and markets in their territories and spheres of influence, except in strategic areas such as Panama and Suez; . . . abolition of the British exclusion policy preventing ownership of petroleum lands, and equitable division or joint exploitation by British and American companies of new foreign fields.

In less aggressive vein John Carter saw the United States creating an economic empire over most of the planet by entirely peaceful means, dispensing with politics and trusting to business to settle the question of the survival of the fittest. It would be short-sighted folly, he thought, to challenge British power on the seas: the American answer to strategy was to ignore it, and instead to cultivate such intimate and amiable relations with Britain and Japan that 'there need be no occasion to appeal from the common-sense arguments of national interest to the incalculable dictates of force'.[70]

During the interval between two sessions of the reparations conference at The Hague in 1929, Ramsay MacDonald, the Labour Prime Minister, visited the United States. His purpose was not to make specific agreements but to mark a new atmosphere in relations. To a large extent he was successful. In a statement issued at the end of the visit the two governments declared their resolve to accept the Kellogg pact not only as a declaration of their good intentions but as 'a positive obligation to direct our national policy in accordance with its pledge'. So the character of old problems would be changed and satisfactory solutions made possible. This was not solely the politics of gesture: in talks with the American ambassador in the summer, MacDonald had accepted parity and agreed to reduce the number of British cruisers to a figure well below that claimed two years earlier.[71] This having been achieved, invitations were issued for the naval conference which under the terms of the Washington treaty was to be held in 1930. This proved to be the high point of arms limitation in the interwar period, and the achievements and failures reflected the politico-strategic situation at the time.[72] British policy had changed since the breakdown in 1927. The Labour government was committed to arms limitation in a way that the Conservatives had not all been, and pursued agreement even at a high cost. The Americans were more prepared than before to recognize that Britain had needs that did not directly concern them. The Japanese were still, but only just and for the last time, willing to accept the same ratio of strength as in 1922. Britain, the United States and Japan only threatened each other on the high seas: the limitation agreed between them in all classes of vessel froze their relative situations at a level that left Britain with very little margin over Japan in the Pacific even if she were able to put all her strength there. And having achieved parity with Britain on paper, the United States proved to be in no hurry to realize it in practice. The sting was taken out of the question; there was no strategic need; and the depression took a toll of naval expenditure. Belligerent rights were not discussed at the conference: for the time being their potential for causing Anglo-American discord dropped out of sight. But for France and Italy the problem was quite different. Naval armaments were only part of a larger whole; they were rivals in the Mediterranean and in central Europe. A compromise was only reached between them a year later and disappeared almost at once. Even the balance achieved between the three other powers was precarious. Anglo-American rivalry was disposed of – as it turned out, permanently; but Japan very soon became a cause for anxiety, and in 1935 the whole system came to an end.

By the end of 1930 the power relations between Britain and the United States had been shifted one stage further in favour of the latter, but amicably so that the improvement in general atmosphere may be held not merely to have masked but actually to have softened the impact of the power shift in the world as a whole. The improved atmosphere of Anglo-American relations owed something to the changes of government on both sides. But perhaps the crisis of 1928–9 had not been as severe as some people thought. A naval agreement had to be reached by 1931 in any case, and its outlines could already be foreseen. The relative absence of acrimony, and the silencing of voices prophesying war, were no doubt a great gain. But equally the two countries did not enter a new age of friendship and cooperation. Within a few weeks of MacDonald's visit to the United States, the 'Great Crash' precipitated a general deflationary financial crisis in which war debts and reparations were swept away in default, and as depression covered the world international cooperation went by the board. New causes of trade rivalry and tension appeared. As the international scene darkened in the early 1930s, the question marks over American power remained as prominent as ever.

4
Appeasement, Isolationism and the Approach of War in the 1930s

The depression affected the United States more seriously and for longer than any other country. Whether or not its causes lay primarily there, the weight of the United States in the world economy meant that long and severe depression in that country had a proportionate impact on the rest of the world. In Britain the depression, while painful for individuals and regions and presenting many difficulties for governments, was relatively mild, and Britain emerged from the wreckage of the gold standard as leader of a relatively successful sterling monetary bloc. The long-term trend to American economic preeminence was not reversed; but for a few years the balance moved slightly back in Britain's favour.[1]

The depression had profound effects on the politics and psychologies of individual nations, and at the same time world political stability was breaking down too – the relationship between the two breakdowns was not simple, and cannot be explored here. The foreign policies developed by the British and the United States governments, whilst by no means wholly new, were responses to partly new and difficult situations. In Britain it took the form of appeasement.

Appeasement has a wide range of connotations. Its meaning and its practice in Britain between the wars has been the subject of much discussion.[2] In the most general sense appeasement can be understood as the natural policy for a satiated power with widely scattered interests and obligations, conscious that the prospect of war, even rumour of war, spelled nothing but loss for Britain. In the 1920s awareness that the inherited burdens were too heavy for the country's capacity was not widely spread; but there were many pressures for a pacific policy. They operated to support the more or less active pursuit of a general European settlement that would reconcile former enemies; pursuit also of stability in the Far East and cooperation with the United States, all from a position of confidence. In the early 1930s, the economic pressures for disarmament and the public's passion for peace reached a peak just as world stability broke down and it became necessary to acknowledge that Britain's defences were not in a fit state to meet any single likely threat, let alone a foreseeable combination. The result was a confused and muffled transition. In some quarters the hope of a lasting solution survived for years; in others it became a question more of buying time until Britain should be strong enough – not to fight but to deter, to exercise influence, to prevent others plunging Europe or the Far East into war. By 1936 the hope of a reconciling settlement in Europe was dwindling, but it was still pursued with varying degrees of hope, almost blindly by some of those subsequently condemned for doing so, because any other policy seemed to lead straight to war and ruin. As the pace of events quickened a new element, fear, entered into appeasement. But there was no safe outcome. Appeasement itself carried enormous risks, the loss of strategic assets, the loss of allies, the loss of a short war because one had been preparing for a different kind. The risks were increasingly identified and discussed from 1936 but the government's critics were divided. Until January 1939 rearmament was not allowed to disrupt the peacetime economy, partly because war was not certain, partly because financial and economic strength were the 'fourth arm' which would enable the country to fight a long war if it had to. In early 1939 financial prudence was relegated to second place; the risk of bankruptcy was accepted as preferable to the position of second in a German-dominated Europe; and a pacific public's outrage at Hitler's wanton aggressions impelled into action a government that, whatever its appeasing proclivities, still assumed that Britain could act as a world power.

Just as appeasement was a natural policy for a satiated and over-extended empire, so isolationism was a natural policy for the United States in the 1930s, reversing a trend that for a few years had appeared to be leading in the opposite direction, towards international cooperation. Isolationism reached its height about 1935–7 and remained powerful until 1941.[3] Isolationism in the 1930s was a combination of unilateralism and pacifism, based on beliefs that international politics were at best amoral (and probably immoral), corrupting of American values; that peace-loving states became involved in war by the machinations of selfish interests; but that the western hemisphere was invulnerable, so that the United States both could and should remain aloof from any form of involvement. Earlier American unilateralism had been self-confident and even at times aggressive: now the depression had shaken confidence in American strength. Earlier devotion to the cause of peace had led some Americans to support the League of Nations and cautiously to adopt ideas of collective security. But as clouds of real war gathered in Europe and the Far East, so grew a passionate desire to avoid involvement. Far from aspiring to greater world power and leadership, Americans tried to withdraw from the world.

The early 1930s saw the highest level of American interest in international cooperation and its most disappointing setbacks.[4] Coming into office in March 1933 at a moment of national near-despair, Franklin D. Roosevelt was not by temperament or conviction an isolationist; but in his first term his priorities were domestic and he never wished to involve the United States unnecessarily. After raising foreign expectations about a debt settlement and currency stabilization, he found himself unable to do anything about debts and torpedoed the World Economic Conference meeting in London in June. Roosevelt's Secretary of State, Cordell Hull, never made policy except on the liberalization of trade, to which, believing that international economic cooperation would save the cause of peace (and benefit the American economy), he devoted much of his energy.[5]

In the first two or three years after its signature, debate on the implications of the Kellogg pact for United States policy was largely abstract.[6] The problem became actual with the approach of the Disarmament Conference. In August 1931 Henry L. Stimson, the Secretary of State, told MacDonald privately that he:

could not believe that any American Government would seek to use our Navy to enforce an extreme doctrine of neutrality under which American merchants were seeking to trade with an aggressor nation so declared by the League and against whom Britain and British public opinion were sanctioning the use of the Royal Navy.

The American representative with the Preparatory Commission, Hugh Wilson, told Cecil in September that his government might offer to give no aid or comfort to a country that broke the Kellogg pact, or might even agree to consult if war threatened.[7] But no prospect was held out of any American contribution to European security.[8] Finally in August 1932 Stimson made the possibilities and the limits of American cooperation reasonably plain in an address to the American Council on Foreign Relations. This was an important occasion, intended by Stimson to proclaim the United States' commitment through the Kellogg pact and to rally the European countries round it. The pact, Stimson said, had changed the whole doctrine of neutrality. War was now illegal, no longer a source of rights of belligerents and neutrals: new rules would have to be worked out. The pact did not provide sanctions of force against a violator, but it contained definite promises and it rested on the sanction of world opinion. To invoke that opinion effectively postulated discussion and consultation among signatories, and this would take place so long as other signatories supported the policy the United States had tried to establish. Stimson was, he told a British friend later, at this time trying to work out a remedy for the difficulty of Senate power in foreign policy by building up a series of precedents in the shape of executive action, to the ultimate point of establishing a practice in international affairs that would be almost as binding as a treaty.[9]

Stimson's address was regarded as a real step forward in the organization of peace. The *Economist*, for example, thought it meant that 'America is prepared to insist on the League's verdict on the Manchurian question being carried out, cost what it may', but then revealed some uncertainty as to what the United States might actually do 'when the time comes'. Raymond Buell of the Foreign Policy Association, however, thought that the principle of consultation would not succeed in maintaining peace unless given life by procedures: shouting moral disapproval merely strengthened nationalistic antagonisms. Frank Simonds awaited the arrival of a president or secretary of state 'with the courage and capacity to explain to the American public that the profits of international peace can only be shared by peoples prepared to pay the tax of international responsibility'.[10] Procedures were just what the United States could not join. In the crisis of the Disarmament Conference in the autumn Norman Davis, the American delegate, made it plain that his country could not undertake to concert measures in case of a breach of the Kellogg pact, still less promise in advance to adopt any measures.[11] However in May 1933 Roosevelt approved a further step. He coupled a message urging the abandonment of offensive weapons with a statement that the United States would consult in case agreements were broken. And on 22 May Davis declared at Geneva that if a general disarmament agreement were reached, the United States would consult in case the Kellogg pact were broken. Furthermore, if the United States concurred with the collective identification of a peace-breaker, it would not obstruct a collective effort.[12] This statement, although containing no commitment to any action, was farther than Congress was willing to go. Within a week the Senate Foreign Relations Committee amended a resolution on shipment of arms in such a way as to prevent discrimination in favour of a victim of aggression. Since no general disarmament agreement was reached, the undertaking fell in any case; and with the failure of the Disarmament Conference and the darkening of the international scene, so grew American determination to prevent by legislation the kind of activities that had jeopardized complete neutrality in the First World War.

The experience of the Far East crisis of 1931–3 helped to disillusion Americans about cooperation with cynical European powers.[13] The question of Anglo-American cooperation was controversial at the time, and gave rise to later mythology, compounded by vagueness or confusion over the meaning of the word 'action'. Later denunciations of British failure to follow an American lead or, worse, refusal of an offer of cooperation, came close to suggesting that Stimson had been prepared to take some action against Japan. This was not the case. Stimson was readier than Hoover to utter statements of principle in the American tradition, and even to cooperate with the League. He trusted, like so many others at the time, in the moral power of world opinion to check aggressors. At no time did he contemplate anything more concrete; but then and later he regarded his proposal of joint representations to Japan as 'action'.

The fact of any American initiative at all was new and potentially important. It aroused expectations in sections of British opinion. The *Manchester Guardian* thought the statement about non-recognition, made to the Japanese and Chinese governments on 7 January, might be a prelude to firmer action; the *Economist* considered that leadership of the English-speaking world in the Pacific was passing from London to Washington.[14] As late as 1937 Sir Norman Angell thought that acceptance of Stimson's offer (about the nature of which Angell was vague) would have made the Kellogg pact a political reality and ensured American acquiescence in Britain's view of belligerent rights.[15] At the point when Stimson made his proposal of joint representations, the British were involved at Geneva in League efforts to get the Japanese to withdraw from Manchuria and to affirm the principle of non-recognition. The government's response to Stimson was therefore hesitant, and helped to confirm American perceptions of British policy as timid and tricky. Combining action within the League with cooperation with the United States was not simple. Desire for cooperation was not lacking in the government, but there were other considerations as well, notably a real fear of antagonizing Japan, some pro-Japanese feeling, and a conviction that the United States could never be relied on for more than words and would leave Britain to bear the brunt of any repercussions. Sir Ronald Lindsay, who had succeeded Howard as ambassador in Washington and who thought there could be no question of preferring Japan to the United States if it came to a choice, admitted:

> I know the Americans are dreadful people to deal with – they cannot make firm promises, but they jolly you along with fair prospects and when you are committed they let you down. Taking a short view it is hard to remember a bargain with them that has been really satisfactory to us in itself.

But, he went on, 'on the long view there has never been a case where we were not right to have made the bargain'.[16]

There was no doubt that the events of 1931–3 enhanced Japan's position, nor that Britain's position in the Far East was weak. Before the crisis erupted the British government was aware that the Singapore base was not ready and its defences hardly existed, and also aware that if the fleet had to be sent to the Far East there would not be enough ships left in home waters to meet a European emergency. Throughout the crisis officials in the Far East and in London emphasized the damage that Japan could do to British interests. The Chiefs of Staff reported on 22 February: 'The position is about as bad as it could be . . . The whole of our territory in the Far East, as well as the coast-line of India and the Dominions and our vast trade and shipping lies open to attack.'[17]

In the United States too the crisis revealed that naval re-sources were inadequate: naval building, despite the rhetoric about parity, had fallen short of the tonnages allowed under the treaties of 1921 and 1930, and there was no clear idea what the resources were for. The navy had no realistic plan for war with Japan. But there could be no question of large expenditure at present: Stimson's threat to reconsider the Washington treaty remained unrealized. American policy in the Far East for the next few years was entirely passive.

It was the Far East crisis that precipitated the end of the Ten-Year rule, but well before Hitler took Germany out of the disarmament conference and the League in October 1933 the pace of German rearmament was hardly disguised, and in London the gloomiest forecasts were being made of an arms race and war within four or five years. Attempts to find ways of bringing Germany back continued: MacDonald was still devoted to the cause of disarmament, and other ministers were so alarmed at the thought of an arms race that they would try almost any alternative. Nevertheless it was clear that a defence problem in Europe had to be added to the one in the Far East. Tackling it, however hesitantly at first, raised major issues about Britain's strategic position and priorities.[18] The trio of top civil servants – Hankey, Sir Warren Fisher (Permanent Secretary to the Treasury) and Sir Robert Vansittart (Permanent Under-Secretary of State at the Foreign Office) – who with the Chiefs of Staff were set in November 1933 to examine what was needed to make good deficiencies in the existing defence programmes, soon concluded that Germany was the most serious long-term threat. This suggested a search for a new policy in the Far East and the committee recommended 'getting back, not to an alliance (since that would not be practical politics) but at least to our old terms of cordiality and mutual respect with Japan', and saw no insuperable difficulty in doing so.[19] This piece of optimism was due to Fisher, who with Neville Chamberlain, then Chancellor of the Exchequer and from 1937 Prime Minister, retained for several years an unfounded faith in the possibility of an Anglo-Japanese understanding that would maintain Britain's interests in the Far East.[20]

Those interests were both imperial – British possessions and communications, and economic – trade and shipping in the entire region, including China. There were two formidable obstacles to an understanding with Japan: the United States, and Japanese policy. The United States was known to be very suspicious of Japan, and of anything that looked like a return to the Anglo-Japanese alliance. Japanese naval policy was thought to be governed by fear of an Anglo-American combination, and thus capable of modification if the combination were dissolved. Chamberlain and Fisher argued that American resentment at dissolution would not matter: the Americans were always anxious to push Britain into the forefront in the Far East and ready to leave her to bear the brunt of Japanese hostility; they could moreover not be relied upon to support Britain in Europe. Fisher revealed a strong anti-American streak, writing of 'the braggadoccio of Yahoodom', 'childish amour-propre', and 'their quaint theory of civilization'.[21] Others, including Vansittart, while agreeing that the United States was not reliable, continued to think that recent advances in Anglo-American relations should not be jeopardized. Some degree of American support, or at least benevolent neutrality, in Europe was necessary and possible; and public opinion would criticize any government that allowed relations to deteriorate.[22]

Even if the American difficulty could somehow be overcome, there remained that of Japanese policy. It was increasingly clear, especially after a Foreign Ministry statement of April 1934 claiming for Japan the controlling voice in foreign assistance to China, that Japanese policy in China was aimed at domination. Assurances about respect for foreign interests were belied by experi-

ence in Manchuria and north China. An Anglo-Japanese understanding would be bound, according to all the China experts,
to arouse Chinese resentment; and the consequent damage to
British interests would more than outweigh temporary gains
from Japanese favour. Despite a continuing tendency to regard
China as a semi-dependent territory, British advisers never
thought total Japanese domination possible. British commercial interests and investments in China were commonly described
as 'vast'. This was an exaggeration. China took 2.5 per cent of
Britain's exports, coming sixteenth on her list of customers.
Britain's investment in China was less than what she had in
Argentina. Still, important sums were involved, and were not
lightly to be jeopardized in times of depression. Chamberlain
never advocated abandoning British commercial interests.

In the summer of 1934 the government announced a new
air programme for home defence, and postponed decisions on
the navy and the army. The considerations were largely those
of public and parliamentary opinion. The implications for imperial defence were shelved. Chamberlain, with ruthless logic,
would have been ready to abandon the idea of sending the
fleet to Singapore. His colleagues did not agree; but whilst
Hankey, who was about to go on a Commonwealth tour and
discuss defence matters, secured from Baldwin an assurance
that it was still assumed that the fleet would be sent to Singapore in the event of a major emergency in the Far East, there
was at present not much for the assumption to rest on.[23]

One reason for postponing a decision on naval building was
the prospect of a new naval conference in 1935. Preliminary
conversations to explore the ground took place in London with
both the Americans and the Japanese in the second half of
1934. The Americans' position bore little relation to the state
of the world. They were anxious to achieve actual tonnage
reductions, as well as determined not to concede parity to Japan. In London they did not deny the strength of the British
case for more cruisers, but were extremely reluctant to accept
it, because of domestic considerations and for fear that it would
encourage further Japanese building. They refused to consider
a British compromise aimed at keeping Japan bound by qualitative limitations and voluntary acceptance of a programme based
on minimum security needs. The Japanese conceded that actual

British needs were greater than their own, but insisted on formal parity; and on 30 December they gave notice to terminate the Washington treaty.[24]

The chief American negotiator, Norman Davis, was anxious for Anglo-American friendship and well aware that his country's refusal to make any commitments was no help. He at least professed not to be greatly disturbed at the talk there was in London in the autumn of a new Anglo-Japanese agreement. But American suspicions were roused, reminiscent of 1920–1. Roosevelt told Davis to impress on the British that if they were even suspected of preferring Japan to the United States he would appeal to public opinion in the Dominions.[25] As Walter Lippmann explained a few months later, the United States disliked intensely:

> any British disposition to act as intermediary, honest broker, arbiter or judge between Japan and the United States. The British interest in China is far greater than the American, and America does not desire to be manoeuvred into a position where it opposes alone the Japanese advance, while Britain assumes the role of friend of all concerned.[26]

Liberal and pro-American groups in Britain were also alarmed, and a press campaign was mounted. Lord Lothian (Philip Kerr had succeeded to the title in 1930) called in the *Round Table* for a common Commonwealth–United States policy. Walter Layton wrote in *The Economist* that a deal with Japan at the expense of China would destroy fundamental British interests, cause bitter estrangement from the United States, and result in the loss of Canada. General Smuts (who wanted the Empire to remain a first-rate naval power and to build against Japan) said in a much-publicized speech at a Chatham House dinner that the future policy of the Commonwealth lay more with the United States than with any other group in the world.[27] This mobilization of opinion illustrated how unpopular an Anglo-Japanese understanding would have been. It was hardly necessary, for the Japanese declined the British naval proposals, denounced the Washington treaty, and said that their proposal for a non-aggression pact had never been firm.

The prospects for an active Commonwealth policy, let alone

a common one with the United States, were very poor. In September 1933 an unofficial conference on British Commonwealth relations was held at Toronto, bringing together British and Dominion members of the Chatham House/Round Table network. It was immediately clear that underneath a broad consensus that foreign policy must be based on support of the collective system, and the closest possible cooperation maintained with the United States, lay sharp divergences about what the collective system was, and even about what cooperation with the United States meant. There was no desire for any kind of Commonwealth machinery, and much emphasis on diversity.[28] According to one Canadian writing at the time, since Britain could hardly escape participation in European affairs, the dominating voice in foreign policy 'must no longer be left with that section of the Empire which is most likely to embroil the remainder'. Britain must be prepared to give up the power of decision (he did not say to whom), must at all costs be kept out of European quarrels, and must adopt a policy 'unpleasantly close to peace at any price'.[29]

Lothian, calling for reconstruction of the League of Nations after the departure of Japan, envisaged as an alternative a security system of the 'oceanic' powers which would have enormous resources, a common understanding on the use of sea power, and no military commitments.[30] But Lothian had to admit that there was little likelihood of the United States joining any system in the near future, and J.W. Dafoe, veteran editor of the *Winnipeg Free Press*, could see no way out of the difficulty in the short term. Britain, he wrote to Lothian, was inextricably involved in Europe but the Dominions feared and loathed it. If Britain were involved in a European war, Canada would be deeply split. Australia and New Zealand were more alive to the Pacific dangers, but their answer seemed to be an armed Empire alliance, something that Canada would not countenance:

> Of course if the United States would step down from its citadel of pride and selfishness the whole situation would change ... If they made an agreement with Great Britain about the Pacific Canada would sign on without question ... A Pacific understanding to which the United States was a party would be an understanding really dominated by United

States policy which would correspond pretty closely to the Pacific policies desired by the Dominions with a Pacific frontage.

But Dafoe knew that this was hankering after the impossible: 'Uncle Sam is wedded to his idols and will not, I fear, come out of his trance until the guns begin to go off.'[31]

The mid-1930s were the high point of isolationist success in the United States. In January 1935 the Senate failed to produce a sufficient majority to approve United States adherence to the World Court.[32] At the end of August, with war looming over Ethiopia and driven by the widespread conviction that the United States had been mistakenly drawn into the First World War by, on the one hand, supplying arms and finance to belligerents and, on the other hand, insisting on full neutral rights to trade and travel, the Senate approved a bill placing a mandatory embargo on the supply of arms to all belligerents and prohibiting American ships from carrying war materials to belligerent states. The President was given power to define munitions of war and to bring the embargo into effect, and was given discretion to withhold protection from Americans travelling in belligerent ships; but he was not, as Roosevelt had wished, given discretion to discriminate between aggressor states and victims. In February 1936 this law was substantially reenacted for another year, with the addition of a ban on loans to belligerents. A new permanent act in 1937 gave the President discretion to withhold raw materials from belligerents (it had proved impossible to prevent increased exports to Italy of such material as scrap and oil in 1935–6), and added a provision, valid for two years, that belligerents must pay cash for non-embargoed goods purchased in the United States and transport them in non-American ships.

The neutrality laws put any idea of positive American cooperation with other signatories of the Kellogg pact out of the question; but equally they reduced the prospect of attempts to interfere with League action on the score of neutral rights, and with it the British nightmare of the 1920s. Those who advocated the neutrality legislation were prepared for a considerable sacrifice of trade. They were not for the most part motivated by Anglophobia, but advocacy of Anglo-American cooperation roused suspicions about Britain's motives, and Lothian's talk of an alliance was regarded as hardly sane.[33] Some, like Walter Lippmann, admitted sympathy for the powers aligned for the status quo, 'not because they are for the status quo, but because they are free nations and are resisting the spread of tyrannical government'. But sympathies did not make a national policy, and Lippmann calculated that it was in the United States' interest to stand apart from European policies. He comforted himself with the thought that by devoting their efforts to domestic economic recovery Americans would promote world recovery and so relieve political tensions. 'By proceeding with our own social reconstruction we can, by its example, hearten the supporters of freedom and peace throughout the world'.[34] The historian Samuel Flagg Bemis thought that:

> when the proof comes that the great powers are willing to sacrifice lives and treasure for peace in regions of the world where their interests are not vitally concerned, but only when that day comes, the United States may well join them and contribute its sacrifices too.

But meanwhile neutrality legislation, an autarchic commercial policy, and a navy 'adequately superior' to Japan were what was required.[35] The prospect that mandatory embargoes on war materials could work to the detriment of victims of aggression caused some discomfort, but at least the prospect of interference with League sanctions was removed. Only a few continued to advocate cooperation for the prevention of war.[36]

The isolationists' fears mainly concerned Europe, which was where the United States had become involved last time and where involvement was bound to mean entanglement with allies. The Far East, to many, was less worrying. The threat of an actual war with Japan was remote. It could be avoided by refraining from meddling in the affairs of east Asia; but if it came, it could be fought at long range by naval means without the need to mobilize large armies. After the Japanese gave notice of termination of the Washington treaty there was no fear that naval competition could not be sustained; but there was opposition to increased naval spending and some calls for concessions to Japan. American opinion continued to disapprove of Japanese activities in China; but there was little support for practical action to help China, and considerable fear of being pushed into the forefront by Britain, whose interests in China were larger than American ones and who was suspected of wishing to use the United States to pull chestnuts out of the fire. Anglo-American agreement to restrain Japan was considered hardly practicable even by the few who thought it desirable.[37]

The essentially passive character of American policy was illustrated by Roosevelt's notion of neutralizing the Pacific, a proposal that would mean dismantling the defences of Hong Kong. As Lindsay commented, neutralization would not hurt the United States once it was free of responsibility for the Philippines (and the date for independence was now thought likely to be advanced to 1938 or 1939) but would harm Britain unless neutralization were jointly guaranteed – and of an American guarantee there was of course no sign.[38]

On the British side officials regarded hope of Anglo-American cooperation in the Far East as futile. The idea that it was possible to cooperate with Japan for the benefit of China was pursued by the Treasury until one of its officials, Sir Frederick Leith Ross, discovered the difficulties for himself. There was little Britain could do to protect her interests in China, but no disposition to abandon them, not so much for their actual value as for the deductions about British power that would be drawn throughout Asia: as an official noted, 'On intrinsic merits these are not worth a war, but what will be the effect on the world in general if we are no longer willing or able to defend our interests. That becomes an imperial question.'[39] The Japanese more than once held out the prospect of a political understanding, but each time the price seemed likely to be too high or the offer proved meaningless. In a memorandum on British policy in the Far East written just before the opening of the Imperial Conference in May 1937, the two main aims were stated as, first, the essential one of safeguarding Malaya and the East Indies colonies together with communications to Australia and New Zealand, and, secondly and less vitally, the maintenance and increase of British trade and commercial interests in China, Japan, Siam and the Netherlands East Indies. Malaya was of paramount importance to both defence and economic policy. Since the only threat to the British possessions in the Far East came from Japan, Japanese offers to protect them were valueless.[40]

During 1935 the government's advisers continued to stress Britain's unfavourable strategic position. 'We consider it a cardinal requirement of our national and imperial security', the Defence Requirements Committee stated:

> that our foreign policy should be so conducted as to avoid the possible development of a situation in which we might be confronted simultaneously with the hostility, open or veiled, of Japan in the Far East, Germany in the West, and any Power on the main line of communication between the two.

A simultaneous or practically simultaneous threat on the two fronts could not be excluded, and the double emergency was the more likely to occur if naval forces were not sufficient to provide a deterrent:

> If there is danger from Japan at all, it reaches its maximum from the point of view both of probability and extent when we are preoccupied in Europe. Unless we can provide a sufficient defence for that emergency Australia, New Zealand, India, Burma, the rich Colonies East of Suez and a vast trade will be at their mercy, and the Eastern half of the British Empire might well be doomed.[41]

The committee recommended balanced forces, but in the circumstances of the winter of 1935 the proposals for both the army and the navy were again cut down. Public opinion was intensely opposed to the idea of sending an expeditionary force to Europe, so political considerations reinforced the Treasury's hostility to providing reserves for such a force. Within days of the Cabinet deciding to equip a small field force but no reserves, the German army moved into the demilitarized Rhineland and demonstrated Britain's inability to face war or reinforce a continental ally.[42] Similarly the new naval standard, whilst accepted in principle, was never achieved in practice. Only the RAF was promised as much as it could absorb. The decisions taken in early 1936 thus emphasized the defence of the United Kingdom above everything else. The RAF might deter Germany from attacking the United Kingdom, but could not do much to influence German actions on the continent of Europe; and the Pacific Dominions and British interests in the Far East were still to be left without naval protection. Now Italy had to be included in the list of potential enemies as a result of British support (qualified though it was) of the League of Nations over Ethiopia.[43]

In 1936 burgeoning and uncoordinated demands from the services aroused concern about costs and about production capacity, and led to a system of rationing within a global sum. The government was committed to rearmament, but for deterrence rather than preparation for war; so it was generally agreed that defences should not be expanded beyond the level at which the ordinary economy could sustain them. Within the global total, decisions about priorities had important implications for Britain's world position. While the idea of even a limited liability on the continent was being reduced to vanishing point by the end of 1937, no one seems to have faced the thought that the smaller Britain's European contribution was, the smaller would be her voice in deciding allied strategy. Public opinion was divided and confused. With the tacit, if unwilling, acknowledgment in the summer of 1936 that collective security under the League of Nations was effectively dead, the principles on which Britain's attitude to Europe should be based were left in doubt.[44] There was no question of returning openly to a policy of maintaining the balance of power: that concept was discredited or at best regarded as archaic. The influential military correspondent of *The Times*, Basil Liddell Hart, expatiated in articles and books on the unwisdom of sending a field force to the continent.[45] Liberals and the Left continued to hanker after the collective system, and some supposed that the Dominions were devoted to it.[46] The *Spectator* ran a series of articles on what in the last resort Britain should fight for: most of the contributors, from various parties, were ready to contemplate fighting for the Empire, but there agreement ended. Beaverbrook, the newspaper proprietor and campaigner for 'Empire Free Trade', would fight only for the Empire; A.L. Rowse for no purpose at all under the present government; Arnold Wilson for Scandinavia and western Europe; Norman Angell (and in another periodical Vernon Bartlett) for principles.[47] Elsewhere Sir Charles Mallet wanted to 'limit our risks, . . . to eschew additional entanglements and yet to remain essentially good neighbours and good friends to any Government which will walk with us along the road to peace'.[48] Lothian called for reform of the League and a 'Monroe system' joining the Empire with the United States in a bloc detached from any other continental system, so strong that no other country would dream of attacking it, and 'economically and politically so stable that it could stand outside a European war, in isolating it if it broke out, and in ending it quickly and on reasonably just terms'.[49]

Lothian knew the United States well enough to be aware, and occasionally admitted, that Americans were not in a frame of mind to cooperate in keeping or enforcing the peace. His willingness to scrap the League was not shared by all his friends. His acceptance of a British interest in the security of France and Belgium was not shared by all the Dominions, as the Imperial Conference of May 1937 showed. They no longer all believed even vaguely in a collective system. Whilst the New Zealand Prime Minister, Savage, reproached the British government for not following a 'League policy', Mackenzie King said plainly that Canada did not believe in collective security. Imperial solidarity too was in question. British ministers desired a statement of unity to impress potential opponents; but whilst Australia and New Zealand were concerned with Japan, South Africa and Canada did not believe in a German threat. General Hertzog warned that South Africa would not support Britain in a war that might arise out of her continued association with France in a 'policy calculated to threaten Germany's existence through unwillingness to set right the injustices flowing from the Treaty of Versailles'. Nor were the British more successful in getting a general promise of defence cooperation. They explained the seriousness of Britain's position and received undertakings from Australia and New Zealand, worried about the fulfilment of the pledge to send a fleet to Singapore; but Mackenzie King would not say that Canada would even consider cooperation in expanding war industry. The final communiqué taxed the ingenuity even of British draftsmen, and emerged as no more than a statement of support for peace.[50] Dominion leaders were not yet ready to expose their disunity in public; and the possibility that in the last resort they would refuse to support Britain was not yet thought very serious. But no British minister could feel encouraged to act in such a way as to risk the test of imperial unity.

During 1937 the issues of peace and war gradually became clarified. The hope of a new settlement in western Europe finally evaporated after months of fruitless negotiation. The civil war in Spain sharpened the ideological division of Europe and increasingly locked Mussolini into association with Hitler. Italy joined the anti-Comintern pact in November, the month in which Hitler declared to his associates his intention of acting against Austria and Czechoslovakia in the following year if conditions were right. The outbreak of the Sino-Japanese war gave a further downward turn to relations in the Far East. In Britain, Neville Chamberlain took over from Baldwin as prime minister and stepped up the active search for ways of reducing the number of Britain's potential enemies.

In a report of 12 November the Chiefs of Staff drew the attention of ministers to the 'increasing probability' that a war started in Europe, the Mediterranean or the Far East might extend to one or both of the other areas. They could not, they said:

> foresee the time when our defence forces will be strong enough to safeguard our territory, trade and vital interests against Germany, Italy and Japan simultaneously. We cannot, therefore, exaggerate the importance, from the point of view of Imperial defence, of any political or international action that can be taken to reduce the numbers of our potential enemies and to gain the support of potential allies.[51]

Looking at the defence problem from the other end Sir Thomas Inskip, the Minister for Coordination of Defence, tried in a report of December to balance the need to maintain economic stability, as one of the country's chief resources, as a deterrent to an enemy, and as a necessary means of sustaining a long war if one came, against the need to be strong enough to withstand a knockout blow. Everything, he wrote, indicated that the cornerstone of imperial defence policy must be the security of the United Kingdom. Two months later Inskip admitted, in effect, that the present rearmament programmes could not secure Britain's safety. Proposing to look no farther ahead than another two years, during which efforts must not be relaxed, he effectively gave diplomacy that period in which to find the solution. 'The plain fact which cannot be obscured', he wrote:

> is that it is beyond the resources of this country to make proper provision in peace for the defence of the British Empire against three major Powers in three different theatres of war. If the test should come, I have confidence in the power and inherent capacity of our race to prevail in the end. But the burden in peace time of taking the steps which we are advised . . . are prudent and necessary in present circumstances, is too great for us. I therefore repeat with fresh emphasis the opinion which I have already expressed as to the importance of reducing the scale of our commitments and the number of our potential enemies.[52]

Since all those enemies had ambitions to which Britain was an obstacle, the task of reducing their number was not simple. Within another month the objective in relations with Germany was no longer general appeasement but avoidance of war. What turned out to be the last proposals for a general settlement failed to divert Hitler's attention from Austria. Chamberlain was rather more successful with Mussolini, at the cost of losing his foreign secretary.[53] No other allies were in sight. France, it was assumed, would defend herself in any case and her eastern allies were her responsibility. The strength and willingness of the Soviet Union were not rated highly. American good will was greatly prized, but there was no way of securing actual assistance. Cooperation improved during 1937. To British visitors such as Walter Runciman, President of the Board of Trade, Roosevelt was full of friendly words and hopes of promoting exchanges of information.[54] Henry Morgenthau, the Secretary of the Treasury, sought Chamberlain's views on reducing arms expenditure and preventing war. He received a plain reply that Britain could not halt her efforts to close the gap between her material strength and her obligations, and the greatest contribution the United States could make was to amend the neutrality laws.[55] Asked what Britain could do to retain American good will in the event of a major European crisis, Lindsay advised that at present nothing could draw Americans from isolationism, and an approach on a major political issue would only arouse the suspicion that Britain was trying to entangle the United States in war. But the Administration was well disposed, and any offer from it of cooperation should not be refused despite the perennial danger that the Americans 'lead you down the garden path until you are committed, and then you suddenly find yourself left all alone'. The best prospects for cooperation might be in the economic field, and a trade agreement might be of decisive importance.[56]

Cordell Hull had been pressing for trade negotiations for over a year. He believed, in a Cobdenite way, in the pacifying value of economic internationalism and its ability to transcend power politics among nations. He had been working since 1934 on a trade agreements programme. Hull strongly disliked all economic blocs, and in particular the system of imperial preferences set up by the Ottawa agreements of 1932. In the eyes of British imperialists such as Amery this had been a step towards an imperial economic system, which was seen as a natural alternative to national self-sufficiency (impossible for Britain) on the one hand and internationalism on the other. But the imperialists were not in control of British policy, still less of Dominion governments, which aimed at developing their countries' manufactures and securing free entry for their products into the United Kingdom. At Ottawa the Dominions proved the more successful bargainers. The outcome was not lower barriers to inter-imperial trade, but the diversion of trade. Ottawa did not help Britain recover its previous financial or trade position in the world. Non-Empire borrowers found it more difficult to service their sterling debts by export earnings, and suppliers of foodstuffs such as Argentina, the Scandinavian countries, and the United States suffered.[57]

The results of the Ottawa system may have been relatively unimportant, but Hull's policies raised serious problems for Britain. How far the Americans understood and intended the potential threat to Britain's international position is not clear. That they aimed at a formal economic hegemony is unlikely, even if they thought one possible without a political leadership that they did not want; but they felt no greater interest than they had ever felt in the past in sustaining Britain's position.[58] The danger was recognized in London, and in consequence the response to Hull's urgings towards negotiations for a trade agreement was hesitant. By the end of 1936 it was agreed in London that a trade agreement was desirable, mainly on political grounds. The problem remained whether there would be any political gain to justify the commercial price. Negotiations began in the winter of 1937–8.[59] Meanwhile Roosevelt, in a further gesture of cooperation, invited Chamberlain to visit the United States.[60] Chamberlain's reluctance to go, in the absence of any prospect of concrete results, has been taken as evidence of a failure to take the United States seriously, or even of anti-Americanism. But it seems clear that Roosevelt had no clear object for a visit, and unlikely that one would have made any difference to subsequent events. Eden was ready to pay a visit, but that was not Roosevelt's purpose; and although the Foreign Office continued to canvass the possibility of a Cabinet minister going to Washington to sign the trade agreement when it was ready, the negotiations were so long drawn out that the eventual success had little political value.

Over the war that broke out in China in July 1937 Roosevelt was ready to show an active interest, and was disposed to cooperate with other countries. Having delivered his 'Quarantine' speech at Chicago on 5 October, he sent a delegation to a conference at Brussels in November of the signatories of the Nine-Power Treaty of 1922.[61] What Roosevelt was hinting at in calling for a 'quarantine' of nations spreading the 'disease' of 'world lawlessness' is, like so many of Roosevelt's intentions, not certain. He may well not have had a clear idea himself. It seems most probable that the speech was meant as a step in his gradual education of American public opinion and an expression of his desire to exert influence. At the time the speech seemed to some observers to be an attack on isolation and a suggestion of something like economic pressure on Japan. This aroused mixed feelings not only in the United States but in London. Any prospect of closer Anglo-American cooperation was welcome, but concrete action was not expected, and some feared that having encouraged anti-Japanese enthusiasm the Americans would then pull back.[62] Chamberlain, although prepared to welcome the speech as a sign that America was abandoning the attitude of complete detachment, wrote to his sister:

'I very much fear . . . that after a lot of ballyhoo the Americans will somehow fade out and leave us to carry all the blame and the odium.'[63] The Brussels conference was not intended to plan action against Japan, and the Americans had no intention of taking a lead in it; but Japanese air attacks on HMS *Ladybird* and USS *Panay* on the Yangtze in December led to talk of a joint naval demonstration in the Pacific. Roosevelt even talked of a long-distance naval blockade of Japan which, he thought, would not involve a risk of war, and sent a naval officer to London to talk about technical cooperation; but when the Japanese apologized about the *Panay* the activity subsided.[64]

Roosevelt was certainly looking for some sort of programme by which he could exert United States influence in world affairs to halt the visible slide towards war in Europe and the Far East. American opinion was uncertain, but there was some demand for a more active peace policy.[65] Roosevelt was attracted by an idea of Sumner Welles, who had become Under-Secretary of State in the summer, that the United States should call a conference on standards of international conduct and on access to raw materials. Welles was looking to an international economy based on reduced armaments and equal access to world resources; and his plan was intended to appeal to German 'moderates' such as Schacht, the president of the Reichsbank.[66] Roosevelt took up Welles's plan in January 1938, and agreed to propose to all the countries with representatives in Washington discussion of the principles of international conduct, reduction of armaments and equality of economic opportunity. If the response was favourable, Roosevelt would invite representatives of nine small countries to join the United States in drawing up recommendations. Informing the British government, only, of this plan, Roosevelt added that if Chamberlain did not express wholehearted support within five days, he would abandon it. Chamberlain's reaction was, as is well known, unfavourable. He believed that Roosevelt's plan would cut across and confuse the delicate negotiations he was about to take up, or try to take up, with Hitler and Mussolini; and he did not believe that it could have any useful result. He was persuaded to reverse his initial rejection to the extent of offering to support the plan whenever it was announced, but Roosevelt now dropped it.[67]

It is highly unlikely that Roosevelt's proposal would have had any effect on the course of events in Europe or the Far East. It is, for example, hard to imagine Hitler taking seriously recommendations on disarmament or international behaviour from a group of small states (or one large one), and the governmental and army changes in Germany in February 1938, when Schacht was dismissed, demonstrated how little he was interested in ideas about access to raw materials. The degree of Roosevelt's disappointment at Chamberlain's rejection is disputed. He had shown no inclination to support British initiatives previously, and presumably felt less now; but he would not object to Chamberlain's policy of appeasement since he wished for appeasement himself. His distrust of Chamberlain may well have increased: American suspicion in general of British policy as selfish and immoral was certainly enhanced by Eden's resignation. For the next eight months Roosevelt was content to observe European events without attempting to take part. He had nothing to offer from the United States, and Chamberlain, despite his belief in the power of Anglo-American cooperation to impress the dictators, was well content to go it alone.

British policy in the critical year 1938 has been examined thoroughly.[68] With French policy paralysed in the nightmare possibility of having to go to war with Germany on behalf of an eastern ally and otherwise almost alone, Britain's role was crucial. Chamberlain, and the Cabinet, the Chiefs of Staff and the Foreign Office, shared in the public's wish to be spared war and were acutely aware of the state of the country's defences. In 1938 Chamberlain wanted to reach a general settlement with Germany and to resolve the Czechoslovak crisis without war, both because a peaceful solution was good in itself and because if there were a war now Britain might well be defeated. In this policy the government had the broad support of public opinion. Dissentient voices were at first not numerous, and on the whole criticized the government for having got the country into this situation: few, however, proposed a clear alternative. The Commonwealth was even more determined on appeasement than were the British people. Some imperialists in London realized that the League had masked the drifting apart of the Dominions' policies, and feared that there were not now sufficient common interests on which to build. A Canadian saw no possibility of a common Commonwealth foreign policy. Britain's policy, he thought, should be shaped in the light of her decline in power. Leadership would have to be left to those who were weightier. The Dominion high commissioners in London were urgent against war, and the Dominions Secretary, Malcolm MacDonald, genuinely feared the break-up of the Commonwealth if war came. The Cabinet's decisions were not governed by knowledge of this imperial weakness, but it was very present in their minds.[69]

On the American side the desire to keep out of war was still virtually unanimous. Sympathy for Czechoslovakia was strong, sympathy for Germany non-existent, sympathy for the western democracies was not as strong as suspicion of their supineness.[70] Roosevelt toyed with the idea of mediation, feared the consequences for the United States of a grave diminution of British power, issued general appeals, contemplated calling a conference, expressed distrust of Chamberlain, assured a French visitor that the United States could be relied on for everything except troops and money – in short, was at a loss to know what could be done.

Once the first relief at the removal of the imminent danger of war was absorbed, it was clear that British prestige had been severely damaged all round the world. In the United States, contempt for what was seen as British pusillanimity grew. For example, on 30 September Harold Ickes, the Secretary for the Interior, refrained from passing judgment on Britain and France and expressed respect for Chamberlain's persistence and courage. Early in November he at least half believed rumours that Chamberlain and Hitler had had the whole crisis fixed up in advance.[71] In this uncertain climate the Anglo-American trade negotiations finally came to a conclusion. They had been continuing all year, hampered by the system in which American interest groups could make repeated demands of their government. It was thought in London that the Americans were taking advantage of Britain's political need for an agreement to drive an unfair bargain. On their side the Americans became suspicious of suggestions, being explored in London, of Anglo-German trade cooperation.[72] They accepted the final British offer on the trade negotiations and the agreement was signed on 17 November. By this time no one expected great things of it, commercially or politically. Failure would have been politically very unfortunate; success was generally welcomed in Britain as likely to further Anglo-American friendship, but without expectations of diplomatic reinforcement, still less of a change in American foreign policy.[73]

Munich, with the disappearance of 35 well-equipped Czech divisions from the forces which could have been expected to meet Germany on land, transformed the strategic situation for Britain as well as for France. The implications were not absorbed for several months, but even while hopes of genuine cooperation with Germany remained alive in some quarters, the Chiefs of Staff were forced to recognize that France, faced with Germany and Italy, might give up the unequal struggle unless assured of the utmost British support. Rumours in January 1939 of an impending German attack on the Netherlands, which the Cabinet accepted would necessitate British intervention, combined with the newly felt need to take French pressures seriously to bring about a decision on 22 February to equip reserves for a field force destined for the continent.

The 'fourth arm' of defence was perforce being downgraded in importance. Treasury officials continued after Munich to point out the effects on the economy of greater borrowing for defence purposes. One wrote at the end of October, concerning proposals for reaching air equality with Germany by 1942:

> The difficulty ... is that we cannot say whether we shall be able to afford it. Indeed we think that we shall probably not be able to afford it without bringing down the general economy of the country and thus presenting Hitler with precisely that kind of peaceful victory which would be most gratifying to him.

Another worried in January that:

> Defence expenditure is now at a level which must seriously call in question the country's ability to meet it and a continuance at this level may well result in a situation in which the completeness of our material preparations against attack is frustrated by a weakening of our economic stability which

renders us incapable of standing the strain of war or even of maintaining those material defences in peace.

In the Cabinet at the beginning of February, Chamberlain spoke of finance as 'one of our strongest weapons in any war which was not over in a very short time'. But three weeks later he admitted that he could see no alternative to paying for an army to serve on the continent, and Simon, the Chancellor of the Exchequer, agreed that 'other aspects of the matter outweighed finance'.[74]

Meanwhile in the United States, British and French prestige remained low, and suspicion that appeasement might be renewed continued even after the guarantees to Poland, Romania and Greece in March–April 1939. Perceptions of British decadence did not lead Americans to conclude that their country must show leadership. One visitor noted that: 'If one partner believes, however untruly, that the other is not pulling his weight, he will be disinclined to accept responsibility for the other's commitments.' Hardly anyone chided American moral indignation as did the philosopher Bertrand Russell (a pacifist). 'It is difficult', he wrote in the *Nation*, 'to feel much respect for those who say: "This is a holy cause, therefore you ought to fight, but we ought only to look on and make money out of your necessities".'[75]

Roosevelt shared the impression of British moral weakness and did not at all relish suggestions that the United States should take up the burden. Setting off for a visit to America in January 1939, Lothian took with him papers on what the effect would be on the United States if the British Empire collapsed. In one of these Hankey argued that the United States would lose the position it now enjoyed of holding the balance of power throughout the world. Lothian told Roosevelt that Britain had defended civilization for a thousand years; but her arm was now weaker and the task was passing to the United States. Far from gratifying the President, this kind of talk angered him and he wrote to friends and spoke to associates of British cowardice[76] As with the Dominions in 1937, the problem was to convey the seriousness of the position without giving an impression of defeatism, and it appeared that Lothian had got it wrong. The episode worried the Foreign Office, as Lothian was being considered for the embassy in Washington; but Lindsay did not think Roosevelt was seriously put off. He talked positively to other British visitors about assistance if war came, and Lothian came home soberly optimistic about American policy. He was at pains, however, to convey to readers of the *Observer* that there were many obstacles to repeal of the neutrality laws, that if the United States acted at all it would be for her own interest and not from sentiment, and American support was more likely if Britain showed herself independent and vigorous.[77]

Roosevelt's advisers were divided, and torn in their own minds, as they contemplated the European situation. Adolf Berle, Assistant Secretary of State, considering the courses open to the United States at the beginning of April, saw great objections (apart from the difficulties about public opinion) to promising support to Britain and France. At the end of June, Berle confessed to mixed feelings: 'readjustments' in central Europe were 'apparently necessary', but would be the basis for further German expansion and an eventual challenge to Britain:

> We have no necessary interest in defending the British Empire, aside from the fact that we prefer the British as against the German method of running an empire. But we do have a very solid interest in having the British, and not the Germans, dominant in the Atlantic.

The latter would force the United States into military power or, 'still worse', into empire to preserve itself.[78]

In this very uncertain world situation and domestic state of mind, the Administration and Congress approached the question of revising the neutrality laws. Roosevelt's hold over Congress at the time was weak. Various bills and amendments dragged on through the Senate and the House of Representatives until the latter, on 30 June, voted by a narrow margin to maintain the embargo on arms and munitions (though not on 'implements of war') and the former refused to move at all in the present session. Whilst those like Hull who maintained that repeal would have affected Hitler's plans were certainly mistaken, it would as certainly have been an encouragement to the British and French. The outcome confirmed R.A. Butler, Under-Secretary of State in the Foreign Office, in his long-held opinion that 'we can no more count on America than on Brazil'. Publicly the reaction was muted, since the Administration's good will and efforts were recognized. The visit to the United States in June by the King and Queen had been a great success. *The Times* was careful to report the Congressional saga in purely factual terms. The *Economist* concluded that there was no reason for despair, as American public opinion would not allow the European democracies to be destroyed unaided.[79] The position in August 1939 thus was that the mandatory embargo on the export of arms, munitions and implements of war remained; the cash and carry provision, originally valid for two years, had lapsed; and since Britain was in default on the First World War debts the government was precluded from raising a loan in the United States.

In the Far East, Japanese pressure on British interests in China continued. The only possible responses seemed to be either to reach an accommodation with Japan or to play for time. The second was in many ways the easier policy to choose, since there was no immediate prospect of a direct Japanese attack; and as most expert advice agreed that Japan could not win in China, this was the path taken. In the summer of 1938 Craigie, the ambassador in Tokyo, had discussions with the Japanese Foreign Minister about possible cooperation, but they came to nothing and in the September crisis the Japanese position was unequivocally pro-German. Munich temporarily eased the tension; but at the beginning of November the Japanese government announced the founding of a new order in east Asia, aiming to minimize or exclude western influence in China and build a tripartite Chinese–Manchukuo–Japanese movement under Japanese leadership. Soon afterwards reports began to appear that the anti-Comintern pact was to be converted into a military alliance. The prospects either of such an alliance or of a new order covering a willing China and extending to Indo-China and Malaya seemed almost equally unwelcome and dangerous. Craigie thought that Britain must do something positive to stave off the dangers, and suggested that he should try to find out whether a tripartite alliance could still be averted, and at what price. Once again, however, the conclusion in London was negative. It seemed unlikely that Japan could be bought off by any price that Britain could safely pay, and the

hope of American collaboration in Europe was more important than ever. To Cadogan, Vansittart's successor as Permanent Under-Secretary in the Foreign Office, 'the overriding
consideration is the danger of alienating the United States'.[80]

In the summer of 1939 the Japanese blockaded the British
concession at Tientsin. To settle the crisis the British were obliged
to yield some rights. It was no longer a question of inducing
Japan to pay greater regard to British interests in China nor,
as had been discussed in the winter, of whether sending a naval
squadron to Singapore would prevent Japan:

> creating a vast closed area from which she would be able to
> draw nearly all the raw materials which are essential to her
> and thereby attaining such strength as might enable her sub-
> sequently to absorb into that area other territories produc-
> ing two at least of the other raw materials of really vital
> importance to her, oil in the Netherlands East Indies and
> high-grade iron ore in Malaya

and thus presenting, alone or in combination with Germany
and Italy, a permanent threat to British interests throughout
the eastern hemisphere.[81] Instead, in the first months of 1939
the principle that, if necessary, the Mediterranean should be
abandoned in order to send the fleet to Singapore had come
under serious question in the light of the growing prospect of
war in Europe and the situation in the Middle East. The strategic problem, reduced to its simplest terms, was whether defeat in the Far East should be risked for the sake of knocking
out Italy. Defeat in Europe, it was accepted, would mean the
defeat of the British Empire as a whole; but would victory in
Europe ensure that initial defeat in the Far East could be re-
trieved? The effect on Britain's imperial position of failing to
support Australia and New Zealand would be grave, but de-
nuding the Mediterranean also had imperial implications in
Egypt, Palestine and, eventually, East Africa.

The Committee of Imperial Defence accepted in May 1939
that it was impossible to say how soon after a Japanese intervention a fleet could be sent to the Far East, and accepted
that there had been a 'considerable scaling down of our undertaking to the Dominions to send a fleet to the Far East in all

circumstances'. That undertaking had hitherto been repeated, most recently at the Imperial Conference of 1937, despite recognition that its fulfilment would depend on conditions in Europe, and now the Australian High Commissioner in London, Stanley Bruce, was alarmed. Chamberlain reassured the Australian government that Britain was not reneging on her promises, but the truth was that if Great Britain and France were engaged in war with Germany, Italy and Japan at the same time, their situation would be desperate. Moreover Britain's financial reserves were inadequate for a long war, and unless the United States intervened success could hardly be hoped for.[82]

In the final stages of the crisis in Europe, Roosevelt sent messages to Mussolini, Hitler and the Polish President appealing for peace. They were sent largely for domestic purposes. On the recipients, as Berle observed, they would have 'the same effect as a valentine sent to somebody's mother-in-law out of season, and they have all that quality of naïvete which is the prerogative alone of the United States.'[83] Roosevelt had no intention of asking the American people to remain neutral in thought, and would apply the neutrality laws in a manner as favourable to the allies as possible. The position was quite different from that in 1914. But both the people and the President were determined that whilst the United States might sell supplies to one side only, it should keep out of the impending European war. Distrust remained at all levels including the highest, born on the British side of a conviction that whatever the professions of shared principles the American government was not capable of international action, and on the American side of residual Anglophobia and a suspicion that British policy was selfish and tricky. Policy-makers on both sides still lacked the kind of half-instinctive understanding of what Lord Tweedsmuir, the Governor-General of Canada, called 'the things at the back of each other's minds',[84] that comes from continuous interaction over a long time on common activities. Such understanding does not necessarily mean agreement, as Anglo-French relations showed; but without it talk of shared principles could be misleading.

5
The Second World War and American Predominance

It was during the Second World War that the United States emerged as an active acknowledged world power, able to develop and harness enormous productive capacity that had lain idle through the 1930s, raise very large armed forces, and apply this strength all round the world. The Soviet Union too became, at appalling cost, a major power on the world stage. By the end of the war Britain, which with the Dominions was the only belligerent to have fought from first to last, was relegated to second or perhaps third place. Whilst involved with and obliged to take account of the Soviet Union as a vital ally, Britain became to a greater degree dependent on the United States.

Dependence on American money and supplies was already substantial before the United States entered the war in December 1941. Although its benevolence was regarded from the start as of the utmost importance, there was little prospect of much material help even when the neutrality law was revised in November 1939, repealing the arms embargo and reinstating the cash and carry provision of the 1937 act. The British and French governments did not instantly multiply their purchases of munitions. In any case American productive capacity at present was small: the British government had not been able to envisage the United States as a major source of war supplies and had had little idea of helping to create a capacity in advance of need.[1] Even so, dollars had to be husbanded, and spending was switched to war supplies from farm products and tobacco which could be bought elsewhere for sterling. American farmers complained loudly, and resentment of British blockade measures mounted in early 1940 to an outbreak of public ill feeling, official protests, and accusations that Britain was using the war as an excuse to divert trade away from the United States.[2] It began to look like a rerun of difficulties in the First World War.

The German victories in Scandinavia and western Europe in April–June 1940 altered all expectations. Hitler became master of the resources of Europe, and the naval situation in the Mediterranean and the eastern Atlantic was transformed. The German victories were as great a shock to the Americans as to the European peoples. Hitherto the war had seemed far away and of little concern. Even in circles where doubt had been felt about an Allied victory, few had expected Allied defeat. The prospect of American security being threatened had hardly entered any minds. When the blow fell the United States was in no position to act effectively, even if the Administration and the people had been willing to do so. Public opinion was fully behind efforts to put the national defences in order, and increasingly willing to supply material aid to Britain, but the relationship between the two objectives presented problems. At Charlottesville on 10 June, the day Italy entered the war, Roosevelt promised to extend the country's resources to the opponents of force; but there were few spare stocks and the transfer of material belonging to the armed forces was forbidden unless the Chiefs of Staff certified that it was not necessary to the defence of the United States. If Britain too were going to be defeated prudence indicated keeping all available resources for the United States itself. The military authorities were naturally inclined to play safe, one remarking that if mobilization were not needed for two years weapons could be spared for Britain, but if it became necessary sooner and needed artillery had been let go, anyone who had been party to the decision might expect to be found hanging from a lamppost.[3] On the other hand powerful voices in the Administration – Morgenthau, the new Secretaries for War and the Navy Henry L. Stimson and Frank Knox – and groups such as William Allen White's Committee to Defend America by Aiding the Allies and the Century Group, argued that Britain was America's first line of defence, so that it was worth running risks to send the British all that they could use now.

On the British side there was no doubt of the vital necessity of American help. In a memorandum of 25 May on strategy in the event of a French collapse, the Chiefs of Staff wrote that without full American economic and financial support, 'we do not think we could continue the war with any chance of success'. Arthur Greenwood, a member of the War Cabinet and chairman of a newly established Production Council, reported on 16 June: 'However admirable the spirit of the country, the task of maintaining a prolonged resistance . . . will be well-nigh insupportable unless we are able to draw assistance on a large scale from the New World.'[4] There was less unanimity on whether American belligerency was desirable. Chamberlain had doubted it in January.[5] Now in that desperate summer the moral effect would certainly have been great, even if hopes of immediate action were illusory. The press was careful not to ask for American intervention. Churchill would not countenance any suggestion that American supplies alone would be preferable.[6] Later, to encourage the passage of the Lend-Lease bill, Churchill might tell Americans: 'Give us the tools, and we will finish the job.' In fact, it was soon recognized that even given the tools Britain and the Commonwealth could never hope to arm and put in the field forces large enough to defeat Germany.

One weapon for which the British (and the French, while they were able) appealed repeatedly in the summer was destroyers. Churchill first mentioned them in a message to Roosevelt on 15 May,[7] and went on asking over the next weeks; but Roosevelt was loath to seek Congressional approval, and Admiral Stark, the Chief of Naval Operations, was opposed to releasing any ships. A solution was eventually found in the suggestion of a deal that would obviously enhance the security of the United States, the grant of bases in the West Indies, Newfoundland and Bermuda. This, Halifax told the War Cabinet, 'corresponds to a realistic view of Anglo-American relations both in the present and in the future'. For nearly a century the British Empire had almost alone guarded the English-speaking peoples by sea. 'But in future we may well neither be capable of performing these functions unaided, nor can we reasonably hope for cordial collaboration from America unless we share with her the strategic facilities which these duties will require.'[8]

Linking the offer of bases with the transfer of ships took

another month of negotiation.[9] Roosevelt was still slow to move, fearful of isolationist and Republican reaction and anxious to counter it by getting not only the largest number of bases but an assurance on the future of the British fleet – a subject of as much or greater American anxiety as the fate of the French fleet had been to the British in June. The British government on its side was worried about the effect on public opinion of the appearance of an unequal bargain, about mentioning the possibility of defeat in connection with the fleet, and about allowing the Americans to think that they could get the benefit of the fleet while remaining neutral. On one calculation the United States got a very good bargain: as the *Economist* put it, 'the price of fifty destroyers for a century's lease of six bases might even be called cheap'. On another calculation it was not only a step away from neutrality but the beginning of a process by which, as Churchill put it to the House of Commons, the British Empire and the United States would 'have to be somewhat mixed up together in some of their affairs for mutual and general advantage'.[10]

By the end of September the immediate threat of disaster had lifted. The great air battles over England had not given Hitler the air mastery he needed to launch an invasion. It was again possible to envisage a long war in which material American help would be well spent. But with a growth of American confidence in Britain's survival came worrying evidences of complacency. Roosevelt's re-election as President in November was greeted with enthusiasm, and some expectations of early American intervention in the war. When nothing happened, it was decided to address to him a full statement of Britain's needs. Among these was money. Once financial prudence was abandoned in May, Britain's dollar resources began to drain away at speed, and massive financial assistance was likely to be needed by the middle of 1941. It took months to convince the Administration. Morgenthau had to be convinced, and then had to be able to convince a sceptical Congress, that Britain was doing her utmost and was not trying to inveigle the United States into the war by means of loans as – it was still believed – she had been inveigled in 1917. The conviction that Britain had enormous overseas assets was universal, shared not least by Roosevelt: the difference between, say, tin mines in Malaya or railways in Argentina and liquid dollars was not readily understood; the difficulty of selling even investments in the United States at a useful price was underestimated.[11]

Lothian, returning from London after the election, opened up public debate by telling the press that Britain's resources were running low. The long letter which Churchill addressed to Roosevelt on 8 December presented the whole picture of the interconnected problems of merchant shipping, naval escorts, munitions and money. 'The more rapid and abundant the flow of munitions and ships which you are able to send us', the letter ended:

> the sooner will our dollar credits [i.e. credit balance] be exhausted . . . Indeed as you know orders already placed or under negotiation, including expenditures settled or pending for creating munitions factories in the United States, many times exceed the total exchange resources at the disposal of Great Britain. The moment approaches when we shall no longer be able to pay cash for shipping and other supplies.

Roosevelt had begun to think about the financial problem but still believed that Britain had enough assets to finance actual munitions purchases if his own authorities took over the capital cost of creating plant. Now made aware of the urgency, and of the obstacles arising on every hand in the way of current measures, he returned from a cruise in the Caribbean with the idea of 'eliminat[ing] the dollar sign' from British orders. In his press conference on 17 December Roosevelt used the analogy of lending one's hose to a neighbour to put out a fire; and in his fireside chat broadcast of 29 December he called on the nation to make itself the 'great arsenal of democracy'.[12]

Thus Lend-Lease was born. The precise form was not known until the bill – entitled one 'To Promote the Defense of the United States' – was published on 9 January. Even then the principle received less attention in the press than the projected increase in production; and the enthusiasm in Britain was tempered by a realization of how long it would take for supplies to grow from a trickle to a flood.[13] Opposition in the United States came from varied quarters, traditional isolationists, believers in hemispheric defence, constitutionalists who feared that the powers to be given to the President amounted to dictatorship, others who feared that war would be made more likely. Col. Charles Lindbergh could still see no advantage to the United States in a British victory over Germany. Lend-lease was not a blank cheque. The United States was not committed to paying all Britain's dollar costs from a given date; difficulties over financing continued in the period before the bill became law, and Morgenthau continued to insist on the sale of British assets.[14] Nevertheless Lend-Lease really was an 'unsordid act', and whatever Roosevelt said – and genuinely meant – about it helping to keep the United States out of war, full participation was brought one step nearer.

At the same time the two governments were exchanging ideas on strategy. This had begun in the summer, arising from American anxiety about the future of the British fleet and British anxiety about American intentions in the Pacific. In November, Admiral Stark produced an appreciation, the conclusion of which was that America's future was tied to Britain's defence. If Britain were defeated the military consequences for the United States would be serious: she might not '*lose everywhere*' but might well not '*win anywhere*'. The United States therefore could not afford to see Britain defeated, but Britain alone might be defeated and at best she had neither the manpower nor the means to conduct the land offensive in Europe which was the only way to defeat Germany. Therefore the United States must help with men, munitions and supplies, concentrating on the Atlantic. If Japan entered the war, Admiral Stark suggested a limited defensive war in the Pacific in collaboration with the British and the Dutch.[15] Staff talks were held in Washington in January–February 1941. They were mainly concerned with the Pacific, and not much was achieved there. Almost all the American military and naval staffs were suspicious of the British in general, and of British motives in seeking American reinforcement of Singapore in particular. They refused to plan to send ships to Singapore and left the British to face another nine months of uncertainty whether a Japanese attack on British possessions alone would bring them into the war. On the other hand the Americans, while stressing that no commitments could be made, were clear that if the United States entered the war the main objective would be the defeat of Germany.

This proved in the end the most important and far-reaching strategic decision. The United States turned away from concentrating on the Pacific, where the army had no role and the British would happily have left American naval power predominant, and accepted, even claimed, a major role in the Atlantic.[16]

What form, if any, American political involvement in world affairs might take was at this time discussed only in the most general terms in Britain and hardly at all in the United States.[17] But Keynes, representing the Treasury in Washington in the summer of 1941, found Roosevelt determined that the United States would not pull out after the war. He refused, Keynes reported, 'to consider the possibility that America would not take her full share of responsibility for the postwar situation in Europe, political as well as economic'.[18]

At this stage such determination on Roosevelt's part was more important than details of a future international organization or the like. And by the summer of 1941 America's contribution to the war, as well as her ultimate power, had justified the claim to a voice. The Atlantic Charter issued by Roosevelt and Churchill at their meeting at Placentia Bay, Newfoundland, in August was a kind of commitment to share in providing postwar security. In this respect, and in being a joint statement, it was more than an updated version of Woodrow Wilson's Fourteen Points. The declaration was generally welcomed in the United States as a high statement of principle. It was also greeted as an Anglo-American alliance, welcomed as such by some, and criticized by others. But Roosevelt meant what he said on his return, that the United States was no nearer to war than when he had set out. He had avoided giving Churchill an assurance that a Japanese attack on British possessions would bring the United States in, and the stages of American involvement in the Atlantic, which in retrospect seemed so inexorable, were still slow and hesitant.

There was little military discussion at the Atlantic meeting. Churchill gave one of his surveys of the state of the war, and the British Chiefs of Staff gave their American counterparts a strategic review.[19] It did not breathe great optimism or vigour. American assistance was thought of more in naval terms than for the prospect of large armies. The effort involved in shipping modern armies was regarded as so great that it was vain to think of building up on the continent a force large enough to defeat the entire German army in the field. The German war machine would have to be worn down by attrition before more limited land operations became possible. The essential British dilemma remained: inadequate means for the intended purpose; but no other means were available or could become so until the terms of the problem had changed.

By the time of the Atlantic meeting such a change had begun with the German attack on the Soviet Union, which was in the end to do so much to destroy the German war machine. But at this point the outcome was wholly uncertain: neither the British nor the American staffs thought Soviet chances good, and the prospects for anything other than immediate aid were not discussed. The American Chiefs of Staff were not greatly impressed by the British review, but they were not yet in a position to offer an alternative. They were convinced that Hitler could only be defeated by a large-scale invasion of Europe, and that the United States would have to enter the war. They were thinking of war with Japan as well. But their present plans were directed almost exclusively to the defence of the western hemisphere: there was no equipment for more. For the immediate future Britain and Russia should be supported and reinforced, with the emphasis on blockade, bombing and peripheral operations, while Japan was held in check. Land armies must, however, be built up: 'It should be recognized as an almost invariable rule that only land armies can finally win wars.' If all this were to be done and victory achieved, previous American production programmes would have to be at least doubled.[20]

Whilst American strategic influence could not be great in advance of active belligerency and large forces to put into the field, Lend-Lease already offered the Americans an opportunity to influence Britain's postwar economic policy. After the Lend-Lease bill became law, negotiation of an agreement on implementing it was delayed by disputes between the United States Treasury and the State Department on who should be responsible and the basis of the terms to be asked of the British. No one wished to recreate the debt problem of the interwar years: the State Department wanted to commit Britain to abandon imperial preference and join in promoting an 'open world' economy of a kind that would further American commercial interests, while the Treasury thought more in terms of material compensation.[21] When negotiations began the British were not inclined to hurry. They were ready to promise to discuss future cooperation in general terms, but there were suggestions that it would be worth playing for time, in the expectation that if the United States came into the war better terms would be available. There was strong opposition from some Conservative ministers to any sacrifice of imperial preference: other groups, not opposed to liberalization, were very reluctant to undertake to abandon economic controls before knowing what postwar conditions would be. British views on postwar economic policy were largely governed by fear of a huge adverse balance of payments, struggle to rebuild exports, and shortage of dollars. American views were greatly affected by fear of a postwar slump. Both were affected by past commercial rivalry, a factor which, when combined with the scale of the aid given, made it natural for business and Congressional opinion to find it hard to see why Britain should need to export at all and retain a measure of independence. The terms ultimately agreed were harder for Britain than those required of other recipients of Lend-Lease.

Neither Roosevelt nor Churchill wanted to include detailed formulations in the statement of common principles which became the Atlantic Charter. The fourth point simply promised that the two countries would 'endeavour, with due respect for their existing obligations, to further the enjoyment by all States ... of access, on equal terms, to the trade and to the raw materials of the world which are needed for their economic prosperity'. Even this was farther than the Cabinet wanted to go, but it safeguarded Britain's relations with the Dominions while for the Americans it secured a promise of movement towards equal trade. Negotiations about the Lend-Lease agreement dragged on until February 1942. The Americans continued to press for a British commitment to abolish discrimination. They professed to be bearing British anxieties about postwar conditions in mind, and to be convinced that freedom of trade was the best possible solution; but some of their actions were incompatible with these professions, and some of their demands were seen in Britain as hypocritical and greedy. Eventually Roosevelt gave an assurance that the Lend-Lease agreement did not contain an advance commitment to abolish imperial preference but only one to hold discussions on agreed action. It has been suggested that Churchill accepted the assurance under a mistaken impression that imperial preference had been excluded altogether. This seems unlikely. Roosevelt's assurance did soften the State Department's position; it gave the British a little more room to manoeuvre; and most importantly it enabled them to get out of a position that was becoming seriously embarrassing to cooperation with the United States in what was now a common war.

'So we had won after all.' Thus Churchill reflected on the news of Pearl Harbor.[22] But there was no expectation of an early turn to the fortunes of war. Quite apart from the naval losses in the Japanese attack, it would be anything up to two years before large American ground and air forces could be fully deployed. There were severe defeats to come. In the Far East, the loss of Singapore was the greatest disaster for the British Empire, and the Japanese took Burma, the Netherlands East Indies, the Philippines, part of New Guinea, and a number of Pacific islands before their advance was stemmed at the battle of the Coral Sea. In North Africa, where a British winter offensive reached the border of Tripolitania, Rommel's counter-offensive captured Tobruk and brought him well into Egypt at El Alamein in June 1942. In Russia, the German summer offensive reached the Volga at Stalingrad, and the doors to the Caucasus, and again raised the spectre of a Soviet collapse. Shipping losses remained dangerously high throughout 1942: the Battle of the Atlantic was not won until the spring of the following year.

American predominance among the western Allies was certain to come, and was already assumed by American opinion;[23] but when Churchill and the Chiefs of Staff hastened to Washington in December 1941 they found their American counterparts inadequately prepared for strategic discussions, although convinced that despite Japan's entry into the war Germany was still the prime enemy.[24] It was agreed to develop offensive action against Germany, and to maintain a defensive strategy in the east. Machinery was set up, in the Combined Chiefs of Staff, for cooperation and decision-making that worked better than anything achieved between the Allies in the First World

War. Conscious of their country's coming preponderance, the American military were determined not to be forced to adopt a preexisting British strategy. Widespread in political and military circles was a suspicion of the British as both effete and wily in playing power politics, actuated solely by British interests while Americans, apparently, had no such mundane motives – it was to be one of Eisenhower's merits as an Allied commander that he recognized that they had. So far as the war with Germany was concerned, British doubts about the feasibility of an early landing in western Europe and desire to exploit opportunities in the Mediterranean were often interpreted as reluctance to meet the enemy head on. In the Far East, almost all Americans believed that Britain's concerns were those of an outdated imperialism antithetical to American principles. Strategic coordination in the war against Japan was never as good as it was in Europe, partly because the Pacific and South-East Asia theatres were widely separated, partly because of the personalities of individual commanders, partly because the Americans did not wish to be closely associated with what they perceived to be British aims. Nevertheless the practice of working together encouraged relationships of trust, not least between Field Marshal Sir John Dill, head of the British Joint Staff Mission in Washington, and General George C. Marshall, the American Chief of Staff.[25]

In the spring and summer of 1942 discussion and differences centred on the question of a landing in western Europe in 1942 or 1943, or a landing in north-west Africa.[26] Marshall and the American army planners were convinced of the advantages of a concentrated attack on France, and wanted to give priority to building up American forces in the United Kingdom in preparation for such an attack in 1943, with if possible a limited landing in 1942 (for which the Commonwealth would have to provide most of the forces) to take some of the German weight off the Russian front. The Russians, and a good deal of British and American public opinion, clamoured for a 'second front now'; Roosevelt and Churchill were determined that something must be done in 1942, and Roosevelt even gave the Soviet Foreign Minister Molotov a half-promise of a landing in Europe. The British Chiefs of Staff agreed about the build-up for 1943, but concluded that lack of landing craft made it impracticable to launch in 1942 a landing that would be substantial enough to help the Russians. In the summer the British came to favour a large-scale landing in French North Africa; Marshall feared that it would absorb too many resources needed for the 1943 landing in Europe. At the end of July Roosevelt ordered the North African landing. It is not clear that either he or Churchill understood that this would make it impossible to build up enough forces in Britain for a landing in Europe the following year.

The fall of Singapore shattered the British imperial position in the eastern hemisphere, and the repercussions spread widely. For Australia and New Zealand it brought to a head developments in relations between them and Britain and the United States that had been long in the making.[27] Both countries had hoped for American involvement but had not bargained for Pearl Harbor and the loss of the Philippines. Both, despite some misgivings, had relied upon British assurances about Singapore and had sent troops to fight in the Mediterranean and Middle East. The exposure of Australia to what seemed for a time a real threat of Japanese invasion, gave rise to accusations about deception and betrayal from the Labour government of Australia which lingered in Australian minds for many years, and forecasts of a turn to the United States. There followed disputes over the return of Australian divisions from the Middle East, and demands for reinforcements somewhat out of proportion to the threat or to overall strategy. The strength of Australian feeling was taken seriously in London, but apart from soothing language and attempts to allay fears about future help there was not much the British government could do.

Nor in fact did the Australians fare very much better with the United States. Even American words were not always encouraging. 'Viewed in the cold, hard light of strategic reality', wrote a columnist in the *New York Times*:

Australasia – except to the Australians – is not strategically vital to the cause of the United Nations. Politically it would be unthinkable to allow Australia, child of democracy, to be ravaged by totalitarianism without aiding her. But militarily, strategically, in this struggle for the world, Australia is an outpost, and one that could be lost without losing the war.[28]

Roosevelt was little better at consulting the Australians than London was: the Pacific Council set up in Washington was purely consultative and was little consulted.

Another consequence of the war in the east was the destruction of the prewar British position of superiority among the western powers in China, and the substitution of American influence. The Americans were quite sure that this was their right, and that they had a special relationship with China which would enable them to secure a better future for Asia and commercial advantages for the United States. They also saw China as the best ally against Japanese attempts to depict the war as one between the white and other races, and as a future partner in maintaining order in the western Pacific. China was built up in the public mind as a true democracy and Chiang Kai-shek as a great statesman. Chiang Kai-shek's regime, which had been at war with Japan since 1937, was not anxious to engage in large-scale fighting but asked for quantities of assistance. Americans on the spot did not harbour illusions about Chinese efficiency or zeal, but were also not impressed by British leadership in India, and assumed, unlike their British counterparts, that British and American interests in the Far East conflicted.

The manner and scale of British defeats in the east activated traditional American anti-imperialism. Amongst a chorus of criticism of the British Empire, now guilty of incompetence as well as inherent sinfulness, Walter Lippmann wrote that:

> the western nations must now . . . identify their cause with the freedom and the security of the peoples of the East, putting away the 'white man's burden' and purging themselves of the taint of an obsolete and obviously unworkable white man's imperialism. In this drastic reorientation of war policy, the leadership of the western nations must be taken by the United States . . . Now it is evident that for the American people the objective of the eastern war is not and cannot be the recapture and restoration of the white man's empire.[29]

On 12 October 1942 the editors of *Life* magazine addressed an 'Open Letter' to the 'People of England'. Americans, they wrote, were not all agreed on war aims but on one point they were unanimous: 'One thing we are sure we are *not* fighting for is

to hold the British Empire together.' They could see no principle in the British presence in India, and entreated the British to forsake 'Your side of the war' and join 'Our side' – that
of freedom.[30] The press gave extensive coverage to the world
tour of Wendell Willkie, who had been the Republican presidential candidate in 1940. In a speech at Chungking, Willkie
called not only for the freedom of colonial peoples but for
timetables for their independence. In a broadcast on his return home Willkie announced that men and women all over
the world were resolved 'as we must be, that there is no more
place for imperialism within their own society than in the society of nations'. Churchill responded with the statement, in a
speech at the Mansion House on 10 November, that Britain
had no acquisitive ambitions anywhere in the world, but 'We
mean to hold our own. I have not become the King's First
Minister to preside over the liquidation of the British Empire.'[31]

Not even all progressive Americans agreed with *Life*. Freda
Kirchwey, for example, the editor of the *Nation*, pointed out
that America could not write the Empire out of existence and
at the same time fight all over the world side by side with its
armies and fleets. Americans could 'ill afford to mutter vague
threats about refusing to fight if the British did not "move
over to our side." They are already on our side, and they were
there long before we were, if you'll forgive the paradox.'[32] Dismantling the British Empire did not become an American war
aim. Nevertheless anti-imperialism remained deeply ingrained
in the American outlook, and a distinction was drawn between
the British at home, admired for their courage and endurance,
and British imperialists abroad. Roosevelt was quite typical in
his anti-imperialism. He never devoted much thought to policy,
remaining at the level of shock at the poverty of the Gambia
(seen on the way to Casablanca in 1943) and reluctance to see
France restored as a colonial power in Asia. He tried to intervene in India in 1942, but having been rebuffed by Churchill
did not again venture into British imperial affairs. American
advisers, on the other hand, began to discuss policies such as
trusteeship, to realize that independence might not necessarily
be appropriate for all colonial territories, and even, by the end
of the war, to see some merit in the continued existence of
the British Empire.[33] And at the same time the expected need

for bases in the Pacific was leading other advisers to advocate taking islands over from allies and exercising general control over wide areas. This would not be imperialism, said the General Board of the Navy, because the islands had no economic value.[34]

For the British, India was a real danger spot in 1942. A mission by Sir Stafford Cripps to negotiate a political settlement ended in failure,[35] but it was clear to all except perhaps Churchill that negotiations for independence would have to start at the end of the war. Colonial officials began to discuss future policy and development. In the east the *status quo ante* 1941 could not simply be restored when the territories were recovered. Attempts were made both to explain the Empire to Americans and to justify American interest to British newspaper readers.[36] The Australian and New Zealand governments came out in favour of applying trusteeship to all colonial territories, not just former League of Nations mandates. As far as the Dominions were concerned, the process of separation continued. The Australians, in particular the ambitious Minister for Foreign Affairs, Evatt, were coming to see a role for their country as a regional power in the Pacific. Canadian hackles were raised by suggestions from Halifax, who had become ambassador in Washington after Lothian's death, early in 1944 that the Commonwealth and Empire might speak with a single voice in the postwar world.[37]

In the summer of 1942 American war production overtook Britain's. There was now substance for the conviction found by Richard Law, Minister of State at the Foreign Office, on a visit to America:

that the United States stands for something in the world – something of which the world has need, something which the world is going to like, something, in the final analysis, which the world is going to take, whether it likes it or not.[38]

Even so, some of the ambitions seemed excessive. Morgenthau, for example, surprised his associates at the Treasury with an idea (which he never developed further) that since the United States was likely to have to pay the cost of liberating and relieving Europe she should take on the whole burden of constructing a Europe that might live at peace for a century, regardless of British, Russian and smaller European Allied ideas.[39]

The Americans did not yet have the dominant voice in western strategy. After the decision for a North African landing, debate continued on the merits of follow-up operations in the Mediterranean and the possibility of an assault in north-west Europe.[40] Underlying the arguments were anxieties about keeping the Soviet Union in the war, and somewhat different British and American conceptions of the possible. The American army's theory of a war of mass and concentration reflected confidence in the apparently unlimited capacity of their country's industrial machine and manpower. For them shortages were not a problem to be put up with (as they were for the British) but a temporary obstacle to be overcome. The British concept was suited to a country with limited resources and widely dispersed interests. At the Casablanca conference in January 1943 the issues were fully debated; the Americans were not overborne, but the British view largely prevailed.[41] General S.D. Embick came away deeply suspicious of British aims in the Mediterranean. The purpose behind Britain's strategy, he believed, was 'not primarily military, but . . . political'.[42]

Fortunately for the working of the alliance some American officers were coming to recognize that strategy was not entirely divorced from politics, and that alliance politics mattered. Eisenhower, now accustomed to working with a combined staff and with British commanders, rebuked a friend in Washington for his attitude. 'I am not so incredibly naïve', he wrote:

> that I do not realize that the Britishers instinctively approach every military problem from their viewpoint of the Empire, just as we approach them from the viewpoint of American interests. But one of the constant sources of danger to us in this war is the temptation to regard as our first enemy the partner that must work with us in defeating the real enemy.[43]

Marshall rebuked Stilwell for objecting to sharing with the British intelligence information in China on the grounds that the Chinese would not like it. 'This matter', he wrote:

> brings up the entire question of cooperation with the British upon which I must give you my frank views. Regardless of

any feeling the Chinese may have . . . the British are our principal ally in fighting this war . . . Any action which tends
toward bringing about a serious cleavage between us and the
British will have a most serious effect on the conduct of the
war.[44]

Nevertheless the American Joint War Plans Committee reported
in May 1943 that Britain:

dominates her empire by controlling the economic destiny
of her dominions and crown colonies. She maintains her
position in the European area by preserving the balance of
power on the Continent. She exploits the resources and people
of other nations to insure her position of dominance. British war policy is influenced by these national policies and
her postwar economic, territorial and political ambitions.

The foremost aims of the United States, on the other hand,
were hemispheric security and improvement of her economic
position by reciprocal trade pacts. These did not depend on
or require a balance of power, so American military policy was
'not strongly influenced by postwar aims'. And Stimson, who
had come to the conclusion a year earlier that the British leadership was tired and defeatist, solemnly advised Roosevelt after
a visit to London in July 1943 that:

We cannot now rationally hope to be able to cross the Channel
and come to grips with our German enemy under a British
commander. His Prime Minister and his Chief of Imperial
Staff are frankly at variance with such a proposal. The shadows
of Passchendaele and Dunkerque still hang too heavily over
the imagination of these leaders of his government. Though
they have rendered lip service to the operation, their hearts
are not in it and it will require more independence, more
faith and more vigour than it is reasonable to expect we can
find in any British commander to overcome the natural difficulties of such an operation carried on in such an atmosphere of his government.

There was a 'vital difference of faith'.[45]

The differences in the summer of 1943 were really more of emphasis than of principle; but the emphasis involved detailed dispositions of forces, and scope for much argument.[46] Marshall, determined on the largest and earliest possible invasion of northwest Europe, felt let down by British aspirations to exploit the overthrow of Mussolini and Italian approaches for an armistice. He was also under pressure from Admiral King to expand operations in the Pacific. Marshall prepared for a showdown with the British at the Quebec conference in August, but they were at last able to convince the Americans of their determination to put their full effort into the cross-Channel attack, and won some understanding of the relation between that and operations in Italy. It was, however, significant that the agreement reached was based on American proposals; and American predominance was confirmed at Tehran in November. In the summer Roosevelt, to Churchill's dismay, had proposed to meet Stalin on his own. That proposal had not come off, but now at Tehran Roosevelt, it seemed, went out of his way to emphasize to Stalin his independence of Churchill and to join with the Russians in teasing the Prime Minister. It was here that Churchill, according to a much-quoted story, realized for the first time what a small nation Britain was, between 'the great Russian bear on one side of me . . . and on the other side the great American buffalo'.[47] It was also here that the date for the cross-Channel assault was fixed for May 1944. After initially showing strong interest in the Balkans, Stalin at Tehran insisted on a definite date for the cross-Channel assault, and favoured a landing in the south of France. This was what the Americans wanted, but the outcome was as much due to circumstances – German resistance in Italy and Turkish refusal to risk German wrath – as it was a triumph for Marshall.

At Cairo after Tehran the combined planners at last agreed on a strategy against Japan, a two-pronged attack through the central Pacific and up the New Guinea–Netherlands East Indies–Philippines axis. South-East Asia was effectively reduced to a secondary theatre. Strategy against Japan involved political considerations for the Americans as well as for the British. William Howard Gardiner, for example, a former president of the Navy League, advised the State Department in March 1943 that:

It would be of very very great postwar importance to the
United States, both politically and commercially, if the war
to crush Japan could be carried on, in the main, by the United
States . . . Such a procedure would improve immeasurably the
peace settlements we would be able to make in the regime
of the Pacific, and our future political standing and commercial opportunities in Asia and in Australasia.[48]

The British too saw their coming contribution to the war against
Japan in a political light, but were not agreed on where it should
most effectively be made. The Chiefs of Staff argued that it
should be a highly visible naval contribution in the Pacific.
Churchill, on the other hand, and a number of his Cabinet
colleagues, believed that it was essential for British prestige
that their possessions in the Far East should be recovered by
British efforts and not just mopped up in the wake of American advances elsewhere.[49] In the end the Chiefs of Staff prevailed, and Churchill at the second Quebec conference in
September 1944 offered a fleet contribution in the Pacific and
an offensive against Rangoon. Roosevelt accepted the fleet at
once; but Admiral King made it very clear that he did not
want it.[50]

Meanwhile the United States government had committed itself to setting up an international organization for peace and
security. There had never been any doubt in Britain that there
should be some such organization. The reasons were simple.
In the first place, Britain could not act as a world power on
her own or even with the Commonwealth. As Eden, Foreign
Secretary again since the end of 1940, put it to the Cabinet in
January 1943: 'We can only hope to play our part either as a
European or as a World Power if we ourselves form part of a
wider organization.'[51] Secondly, despite the failures of the League
of Nations, the notion of an organization to promote international security and cooperation, political and economic, was
not discredited and took on some new life as a counter to the
tyranny of Hitler's New Order.

Discussion moved forward in 1943, on fairly general lines
including great power responsibility for peace, regional groupings, and economic cooperation. In America, a number of individuals and bodies had been studying the future organization

of peace since the beginning of the war. Varied views were put forward, from world federation to Anglo-American partnership.[52] Willkie began to move the Republican Party towards acceptance of responsibility, and the public seemed, albeit vaguely, to accept participation in an international organization. In a Gallup poll of 6 July 1942, 73 per cent of the respondents said they would like to see the United States join a League of Nations after the war; and on 24 March 1943, 64 per cent wanted the government to take steps to set up a world organization. But such figures were indications of good will rather than an informed commitment.[53] Roosevelt, as he told Keynes in 1941, was determined that the United States should exercise responsibility after the war, but did not at first favour an international organization. His prevailing idea was that of the 'Four Policemen' maintaining peace and order, and the only possessors of substantial arms. But he came to accept the idea of a universal organization, and eventually set great store by American membership. At the foreign ministers' conference at Moscow in October a declaration was adopted committing the four great powers (China included) to the establishment of a general international organization based on 'the sovereign equality of all peace-loving states and open to membership of all such states, large and small'. Henceforth the major powers were committed to setting up an international organization, led by themselves. Detailed discussion of machinery took place at Dumbarton Oaks in the summer of 1944. The problem that then arose of voting in what was now to be called the Security Council concerned the weight of the major powers in the organization.

The war was responsible for the start of serious American interest in the Middle East and a breach in near-exclusive British predominance. After the alarms at the end of the First World War about declining domestic oil reserves and British policy, new discoveries in the United States and in Mexico and Venezuela in the 1920s led to a world surplus and falling prices. The bulk of world production was in the western hemisphere: in 1939 the Middle East produced about 5 per cent of the world total, most of it in Iran. American companies had in the 1920s secured a share in the Iraq Petroleum Company and were parties to a comprehensive production and marketing agreement; American interests were also involved in Kuwait and

Bahrain. There was also one wholly American-owned concession in Saudi Arabia, which at the outbreak of war had only just begun to export.[54] The Saudi Arabian concession gave the American government a foothold in the Middle East and it was impelled into activity by the effect of the war on the pilgrim traffic to Mecca and the consequent decline in King Ibn Saud's revenues. The British government paid the king a subsidy, but he demanded help from the oil company and it demanded help from the American government, alleging British designs on the concession. The Administration was at first reluctant to become involved, but gradually became engaged in the whole question of Middle East oil; and the British in turn became uneasy at the trend of American policy.

In December 1943 the Americans proposed talks on oil as a preliminary to an international agreement. The proposal was welcomed in London, but the British did not want the talks confined to the Middle East, where they were in a privileged position and the Americans wished to plead the Atlantic Charter to dismantle restrictions, while the American preferential position in the western hemisphere was not discussed. Anxiety grew when Roosevelt, responding to domestic pressure, announced that the talks would be held at once in Washington at cabinet level instead of being preceded by technical discussions, and when the State Department's draft agenda included concession rights. On 20 February 1944, Churchill took the matter up directly with Roosevelt. 'There is apprehension in some quarters here', he cabled:

> that the United States has a desire to deprive us of our oil assets in the Middle East on which, among other things, the whole supply of our navy depends . . . I am sure these suspicions are entirely unfounded so far as the Government of the United States is concerned . . . [But] I am sure to be asked for an assurance that the question of no transfer of property will arise and I shall be unable to give such an assurance.

Roosevelt's reply was dismissive. He refused to limit the problems to be discussed, or to abandon a top-level start to the talks, and said that against the British apprehensions of American designs, 'I am disturbed about the rumour that the British wish to horn in on Saudi Arabian oil resources.' But Churchill returned to the charge: he feared what might be said in Parliament if an assurance could not be given about property rights, and 'I feel sure that to open up these matters with the maximum publicity without knowing where they will lead us will do real harm to Anglo-American relations.' Roosevelt now took the warning, and replied with a (less than wholly true) assurance that 'we are not making sheeps' eyes at your oil fields in Iraq or Iran', and this enabled Churchill to 'reciprocate by giving you the fullest assurance that we have no thought of trying to horn in upon your interests or property in Saudi Arabia'.[55]

Talks in Washington in April 1944 at a technical level produced a memorandum of understanding which included provision for equitable access to supplies, respect for concession contracts, commitment to the sound economic development of producing countries, and the creation of a joint commission to study and make recommendations on world supply and demand. The British wanted, but did not get, recognition of their country's dependence on imported oil. There were two aspects to this point: the need for a secure supply not subject to restriction by a producers' cartel, and the exchange problem. Ministerial talks followed in July. These were less easy than the technical ones: the British delegation was led by Beaverbrook, who opposed any sacrifice of British interests, and the conversations nearly broke down over British insistence on safeguards for what they called their economic security. Eventually a compromise was reached, and both sides were pleased with the outcome. The British secured at any rate an acknowledgment that they had an exchange problem; but, most important, the agreement seemed to be a constructive step towards long-term Anglo-American cooperation in international economic affairs. For the Americans, the agreement embodied many of the principles on which they hoped to build the postwar world, access to raw materials and markets, and international collaboration. But the terms contained too much governmental control to be acceptable to American oil producers. The agreement had to be revised, but even a second version was never ratified.

The weakening of Britain's financial position was demonstrated by the outcome of discussions about a future world monetary

system. Since 1941 specialists in both Britain and the United
States had been thinking about future international cooperation and monetary stabilization, some new order to prevent
recurrence of the currency disorders of the 1930s and provide
a basis for trade and prosperity.[56] On the British side Keynes
was impelled by the need to find a solution combining stability in the exchanges with domestic expansion, and providing
Britain with sufficient liquidity in a world where the United
States was both a larger creditor than ever and determined on
a policy of non-discrimination in trade and convertibility of
currencies. Britain would face a massive task of reconversion
after the war and would be short of dollars for several years;
but whatever the attractions of trade and exchange controls
and bilateral agreements, no scheme that the United States
government disapproved could hope to work. On the American side the object of Harry Dexter White, Morgenthau's chief
adviser, was largely to use the American holding of gold (about
two-thirds of the world's total) and the power of the dollar to
provide a means for stabilizing exchange rates through an
international fund. Talks led to agreement on a Statement of
Principles, published in April 1944, on the setting up of an
International Monetary Fund to promote cooperation and exchange stability. The statement was generally well received,
although some British papers described the scheme as tanta-
mount to a return to the gold standard, now anathema in Britain.
Opposition also came from the imperial group round Amery
(now Secretary of State for India), who argued that Britain
must be free to make special agreements, control imports, and
strengthen 'that wonderful monetary instrument the sterling
system'.[57] To both these criticisms Keynes replied in a speech
on 23 May in the House of Lords (he had been made a peer
in June 1942). Claiming some authority to pronounce on what
a gold standard was, he said that this was the opposite: it allowed flexibility, and emphasized the obligations of creditors.
As for a closed sterling bloc: 'To suppose that a system of bilateral and barter arrangements, with no one who owns sterling knowing just what he can do with it – to suppose that this
is the best way of encouraging the Dominions to centre their
financial transactions on London, seems to me pretty near
frenzy.'[58]

An international conference was held at Bretton Woods in New Hampshire in July.[59] It produced agreements on the International Monetary Fund and a Bank for Reconstruction and Development, to be set up with funds subscribed by member governments. Restrictions on the convertibility of currencies were to be abolished; outside a certain limit a country might only alter the parity of its currency by permission of the Fund; but there was to be a transitional period of up to five years during which exchange controls might be retained. The total size of the Fund was smaller than Keynes thought right: both it and the Bank were to be based in the United States. In general, indeed, the design of the Fund was very much as the Americans wished, with the possibility of pressure on creditors being reduced to a minimum. American writing on the conference gives an impression of a determination to prevail, and there could be no doubt of American consciousness that their country now held the strings.

Within a few years Bretton Woods was being criticized for failing to anticipate the length and difficulty of the transition period and the severity of the postwar shortage of dollars. Immediate criticism in Britain focused mainly on the credit facilities of the monetary fund and the safeguards for countries which exhausted their balances.[60] American bankers were opposed to the scheme because it was governmental. Congress's approval was not certain, and was not given until July 1945. By that time the war in Europe was over, the dimensions of Britain's postwar problems were becoming clearer, but the decision was no easier. The balance of the economic argument had gone against the monetary fund, but politically almost everything told in its favour. 'How much economic hazard', asked the *Economist*, 'is a reasonable price for continued American generosity and friendship – or at least for the avoidance of American disappointment and resentment?' The decision had to be taken soon 'in almost complete darkness about the nature of the postwar world'. The answer, the paper thought, could not be 'No': 'an outright rejection, at this stage, would do almost irreparable harm to the still very delicate structure of international economic reconstruction'. But the risks were great. Britain might take some comfort from the transition provisions, but five years might not be long enough.[61]

Working out Britain's position was not made easier by the unexpectedly early end to the war with Japan on 14 August 1945, since Lend-Lease also ended immediately. Lend-Lease and Britain's Reciprocal Aid never became thought of in the United States as a pooling of resources for the war. The concept of proportional effort was never accepted by American opinion. British requests were rigorously scrutinized in Washington, and the Treasury used the machinery to reduce Britain's gold and dollar reserves and her financial independence. Rigid restrictions were also maintained over Britain's exports, but did not prevent constant press and Congressional allegations of waste and misuse of Lend-Lease materials. From the early months of 1944 the British authorities had known that it would be necessary to discuss with the Americans the future of Lend-Lease in the period between the end of the war in Europe and victory over Japan – what was known in Britain as Stage II and in America as Phase II – which was expected to last anything up to two years. The fundamental principle of Lend-Lease meant that supplies would be reduced, but beginning the reconversion of the British economy would need American assistance; the people would expect some relaxation of wartime rationing and some improvement in housing; industrial equipment and public utilities needed repair; and rebuilding of export trade was essential. Lend-Lease had enabled Britain to mobilize for the armed forces and war employment a higher proportion of the population than the United States ever did. In the summer of 1944, 22 per cent of the British labour force was in the armed forces and 33 per cent in war employment: the corresponding figures for the United States were 18.5 per cent and 21.5 per cent. Until 1943 Britain's fighting forces were larger than the American ones. Of the Allied forces landed in France on D-Day, Britain and Canada supplied well over half – but then American fighting strength became overwhelming. Britain had been spending over half her national income on the war since 1941: United States war expenditure reached a peak of 43 per cent of national income in 1943. Civilian consumption in Britain fell, between 1939 and 1944, by 16 per cent: in the United States, and Canada, it rose by 16 per cent. Britain's exports shrank steadily from 1940: in 1944 they were less than one-third in value those of 1938. To pay for imports after the war the prewar figure had not only to be regained but increased by as much as 50 per cent, to compensate for the external disinvestment. Some £1118 million in external capital assets had been disposed of, and large debts incurred. At the end of 1944 sterling area debts amounted to £2434 million.[62]

Before the War Cabinet had decided on the best way to approach the Americans, Morgenthau visited London in August 1944. The Chancellor of the Exchequer, Sir John Anderson, explained the situation in detail, and Morgenthau was sufficiently impressed to go home and tell Roosevelt that 'England really is broke'. Roosevelt was surprised. His reaction was covered by the jokey manner with which he concealed his thoughts, a trait that those who worked with him apparently found irresistible and the modern reader is apt to find tiresome. He said to Morgenthau: 'This is very interesting. I had no idea that England was broke. I will go over there and make a couple of talks and take over the British Empire.'[63] When Churchill raised the future of Lend-Lease at Quebec in September, the President was unwilling to make any promise, but he agreed that a joint committee should examine the whole question.[64] Once again the British team in these talks was led by Keynes. The negotiations were not easy. Morgenthau was personally helpful. He had come to the conclusion that Britain must be helped to recover after what she had done in the war; but his position was under attack; other departments and agencies in Washington were opposed to giving Britain any help to recover in Stage II; and the military were opposed to allowing substantial military Lend-Lease – the navy, which did not want a British contribution in the Pacific, was particularly hostile. Keynes provided every possible detail about the British position, and argued the case for a level of Lend-Lease that would allow a beginning of reconversion of the economy and a slight rise in living standards. Agreement was reached on the quantity of Lend-Lease (less than the British hoped for), but Roosevelt was unwilling to have anything put in writing. Once again the British had to rely on American good will.

That they could do so Keynes was convinced. His report to Anderson at the end of the talks affirmed the existence of 'an ever increasing and ever deepening conviction in the minds of all responsible Americans that a strong Britain after the war is a vital, indeed an indispensable requirement of American policy'. Britain could build with safety on this 'sure rock'. She must attain financial independence as soon as possible, but – and here Keynes was surely addressing the anti-American group in the Cabinet as well as sceptics in the Treasury –

> if we can control our suspicions, even though they have some foundation, and our exasperations, for which there will be every cause in the world, if we can overlook their inevitable jealousies and unwarrantable aggrandisements and indefensible intrusions, and if they can do the like . . . the only brotherhood by which civilisation can be held together, already sealed with blood, will become in due time a decent, commonplace, workaday affair, which is taken for granted, as everything must be which is good and durable. On no temptation or provocation or pretext must we allow ourselves to stray, even in thought or hypothesis, along another path than this.[65]

Another demonstration of economic power took place at a conference at Chicago in November on postwar civil aviation. The policies approved were in keeping with the American view of the 'open world' economy and were particularly favourable to American interests. British assent was only secured by threats of reprisals over Lend-Lease.[66] In that field events over the next few months showed that Keynes was over-optimistic. The arrangements of the Stage II negotiations were not fully honoured. There was little understanding of Britain's position. Sympathetic officials were afraid of Congress; others took a hard line; Roosevelt's attention could not be gained. And then the rapid end to the war with Japan left no time to see how the arrangements would work in practice.[67]

As regards politics, by the end of 1944 some of the jealousies and intrusions caused ructions. In the winter there was a spate of American criticism of Britain. Her war effort was described as inadequate; she was accused of trying to compete with American trade and of misusing Lend-Lease supplies. And above all British policy in Italy and Greece (about which much British opinion, fed for three years on propaganda about communist resistance, was also dubious) was attacked as reactionary and playing at power politics in the Mediterranean. No one, of course, defined power politics. Churchill suggested to Halifax that he should ask Stettinius, the Secretary of State, who had himself issued a disavowal of British policy, what it meant:

> Is having a Navy twice as strong as any other 'power politics'? Is having an overwhelming Air Force, with bases all over the world, 'power politics'? . . . Is it giving all the bases in the West Indies which are necessary to American safety to the United States – is that 'power politics'?[68]

In the British press the *New Statesman* pointed out that the United States itself was responsible for a particularly clear and old-established sphere of influence, and was now busy marking out others for itself. The normally Americanophil *Economist* decided on some 'very plain speaking':

> What makes the American criticisms so intolerable is not merely that they are unjust, but they come from a source that has done so little to earn the right to superiority. To be told by anyone that the British people are slacking in their war effort would be insufferable enough to a people struggling through their sixth winter of blackout and blockade and bombs, of queues and rations and coldness – but when the criticism comes from a nation that was practising Cash-and-Carry during the Battle of Britain, whose consumption has risen during the war years, which is still without a national service act – then it is not to be borne.

At the policy-making level the effect was to raise the question of how far British policy could safely be shaped in reliance on American collaboration or even good will. 'Henceforward, if British policies and precautions are to be traded against American promises, the only safe terms are cash on delivery.'[69]

The Administration and press criticism of Britain were part of a general condition of uncertainty in the United States about policy and the postwar world. Some of the difficulties were becoming apparent, and there were calls for something more than general statements about American objectives. The existence of British political influence in Europe was acknowledged, but there was less confidence that it would be used in ways that Americans could approve. The theologian Reinhold Niebuhr attributed the attacks on Britain to covert isolationism, and America's overconfident use of economic power to what he saw as her 'sense of frustration and impotence in dealing with political power'.[70] Roosevelt's chief concern at the beginning of 1945 was to keep American opinion steadily behind involvement in world affairs. Essential for this was the creation of a world body with Big Three cooperation: to achieve it anxieties about particular problems such as Soviet policy in Poland had to be repressed. Publicly, Roosevelt acclaimed the achievement at Yalta of the beginnings of a new structure of peace, and wanted no expressions of doubt. He was less confident in private, and already by the time of his death in April the exultation had vanished; but after years of controversy it is permissible to agree with Roosevelt's claim to Berle that the results of Yalta were the best he could do.[71]

Britain was one of the Big Three at Yalta and Potsdam, but how big? Nothing symbolizes the wartime change in relative power more sharply than the atomic bomb. Britain, in the words of the official historian Margaret Gowing, was the 'midwife' of the bomb. British scientists, and refugee scientists in Britain, did the work in the early years of the war that proved the practical possibility of a bomb, and a British report persuaded the Americans of the urgency of the task. But once the Americans became convinced, their ability to pour enormous resources into the enterprise ensured that Britain, though still a partner, was a junior one.[72]

None of that was yet publicly known. In the last week of the war an assessment of how thoughtful Americans viewed their country's position, and Britain's, came from the embassy in Washington. Enormous pride in the American record of production, achieved at no cost in civilian consumption, was set against a new consciousness of what the war had cost Britain. Russian prestige had grown greatly, and on the basis of statistics Americans were bound to draw unfavourable comparisons between the British Isles and the Soviet Union. The Americans were beginning to think of a world with only two great centres of power, moving away from coequal collaboration between the United States, Britain and the Soviet Union:

towards a new order of things in which Great Britain, whilst occupying a highly important position as the bastion of Western European security and as the focal point of a far-flung oceanic system, will nevertheless be expected to take her place as junior partner in an orbit of power predominantly under American aegis.[73]

Conscious though they were of the power of the United States, neither the British government nor the tired but satisfied British people believed in the summer of 1945 that their country was no longer a world power, or inferior to the Soviet Union except in eastern Europe. The war had released new social energies. The American alliance had grown out of geography and common interests, and was cemented by a common language and shared values in a way that the alliance with the Soviet Union could not be. Fears of a recrudescence of American isolationism persisted, but so did hopes of being able to influence American policy 'for the purposes which we regard as good'.[74] The contribution to this made personally by Churchill and Roosevelt and by the partnership between them seems in retrospect less important than was once represented, not least by Churchill himself. Depicting the wartime alliance as an expression of an underlying unity between the English-speaking peoples, he described his correspondence with Roosevelt as playing a part in his conduct of the war not less important than his duties as Minister of Defence, his relations with the President gradually becoming 'so close that the chief business between our two countries was virtually conducted by those personal interchanges between him and me. In this way our perfect understanding was gained.'[75] This was never true. The correspondence was remarkable in quantity – over 1600 messages between September 1939 and April 1945 – and range, and often brought a resolution of problems that had got stuck at a lower level of Roosevelt's confused and confusing Administration; but it could not be the chief channel of a massive quantity of business. Nor was the understanding perfect. Churchill set out to woo the President; Roosevelt did not reciprocate. There were and remained real differences, arising from real differences of interest between the two countries, and in the last two years of the war from the disparity of power. It is possible to think that relations between the two countries might have been conducted to much the same effect by a different pair of leaders. This is not to deny the importance of these personal relations; but equally important in both the short and the longer runs was the much greater familiarity developed at all levels, and the habit of working together acquired by officials and service men and women from Chiefs of Staff downwards.[76] That experience incidentally largely dispelled the myth of Anglo-Saxon kinship. It did not necessarily bring agreement or even liking. Differences of interest and outlook remained, but the two countries were more 'mixed up together' than they had ever been before, and that experience ensured that the changing alliance would have a distinctive flavour.

6
British Imperial Decline and American Super-Power, 1945–56

For some eighteen months after the summer of 1945 the shape of the postwar world was far from clear. Assumptions that continued cooperation between the three major victors was both necessary and possible were widely held in the west and died hard – it is still not possible to say whether or for how long they were held in the Soviet Union. During 1946 assumptions of hostility between west and east gradually took over, but it was not until 1947 that the world appeared to become locked into the cold war.[1]

Whilst Britain was, as officials admitted, 'numerically the weakest and geographically the smallest of the great powers',[2] there was no disposition to resign from the top table. But since of the three she was the least able to rely on her own strength there were particular reasons for emphasizing collaboration with the others, at the same time attempting to build up her weight by enlisting west European and Commonwealth collaboration.[3] British opinion, too, long remained loath to give up wartime hopes of cooperation with the Russians. Bevin, the Foreign Secretary in the new Labour government led by Attlee, could not openly express the fears that he began to entertain about apparent Soviet probings without upsetting members of his own party and liberal opinion in general.[4] Nor was Bevin much more confident about the United States. Whilst Churchill maintained that a 'special and privileged relationship between Great Britain and the United States makes us both safe for ourselves and more influential as regards building up the safety of others', Bevin feared American economic policies and foresaw world cooperation being replaced by two great equally closed spheres, with Britain left on the outer rim of Europe with the Middle East and the Commonwealth and Empire – 'a tremendous area to defend'.[5] Left-wing intellectuals who called for British neutrality as between the United States and the Soviet Union were not wholly unrepresentative. The anti-Soviet implication of Churchill's speech in March 1946 at Fulton, Missouri, was not welcomed more widely in Britain than its call for an Anglo-American alliance was welcomed in the United States.[6]

On the American side Truman gave assurances in a speech in October 1945 that the United States intended to continue to play a world role; but the principles he enunciated were abstract and the emphasis was heavily on autonomous American power – at one or two removes from Europe but present in bases in the Pacific and Atlantic. There was as yet little thought of conflict with the Soviet Union: America saw no need of allies. Officials accepted that the British Isles were needed for American security (although the Empire was a 'long and sometimes embarrassing attachment'); Britain was expected to continue to defend her traditional interests but to defer to American insistence.[7]

The outcome of the financial negotiations in Washington in the autumn of 1945 provided the British public with one of its first lessons in the country's changed position.[8] In financing the war Britain had in effect disposed of some four-fifths of her prewar overseas assets, and had incurred heavy liabilities. There was no doubt that she needed help to balance the external accounts during the transition to a peacetime economy. The agreement reached in Washington in December was not well received in Britain. The government had been reluctant to accept, and defended it only half-heartedly. The terms of the loan itself were generally acknowledged to be reasonable, and the Lend-Lease settlement generous; but the need to borrow at all was resented. Unrealistic hopes had been raised of a free grant in recognition of the burdens borne before the United States entered the war, or at least an interest-free loan; there were unhappy memories of the war debts controversies of the 1920s and 1930s. 'It is aggravating', wrote the *Economist*, 'to find that our reward for losing a quarter of our national wealth in the common cause is to pay tribute for half a century to those who have been enriched by the war.' The greatest opposition was to the coupling of the loan with the ratification of Bretton Woods and the abandonment of its safeguards. Successful wartime management of the economy had encouraged a belief in controls; scepticism about open multilateral trade was widespread; those who did believe in multilateralism doubted Britain's ability to fulfil these conditions in so short a time. A letter in *The Times* expressed a general view: 'It seems we can only accept the loan, but with a heavy heart.'[9]

On the American side the negotiators were well disposed but were constrained by their understanding of what a conservative tax-cutting Congress would accept. Public opinion had rapidly lost interest in external affairs as soon as the war ended: at the end of September a large majority of those questioned in a Gallup poll thought that Britain should pay in some way for Lend-Lease supplies, and 60 per cent disapproved of the prospect of a loan.[10] When the agreement came to Congress in the spring of 1946 its passage proved as difficult as the negotiators had feared; but soon a new factor tipped the balance: anxiety about the Soviet Union now provided a motive for supporting Britain as an ally.

The war if anything strengthened the British will to retain power over the Middle East. The area had been and was expected to remain a crucial strategic base; it was a hub of communications between the United Kingdom, the Indian Ocean and Australasia; it provided oil and other economic resources. One strategic survey in the summer of 1945 ranked the Middle East after the Indian Ocean in importance for imperial grand strategy; other papers described it as a region of 'life and death consequence for the British Empire'.[11] It was also an area where British interests were directly affected by Russian actions, traditionally in Turkey and Iran, now in southern Europe and possibly northern Africa. Maritime communications through the Mediterranean might no longer be vital, but it was an area of great political and economic importance through which British influence was brought to bear on southern Europe. The Foreign Office was convinced that:

> If in peace time we move out of areas at present under our influence, they are unlikely to remain a vacuum, particularly if they are contiguous to areas under Soviet control . . . We

cannot, therefore, afford to weaken our strategic position in peace time by surrendering our influence in areas of major strategic importance.[12]

The only person to ask radical questions was Attlee. He was not sure whether Britain should any longer be regarded as 'a Power looking eastwards through the Mediterranean to India and the east', rather than as an easterly outpost of the American strategic area. By the end of 1946 Attlee was not only worried about the cost of supporting the Greek government[13] but wondered whether the Russians might genuinely see the British position in Greece, Turkey, Iraq and Iran as a threat. If they did, they might agree to the area being turned into a neutral zone: this 'would be much to our advantage'. Bevin resisted the idea of such a reversal of policy, and did not believe that a neutral zone was possible. The Russians would take over by infiltration. 'Even if we do not believe that the Russians have plans for world domination, I am certain they will not be able to resist advancing into any vacuum we may leave.'[14]

It was possible for the British to withdraw from Greece because by February 1947 the United States Administration was ready to take on the task. During the past year American minds had been focusing increasingly on the Soviet Union as the cause of all the current international problems. They had been less worried than the British in 1945: now American policy all round the world became based on the assumptions and objectives of the cold war.[15] One of the first to provide an explanation of the Soviet Union as enemy was George F. Kennan who, in his famous 'long telegram' from Moscow of 22 February 1946, analysed the Soviet outlook and predicted Soviet policy on the basis of permanent Russian motivations combined with an ideological conviction that there could be no permanent accommodation with the United States. Attempts to seek compromise, Kennan contended, were therefore futile; but the Soviet leaders did respond to strength and so the American government should mobilize the country's energies, educate the public, put forward for other countries a much more positive picture of the kind of world it wanted to see, and face the future with courage.[16] A year later Kennan publicly expounded the doctrine of containment to counter limitless Soviet ambitions in the influential journal *Foreign Affairs*.[17] He had been appointed head of a new Policy Planning Staff in the State Department, and became for a time one of the most influential policy-makers in Washington. Kennan complained later that 'containment' was taken in a more military sense than his essentially political assessment both of Soviet methods and of the means to counter them. But the military needed a basis for their planning, and their concerns were reflected in a report of September 1946 by two of Truman's aides, which gave a cruder picture than Kennan's of Soviet intentions and a more alarming assessment of Soviet strength.[18]

By the spring of 1947 anti-communism was a powerful force in American politics. In its stark black and whiteness this monocausal explanation of the world's ills suited a people accustomed to equating statements of principle with policy, and a government both new to wielding great national power and unused to the compromises of international negotiation. There were few highly-placed dissenters. One was Henry Wallace, the Secretary for Agriculture, a liberal of long standing who still believed in an open world and in a speech of October 1946 (which earned his dismissal) pleaded for compromise with the Soviet Union and warned that toughness on one side would beget counter-toughness. Walter Lippmann too argued that the policy of containment was misconceived,[19] but from then on such voices grew weaker. Strategic considerations about the eastern Mediterranean, similar to those held by the British authorities, impelled the Administration into taking over Britain's commitments to Greece and Turkey: the Truman doctrine was couched in ideological terms to shock Congress and the public into accepting the costs.[20]

The Middle East properly speaking remained a British sphere and one of the three pillars of Commonwealth strategy.[21] But defence requirements, including the maintenance of oil supplies and communications, depended on retaining the good will of the Arab states. The Labour government aspired to transform the old relationship of dominance into one of partnership, by encouraging economic development and social reform, and renegotiating treaties.[22] In the case of Egypt there were two issues. The numbers and role of the British forces in the Suez base now bore little relation to the purposes of the treaty of 1936 and the enclave was a source of endless resentment to Egyptian nationalists. Negotiations in 1946 very nearly produced agreement on a new treaty, providing for British evacuation and a probable right of re-entry in case of war. The sticking point proved to be the second issue, the Sudan, over which the Egyptians were determined to exercise more than nominal sovereignty while the British wished to secure Sudan's right to self-determination. Stalemate followed until 1951, with positions hardening on both sides. Relations with Iraq also needed to be adjusted. A new treaty was signed in January 1948, providing for sharing the previously British air bases and promising general British assistance; but it was immediately repudiated by the Regent. The British had miscalculated the strength of Iraqi nationalism, fuelled by economic discontent and inflamed by the impending crisis over Palestine. This failure was a bad blow, leaving Britain only with a treaty with the King of Transjordan, who was widely regarded in the Arab world as a British stooge.

For the most part Britain enjoyed American support for her position in the Middle East, although there was always some tension in American minds between, on the one hand, a growing recognition that not only the British Isles but the Middle East too was important to American security, and, on the other hand, traditional anti-colonialism and a conviction that the American system was superior. The British were aware of the tension, and tried to improve American understanding. In the 'Pentagon talks', Anglo-American political and military conversations in October–November 1947, the British visitors explained the background to issues in the Middle East; and the State Department recommended that:

> Given our heavy commitments elsewhere and Britain's already established position in the area, it is our strong feeling that the British should continue to maintain primary responsibility for military security in that area.

At the end the delegates agreed to 'endeavour to strengthen each other's position in the area on the basis of mutual respect and cooperation'.[23] What this meant was spelled out by Kennan for the State Department shortly afterwards. 'We have decided in this Government', he wrote:

that the security of the Middle East is vital to our security. We have also decided that it would not be desirable or advantageous for us to attempt to duplicate or take over the strategic facilities now held by the British in that area . . . This means that we must do what we can to support the maintenance of [sic? by] the British of their strategic position in that area. This does *not mean* that we must support them in every individual instance. It does *not mean* that we must back them up in cases where they have got themselves into a false position or where we would thereby be undertaking extravagant political commitments. It *does mean* that any policy on our part which tends to strain British relations with the Arab world or to whittle down the British position in the Arab countries is only a policy directed against ourselves and against the immediate strategic needs of our country.[24]

The American government did not indeed want increased overseas responsibilities. It now accepted that the ultimate Soviet objective was world domination and that the national security of the United States was at stake. It also accepted that a defensive policy would not be enough to check the momentum of communist expansion and induce Moscow to give up its designs: the United States, as the only power capable of organizing effective opposition to those designs, should organize a world-wide counter-offensive, strengthening its own potential and that of other countries, especially in western Europe and the Middle East.[25] But the word to stress here is 'potential': most of the aid given was economic; military spending proposals emphasized air power; and although in the autumn of 1948 Truman endorsed the goal of reducing the power and influence of Moscow, bringing about a basic change in Russian theory and practice of international relations, and the 'gradual retraction' of Russian power and influence from the satellite countries,[26] at the same time he vetoed budget proposals intended to narrow the gap between policy goals and military means.

The great exception to American support for Britain in the Middle East was Palestine.[27] Whilst in retrospect it must seem that the grand idea of transforming relations with the Arab countries by development and reform and still retaining strategic and economic dominance was unrealistic, and that Palestine was not the only or even perhaps the chief cause of failure, there is no doubt that the immediate and long-term effects of events there did very great damage to Britain's position in the region as a whole. And American policy certainly made Britain's position worse.

The war and Hitler's policy of exterminating the Jews of Europe transformed the basis of Zionism, rendering insoluble what had been before 1939 an intractable problem, the reconciliation of Jewish aspirations for a National Home or state in Palestine with the rights of the Arab population. After again failing to find an agreed solution the British in 1947, in conditions of mounting disorder and repression, handed over the problem to the United Nations and announced that in the absence of an agreed settlement they would withdraw. At the end of November the United Nations General Assembly voted in favour of partition. The British then set a date for termination of the mandate, on 15 May 1948, and after some confused attempts to form a temporary UN trusteeship the United States recognized the state of Israel a few minutes after the expiry of the deadline. The Israelis had installed themselves in most of the area allotted to them under the UN partition plan, and held the military initiative. In the next few months, with intervals of truce, they extended their boundaries until an armistice was reached in January 1949. A portion of Palestine smaller than the Arab part under the UN plan was left under Transjordan control, and a small coastal strip in the south under Egyptian control. Nearly one million Palestinians were refugees.

The overriding imperative of British policy throughout was the imperial one of Britain's interest in the Middle East as a whole, with American involvement also taken very seriously. Within this position there were divisions and differences. The British 'official mind' was predominantly pro-Arab. Bevin has gone down in Zionist demonology as an anti-Semite. He was not; but he was anti-Zionist, and tactless, and he believed, for longer than was warranted by the evidence, that the Jews could as well as should be reintegrated into European society. British opinion was torn by feelings of obligation towards the Jews of Europe, revulsion at the spectacle of illegal immigrants being forcibly returned to Europe, and anger at the killing of British servicemen by Jewish terrorists. By 1947 support for withdrawal was strong. The idea of partitioning Palestine had been considered and rejected before and during the war. As late as January 1947 the Cabinet, with much hesitation, decided against, on the grounds that both states would be too small, that the Jews would use their portion as a jumping-off ground for taking over the whole country, and that it would cost too much to enforce partition on the Arabs. 'The risk', Bevin wrote:

cannot be excluded that [partition] would contribute to the elimination of British influence from the whole of the vast Moslem area lying between Greece and India. This would have not only strategic consequences, it would also jeopardise the security of our interest in the increasingly important oil production of the Middle East.[28]

But by this time a bi-national state was no longer a realistic proposition. Handing over the problem to the United Nations was an admission that Britain could not find a solution. Nor could Britain win in a propaganda competition against the resources of world Zionism and anti-colonialism. From the date of the United Nations vote British efforts were mainly directed to damage limitation, refusing to be saddled with responsibility for preventing the expected conflict, attempting to confine its scope, and attempting to rescue relations with the Arab states. Whether a different approach to them earlier would have overcome their and the Palestinians' intransigence cannot be known: the intransigence was very great, and the calculation of the cost of defeating it was not fanciful.

American policy tended from the start towards partition and support for a Jewish state, but its execution was indecisive and there was no disposition to accept any responsibility. Truman was not, it seems, particularly pro-Zionist; but he never understood the Arab dimension. He was subject to enormous domestic pressures and was very conscious of Jewish votes in key areas in 1946 and 1948. The centre of Zionism had moved during the war to New York, and most American Jewish organizations came to support a sovereign Jewish state in Palestine. The State Department, alone among American authorities, considered the Middle East dimension and the position of Britain. In a note just before the United Nations vote in November 1947, Loy Henderson, director of its office of Near Eastern and African Affairs, warned:

> I feel it again to be my duty to point out that it seems to me and all the members of my Office acquainted with the Middle East that the policy which we are following in New York [at the United Nations] at the present is contrary to the interests of the United States . . . It is impossible for the British to remain a force in the Middle East unless they retain the friendship of the Arab world.[29]

The Secretary of State, General Marshall, was adamant that the United States could not contribute any troops to keeping peace or imposing a solution in Palestine, and resented British withdrawals. The Secretary of Defence, James Forrestal, was worried about oil. In the end Truman honoured his promise to the veteran Zionist leader Chaim Weizmann, and announced the recognition of Israel without telling the American delegation at the United Nations. Thereafter the Americans increasingly underwrote the state of Israel. They managed not to forfeit the friendship of King Ibn Saud, and did not have serious stakes to lose in other Arab states.

Beyond the Middle East, India's independence removed in 1947 an enormous piece from the map of imperial strategy, and marked the end of an era in British imperial history.[30] All parties in Britain were pledged to the principle of self-rule for India, although some Conservatives still saw it as only a distant prospect. In Parliament in February 1947, when the government announced the setting of a date for independence in the absence of agreement among the parties, most of the opposition was concerned with the predictable dangers, and Britain's inability to fulfil promises to protect minorities. A few lamented that the British people no longer believed in their moral right to govern India and keep the peace; Churchill spoke of the 'clattering down of the British Empire' and the ruin and disaster that would follow Britain's disappearance from the East. But Halifax, a former Viceroy, swayed a House of Lords full of men with Indian experience, by stressing that it was impossible to stand still or to pretend to have complete power to continue to rule.[31] The press took much the same line. Both India and Pakistan, and also Ceylon which achieved independence in 1948, remained members of the Commonwealth. India became neutralist in foreign policy but Pakistan kept military links with the West. So long as Britain retained Malaya, Singapore, Sarawak, North Borneo and Hong Kong, she did not disappear from the East.

In Africa, meanwhile, the colonial Empire took on added importance after the war. East Africa was seen as possibly providing a new strategic base, with communications running across the continent and on into the Indian Ocean. The economic element was even more important. Colonial development was for the Labour government a matter of principle: it could also contribute to Britain's needs and earn dollars. Cripps, the Chancellor of the Exchequer, stressed this to a conference of colonial governors in November 1947. The need for the sterling group and western Europe to maintain economic independence, he said, made it 'essential that we should increase out of all recognition the tempo of African development... The whole fate of the Sterling Group and its ability to survive depends upon a quick and extensive development of our African resources.'[32] Some of the language, and some of the projects, were such as to give ammunition for accusations of new imperial exploitation. By 1950, however, the most grandiose project had proved mistaken; and while colonial development continued it was in a lower key. At the same time a Commonwealth plan was set up for technical assistance in south and south-east Asia. In many of the colonies steps were taken towards internal self-government, but rapid decolonization was not expected. Malaya and Ghana became independent in 1957, but still in the autumn of that year a Cabinet committee reckoned that only three other colonies were likely to gain independence in the next ten years – rather than the 24 which actually did.[33]

There was never any doubt, from before the end of the war, of western Europe's importance to Britain. In the Labour government Bevin, with the Foreign Office in general, favoured strong political and economic ties, giving Britain the position of a leading European power and a stronger voice among the Big Three.[34] Delays in taking the first steps with France could not be avoided, but in March 1947 the treaty of Dunkirk was signed, ostensibly an alliance against Germany but chiefly important as a symbol of British commitment to the security of western Europe. In that summer new scope for European cooperation arose with Marshall's offer of American assistance with a European recovery plan. Bevin, as is well known, seized on Marshall's speech and was a prime mover in the European response.[35]

With the abstention of the Soviet Union and its east European satellites from the Marshall Plan the continent was irretrievably split, first economically and then politically. At the same time American support was accepted as vital for western Europe, and so American influence there was increased. This influence was exercised in favour of western European unity, but the British were hesitant about the degree and nature of their involvement. Early in 1948 Bevin held out to the Cabinet the prospect of a consolidated western Europe led by Britain:

> Material aid will have to come principally from the United States, but the countries of Western Europe which despise the spiritual values of America will look to us for political and moral guidance and for assistance in building up a counter-attraction to the baleful tenets of communism within their borders and in recreating a healthy society wherever it has been shaken or shattered by the war. I believe that we have the resources to perform the task. Provided we can organise a Western European system . . . backed by the power and resources of the Commonwealth and of the Americas, it should be possible to develop our own power and influence to equal that of the United States and of the U.S.S.R. We have the resources in the Colonial Empire, if we develop them, and by giving a spiritual lead now we should be able to carry out our task in a way which will show clearly that we are not subservient to the United States of America or to the Soviet Union.[36]

For Bevin, then, the main consideration was at this time the enhancement of Britain's position and a vision of western Europe independent of both the United States and the Soviet Union. On 22 January 1948 he announced to the House of Commons that talks on a security pact were to start with Belgium, the Netherlands and Luxembourg, and his speech was welcomed by the opposition and in the press. Bevin, said the *Economist*, had 'set the faltering pulse of Europe beating more strongly'; he had 'scattered a cloud of doubtful hesitations about British policy'; he had 'headed British foreign policy in a new direction'.[37] But Bevin did not contemplate the surrender of British power to centralized European institutions, and his caution was increased rather than diminished by the moves that led to the setting up of the Council of Europe in May 1949. This, as it emerged, was a purely consultative body with wide membership, and demonstrated the differences between those who, like most British and Scandinavians, were opposed to any diminution of national sovereignty and those in France, the Benelux countries, Italy and now west Germany who, for a variety of reasons, saw the best future for their countries in building a closer European unity and had been caused by the war to question the absolute value of the nation state.

All, however, were members of the Organization for European Economic Cooperation, set up to supervise the work of the Marshall Plan. In January 1949 Bevin and Cripps agreed on principles of policy towards that body:

> We can . . . lay down firmly the principle that, while we must be ready to make temporary sacrifices in our standard of living, and to run some degree of risk in the hope of restoring Western Europe, we must do nothing to damage irretrievably the economic structure of this country. The present attempt to restore sanity and order in the world depends upon the United States and the Commonwealth and the countries of Western Europe working together. If, however, the attempt to restore Western Europe should fail, this country could still hope to restore its position in cooperation with the rest of the Commonwealth and with the United States.[38]

During 1949, British preference for cooperation with the United States rather than with western Europe became more marked. Proposals in the Council of Europe for economic unification and supranational machinery were regarded as irresponsible, and caused some to demand British withdrawal. As the cold war was intensified the notion that Britain, with the Commonwealth and western Europe, could constitute a third world power on an equal footing with and independent of the United States was no longer credible. It was recognized that there was no prospect of consolidating the Commonwealth as a single unit, politically, militarily or economically; and there was no immediate or even medium-term prospect of combining Britain and its overseas territories with western Europe without American help. Neutralism was impossible for western Europe, despite its appeal to the Left. Consolidation of the whole of the West, on the other hand, had everything to recommend it; and in such a system Britain could retain a special position 'as the leader of Western Europe, as the link between Europe and the Commonwealth, and as the partner in particularly close relations of long standing with the United States'.[39]

Consolidation of the West took a notable step forward with the formation of NATO.[40] Talks about in some way securing American backing for the Brussels treaty had been going on since its signature in the spring of 1948 and were given greater urgency by the Soviet blockade of Berlin. The purpose of the North Atlantic treaty, signed in Washington on 4 April 1949, was largely political. The treaty did not alter the strategic balance: means to stop a Soviet military advance in Europe were still inadequate; but a treaty commitment was a remarkable departure from traditional American preference for autonomous decision. Victory in the 1948 elections confirmed Truman's faith in his policies. Domestically he called for a 'Fair Deal'; externally he reaffirmed the global struggle against communism, claimed credit for western European recovery, and forecast initiatives everywhere. But the grand language barely concealed gaps and discrepancies. Those between actual military resources, budget limitations and proclaimed objectives were not too serious so long as the promised initiatives concerned aid programmes, and war was not expected in the near future. But in September 1949 the explosion of the first Soviet atomic device forced a reexamination of strategic plans and foreign policy assumptions.

The eventual outcome was a report of April 1950 in which Paul Nitze, Kennan's successor as head of the Policy Planning Staff, called for greatly increased American capability to counter the danger that the Soviet Union, equipped with atomic weapons, would be increasingly inclined to take risks while America's allies would doubt her willingness to risk nuclear war over limited issues. This report, numbered NSC 68, has been described as a turning point in American policy. The assumptions about Soviet aims and American goals were not new: what was new was the call for greatly increased arms spending to fill the wide gap of 'unactualized power' between existing capabilities and those adequate to meet the currently fully mobilized Soviet capacity. New too was the implication that the United States would have to be ready to fight not only a global war but also limited wars in peripheral areas.[41]

The American government wanted to encourage the unification of western Europe, and wanted Britain to play a substantial part. Some senior officials such as Paul Hoffmann, the Economic Cooperation Administrator, and Averell Harriman tried to push Britain in the direction of European union. Kennan, understanding the strength of the British objections, advocated some kind of Atlantic union, with no pooling of sovereignty, as a way of overcoming some of Britain's reservations.[42] This idea received some press coverage,[43] but it never reached the level of serious policy discussion. In September 1949 a new balance-of-payments crisis forced a devaluation of sterling. This was conducted with American support and confirmed Britain's preference for expanding trade with the Commonwealth and supporting the world role of sterling. Dean Acheson, the Secretary of State, now came to the conclusion that it must be for France to take the lead with regard to west Germany, but he continued to press Bevin to do more.[44] At the same moment the Cabinet was agreeing with Bevin and Cripps that Britain should not go beyond the point of no return in involvement with the economic affairs of Europe. Cooperation could be encouraged, but a strict reserve should be maintained over schemes for pooling sovereignty and establishing supranational machinery.[45] The kind of instinctive feeling at work was shown by Hector McNeil, Minister of State in the Foreign Office, who replied to a suggestion that a large body of British opinion would favour union with Europe:

I do not agree. If the alternatives were forced on the U.K. I have no doubt that the overwhelming majority would seek to combine further with the U.S.A. and the Commonwealth. Anti-European feeling is a commonplace of British thought. Everyone has relations in the U.S. and Canada. Most have no one in Europe except the dead of two wars.[46]

The degree to which the Americans would approve of British aloofness from Europe was overestimated in London in the first half of 1950.[47] The Americans agreed that the United States needed Britain's world position but would not accept either that this meant an exclusive partnership or that the British should automatically give priority to Commonwealth interests over the idea of a strong western Europe. Acheson made this plain at talks in London in April 1950, disconcerting people who had expected something rather different. One official who had not made this mistake wrote afterwards to a friend:

Although of course quite willing to subscribe to the doctrine of continuous close consultation in all matters between the two countries, they [the Americans] made it very clear that the value of this country to the United States, apart from our Commonwealth position and our influence in the Far East and other parts of the world, lay in the leadership which we could give in Europe; and they were not prepared to encourage us to think that we could establish, through any special relationship with them, an alibi for our duties in respect of European integration, etc.[48]

In these circumstances it is not surprising that the French Foreign Minister, Robert Schuman, consulted Acheson but not Bevin on the proposal that he launched on 8 May for merging the French and west German coal and steel industries, and those of any other country that wished to join, under a supranational high authority.[49] From the French point of view the importance of the Schuman Plan was that it would control west Germany and guarantee France's coal supplies. From the wider west European point of view it would provide for rational planning of key industries, and mark a practical step towards European unity; and it did not depend on non-European considerations. From the British point of view it destroyed the assumption that Britain was necessary to mediate between France and Germany and that a meaningful customs union without Britain was impossible.

The first British reaction was not hostile. When Jean Monnet, the original author of the plan, came to London in the middle of May, Cripps said he thought Britain should collaborate from the start rather than join later a scheme worked out by others. The *Economist* thought Britain should join wholeheartedly in examining and setting up the proposed council; European-minded Conservatives and Liberals wrote to *The Times*: 'We cannot turn our backs on Europe at this critical moment.'[50] But when the French insisted that acceptance of the principle of a high authority was a precondition for joining in the talks, the Cabinet declined. Public opinion on the whole agreed that the prior commitment was impossible. The Labour Party was opposed to subjecting Britain's nationalized industries to 'undemocratic' outside control. It was, however, an embarrass-ment to the government that the party's National Executive published on 13 June a long-planned document on European unity which rejected the idea of an economic union that was not based on planning for full employment, social justice and stability, and stated:

> In every respect except distance we in Britain are closer to our kinsmen in Australia and New Zealand on the far side of the world, than we are to Europe ... The economies of the Commonwealth countries are complementary to that of Britain to a degree which those of western Europe can never equal.[51]

There was much suspicion (not only on the left) of the largely Catholic Christian Democrat parties currently in power in France, west Germany, and Italy. The Conservatives, while criticizing the government for not joining the talks on the same footing as the Dutch (who had reserved the right to withdraw), were no more ready for a surrender of sovereignty.

Refusal to join the talks on the Schuman Plan did not predetermine later choices. But Britain was now seen to be swimming against the European tide. This aroused little public concern; but the absence, in the discussions in Westminster and Whitehall and Fleet Street, of any thought of the long term is striking. In the defence field Britain remained the leader of western Europe and the most reliable and effective ally of the United States; but in the economic and political spheres she lost the leadership to which Bevin had aspired. Between 1950 and 1955 British policy on Europe was based on the assumption that Britain, as a world power, must not be a unit in a federated western Europe and could not sacrifice any of the sovereign power of Parliament. On the positive side she would not try to prevent integrationist moves by the Six and would wish to be associated with whatever emerged, acting as a link with the rest of western Europe and the Atlantic community if the moves succeeded and being ready with less ambitious plans for cooperation in case the moves failed. This was done, successfully, over the proposal for a European army launched by the French in October 1990 as a means of making German rearmament (on which the Americans were insisting) acceptable to the many in Europe who were horrified at the prospect of seeing arms in German hands again so soon. There was no suggestion that Britain should join the European defence community, but first the Labour government and then the Conservatives, in office after October 1951, pledged British association; and when the treaty was finally rejected by the French parliament in August 1954 Eden rescued the situation by proposing Western Union, a non-supranational extension of the Brussels Pact including west Germany and Italy, and with a British pledge to keep forces on the continent.[52] On all this there was not much difference between the main parties in Britain. While the Labour Party was in power the positive features were often obscured by instinctive 'Little Englandism'. Churchill's interest in European unity while in opposition was based on his desire to see Franco-German reconciliation. Once this was under way, he saw no need for Britain to join. The so-called 'Tory Strasbourgers' were not supranationalists, and remained excessively confident that the Six wanted Britain on her terms rather than theirs. The continuity is exemplified by a report initiated in the Foreign Office under Herbert Morrison (who succeeded Bevin in March 1951) and endorsed by Eden. This did not foresee political danger to Britain from a union of west European countries, nor immediate economic disadvantages. Britain could not join the movement for integration:

Apart from geographical and strategic considerations, Commonwealth ties and the special position of the United Kingdom as the centre of the sterling area, we cannot consider committing our political and economic system to supra-national institutions . . . Nor is there, in fact, any evidence that there is real support in the country for any institutional connexion with the continent. Moreover, although the fact may not be universally recognised, it is not in the true interests of the continent that we should sacrifice our present unattached position which enables us, together with the United States, to give a lead to the free world.[53]

This kind of complacency about British leadership and the true interests of Europe was shown to be misplaced when in 1955 the Six took the next initiative, to set up studies of further integration, a common market, and an atomic energy agency. Britain was invited to join in the studies without precondition, and accepted with the intention of trying to ensure that the actions of the Six were 'as little prejudicial to our interests as possible'.[54] The subject was embarrassing. Officials accepted that for all participants membership of a large common market would be advantageous, and that the transition to it could be painful for all. For Britain the immediate costs, in restructuring industry and perhaps especially in agricultural policy, would present serious political problems while the long-term advantages would be slow to appear. The economic arguments against joining were that Britain's world-wide interests in the sterling area and the Commonwealth trading climate would be hard to reconcile with a common market. The political argument against joining was again the Commonwealth, and the likelihood that a common market would lead on to further integration and eventually perhaps to political federation, 'developments which public opinion in this country is not at present prepared to contemplate'. The best outcome therefore would be for the plan to fail; but Britain must not reject it abruptly and must try to avoid the odium of causing failure. If the Six did succeed in forming a common market without Britain, 'the economic benefits which we should derive from abstaining would be essentially short-term benefits'; prolonged abstention would have increasingly harmful economic effects; it would then be necessary to consider whether Britain could afford to stay out, and she would be in a worse negotiating position. Offered this advice, ministers do not seem ever to have considered participation, taking the objections as axiomatic and asking no hard questions. Having failed to steer the discussions in the Spaak Committee, the British then decided to advocate an alternative plan based on a free trade area.[55] But while this was being worked out, the Six were spurred on to agree to draw up treaties on an economic community and an atomic energy authority. The treaties of Rome were signed in March 1957, by which time the British had devised a plan for free trade (excluding foodstuffs) between the new customs union and the United Kingdom and such other members of the OEEC as wished to join. During 1956 British industry and chambers of commerce came round to the idea of a free trade area, but ministers accepted only reluctantly that the conditions for a commercial policy based on the Commonwealth connection no longer existed, the system of preferences was crumbling, and Britain was too small an economic unit to survive alone. Against warnings that loosening Commonwealth ties would mean the weakening of Britain as a world power, some set a hope of securing continuing status by seizing leadership in Europe.[56] But negotiations in 1957 revealed that the Six did not want leadership of this kind, and Britain's bargaining position was not as strong as ministers thought. Four years later the British government made the first abortive attempt to join the EEC.

Within a few years the British decision of 1955 was recognized as a subordination of economic judgment to political feeling. Whereas for three or four years after the war Britain's economy was stronger than those of her continental neighbours, it gradually became apparent after 1950 that she was not well placed to compete with their recovery. Between 1950 and 1957 Britain's share of world trade in manufactures fell while west Germany's doubled; her industrial production grew at only half the rate of France and west Germany. In the mid-1950s, 45 per cent of her trade was still conducted with the Commonwealth; but markets in the sterling area were growing more slowly than the world as a whole and the OEEC in particular. Commonwealth countries were seeking new markets and sources of capital.[57] Against this background of declining competitiveness came recurring balance-of-payments difficulties. After the crisis of 1949 there was no further devaluation of sterling, mainly because of the Commonwealth – there was strong objection to devaluing their reserves unless it was absolutely necessary – and because in the 1950s still up to half of world trade was conducted in sterling.[58] A balance-of-payments surplus could only be achieved if a higher proportion of resources was devoted to investment and exports, but after years of austerity the British people were not inclined to reduce consumption. Defence spending remained high, taking a greater proportion of GNP than in any European country except France and rising sharply in 1952 and 1953.

The costs of great power status in a dangerous world rose in the early 1950s. For the United States the Korean war proved the point of NSC 68 and set off a programme covering the whole world and requiring increased defence spending over a long period. The point of maximum danger was seen as 1952, when the Russians would have enough atomic weapons to do the United States serious harm and before western forces in Europe were built up. The Americans were determined to seize and maintain the initiative and were confident of their ability to do so, although not without risk. Large new appropriations were approved in the late summer of 1950, but at the same time the National Security Council insisted that military build-up alone would not eliminate the Soviet threat and assure the achievement of American goals. It would be:

> a shield behind which we must deploy all of our non- military resources in the campaign to roll back the power of the USSR and to frustrate the Kremlin design. The United States must at the same time, both by its actions and demeanour, make clear to all that it has no aggressive intentions; that it is not threatening the security or independence of any peaceful country. The United States must also convince the other free nations that this program is the only way, so long as the USSR continues its present policies and practices, to achieve eventually a peaceful and prosperous world.

To this long-term end western Europe must be formed into a continental federal union, and the United States might have to assume some of the obligations of permanent partnership in a looser Atlantic–Commonwealth union.[59] By the end of 1950 the military programme was expanded again, to achieve the 1954 goals by the middle of 1952.

In Britain a large rearmament programme was announced in the autumn of 1950 and it was increased in January 1951. The Chiefs of Staff were agreed that Britain, the Commonwealth and the west European powers could not fight Russia except in alliance with the United States, but they also believed that the latter could not fight Russia alone. Full collaboration in policy and method was therefore essential; but whilst the Chiefs of Staff too hoped for eventual independence from Russia for the satellite states, they were more inclined than the Americans to think in terms of creating 'conditions in which nations with different methods of government can live together peacefully.'[60]

By the end of 1951 the rearmament programme was proving too great a strain and it was soon spread over four years instead of three: the general demands of rearmament had led to world rises in raw material prices and a new balance-of-payments crisis. Even after the slow-down, defence spending was over 10 per cent of GNP in 1952; the disparity between obligations and resources remained; and there was no easy solution. The British people, Eden wrote, might either have to accept a lower standard of living or 'see their country sink to the level of a second-class Power, with injury to their essential interests and way of life of which they can have little conception'. Complete withdrawal from any major commitment was impossible: the Russians would fill the resulting vacuum, and Britain's international status would be affected:

> It is evident that in so far as we reduce our commitments and our power declines, our claim to the leadership of the Commonwealth, to a position of influence in Europe, and to a special relationship with the United States will be, *pro tanto*, diminished ... Finally, there is the general effect of loss of prestige. It is impossible to assess in concrete terms the consequences to ourselves and the Commonwealth of our drastically and unilaterally reducing our responsibilities ... But once the prestige of a country has started to slide, there is no knowing where it will stop.

The answer had to be to persuade the United States to take on a larger share of the burden in Europe and much of the real burden in the Middle East and south-east Asia 'while retaining for ourselves as much political control – and hence prestige and influence – as we can'. But there seemed to be no way of reducing commitments without starting, in the words of the Chiefs of Staff, 'a landslide which we shall be quite unable to control'.[61] Some cuts were made, but the problem of resources remained fundamentally unresolved.

One element in prestige and influence was the possession of nuclear weapons.[62] It is clear that the initial decision to have an independent programme followed naturally from wartime experience. Even while British expertise and resources were being transferred to the United States it was assumed that independent work would be resumed after the war. Continued cooperation with the United States was desired, to save time and duplication of effort; but cooperation effectively broke down at the end of the war, and at the same time there was no assurance of American support for Britain or Europe in case of a Soviet threat. The decision to make a British bomb was formalized in January 1947; but work was slow: the first British device was not tested until October 1952, three years after the first Soviet test; and even then Britain had no independent means of delivering a bomb. There was no real improvement in Anglo-American cooperation until 1954.

The more difficult decisions came with the development of the hydrogen bomb in the early and mid-1950s when defence expenditure was a cause of great anxiety. The argument then for deciding to build British thermonuclear bombs and to order strategic bombing aircraft was largely that it was necessary to be able to influence American strategy. As the Chiefs of Staff wrote in December 1951:

> Recent experience in discussion with them [the Americans] on the policy for the use of the Atom bomb is proof of the grave political disadvantage under which we shall continue to suffer until we are in a position, by virtue of our own contribution, to claim as a right our proper share in the control and direction of what may well be the decisive strategy of any future war.[63]

In July 1954 the Cabinet agreed that a British hydrogen bomb was necessary if Britain were to maintain her influence as a world power. Harold Macmillan, as Defence Secretary, justified it on those grounds, and with general assent, in the House of Commons on 2 March 1955.[64] A year later there was less agreement. Whilst Julian Amery thought the hydrogen bomb would make Britain a world power again by cancelling the advantages of space enjoyed by the United States and the Soviet Union, other MPs suggested that the time had come to recognize that Britain was no longer the power she had once been, and should not try to carry burdens beyond her capacity.[65]

In December 1950 the anxiety was not that the United States might not use atomic weapons but that she might. One area where Britain had had only a minor position and little influence since the war was the Far East, although she retained major commitments in south-east Asia and had been combatting a communist insurgency in Malaya since 1948. General MacArthur ran Japan virtually single-handed, and the United States was almost alone in its policy on China. When in 1949 the Chinese Communists were victorious and forced the Nationalists to withdraw to Taiwan under American protection, Britain recognized the new People's Republic and soon began to advocate allocating to it the Chinese seat in the United Nations, while the United States remained locked in rigid hostility.[66] The Chinese debacle caused enormous feeling in the United States, fuelling conspiracy theories, cold war hysteria, and McCarthyism. There was virtually no coordination of policy between Britain and the United States in the Far East. But when in June 1950 North Korea invaded the south, Truman announced the sending of aid, and the United Nations Security Council – with Russia temporarily boycotting meetings – called on member states to repel aggression, British naval forces in Japanese waters were made available at once. Contributing ground forces was more difficult; but the political argument for behaving as 'the only dependable ally and partner' of the United States, and for fearing the effect of a negative decision on the relationship between the two countries, outweighed military considerations.[67] Parliament and the press took the decision to offer a brigade as natural. But by the winter the position had changed. The invasion of the south had been driven back: MacArthur was advancing into the north, distrust of his declared intentions was widespread, and alarm grew when Truman hinted at the possibility of using atomic weapons. There seemed to be a real risk of being involved by the Americans in the 'wrong' war in the Far East. The argument for keeping in line with the Americans was that:

> Any strong divergence of policy between ourselves and the Americans over the Far East would involve a risk of losing American support in Europe . . . We could not afford to lose America's support in Europe; and on that account we must be prepared, if necessary, to accept American leadership in the Far East.[68]

Some of the press agreed, but in view of great public anxiety, and dissent in his own party, Attlee flew to Washington. He secured a verbal assurance that the use of atomic bombs would not be considered without consultation with Britain and Canada.[69] Then the belligerent American response to Chinese intervention in Korea brought new tensions, and the ambassador in Washington was instructed to warn Acheson that there was a real danger of a rift.[70] The Administration, however, resisted calls at home to escalate the conflict and risk alienating its allies. The United States, warned the Policy Planning Staff, would often find that automatic support from its allies was not forthcoming. On really vital questions it would have to maintain its position; but allies – especially Britain and the Commonwealth – were indispensable, and the number of disagreements must be kept to a minimum 'if we are to have the rest of the friendly world with us when we need them most'.[71] In March 1951 Truman dismissed MacArthur for insubordination. The fighting in Korea ground to a halt around the original 38th parallel dividing line between north and south; in July the two sides began what were to be immensely long-drawn-out armistice talks. Meanwhile two Commonwealth countries, Australia and New Zealand, were given guarantees in return for their consent to the Japanese peace treaty. Britain was excluded from the ANZUS (Australia–New Zealand–US) mutual defence pact, a demonstration of her lack of real power in the Pacific and a blow to imperial pride.[72]

By the autumn of 1951 American planners had accepted that the Russians, far from wanting to start a full-scale war, had not improved their capacity to win one and were showing evidence of restraint. Nevertheless the chances of war by miscalculation were thought to remain high and Soviet aims were assumed still to be the establishment of a communist world in which peaceful coexistence with the United States was impossible. A Russian attack was considered possible before the American build-up was complete, and the United States must continue the process of escalation. If it could do so, it could take initiatives everywhere. This pursuit of preponderance meant eternal vigilance, an unlimited arms race, and unending cold war. As Hans Morgenthau, professor of politics at Chicago, put it, the international system was reduced to the primitive spectacle of two giants confronting one another. To contain or be contained, to conquer or be conquered, to destroy or be destroyed, were the watchwords. Total victory, total defeat, total obstruction seemed to be the only alternatives. To Acheson it was more even than holding the ring: 'we were endeavouring to see to it that freedom of choice rested with us, not the Russians'; and that meant eventually 'rolling back Soviet power to its 1939 borders'.[73]

Increasingly, American policy was taking on a military character, the metaphors of the cold war becoming real. At home, bipartisanship in foreign policy had come to an end in 1949; in the 1952 election campaign the Republicans attacked the Administration bitterly for timid acquiescence in stalemate, and promised a 'New Look' in policy. John Foster Dulles, who had served under Truman to negotiate the Japanese peace treaty but was now the architect of the Republican foreign policy programme, promised, in a much-publicized article in *Life*, a political offensive, making it '*publicly known that it* [the United States] *wants and expects liberation to occur*. The mere statement of that wish and expectation would change, in an electrifying way, the mood of the captive peoples.' The United States did not want bloody uprising and reprisals, but enslavement could be made so uncomfortable that the monster would let go his grip. Dulles was 'confident that within two, five, or ten years substantial parts of the captive world can peacefully regain national independence'. On her side America must develop the will and organize the means '*to retaliate instantly against open aggression by Red armies, so that, if it occurred anywhere, we could and would strike back where it hurts, by means of our own choosing*'.[74] Both these themes, the second soon labelled 'massive retaliation', were repeated in speeches, in testimony to the Senate Foreign Relations Committee, and in writing.[75] Dulles never explained how he thought the 'enslaved peoples' were to be liberated peacefully. Few Europeans thought it possible. The *Economist*, for example, was sure that: 'There is no way in the foreseeable future in which Poland and Czechoslovakia can be released from Soviet bondage except by force of arms . . . "Liberation" entails no risk of war only when it means nothing.'[76] Under the rhetoric there was a basic continuity of aims between the Truman and the Eisenhower administrations. But the rhetoric was different, and mattered. It served to keep the Republicans happy – Dulles was extremely sensitive to the need to protect his rear: he never, for example, tangled with Senator McCarthy on behalf of State Department employees. The rhetoric also frightened America's allies and conveyed a warmongering impression. Dulles threatened the west Europeans with 'an agonising reappraisal of basic United States policy' if the EDC treaty was not ratified.[77] At the Geneva conference on Indochina in 1954 he resolutely refused to shake hands with or sit at the same table as the Chinese delegate. Another *Life* article in January 1956 reported his boast of having three times been willing to bring the United States to the 'brink' of war – and so associated him lastingly with 'brinkmanship'.[78]

The image was to a large extent deliberately created, but Dulles could never resist the temptation to make gestures: he suffered from, in John Lewis Gaddis's phrase, an 'intractable case of pernicious hyperbole'.[79] In practice he was more pragmatic and flexible than the contemporary perception allowed, but the talk of massive retaliation reflected an actual change in American strategic thinking. Even for so rich a country the burden of defence spending was heavy: the new Administration was fiscally conservative and favoured a balanced budget. To prevent costs rising ever further, a new study in 1953 laid greater emphasis on air power and the use of atomic weapons not, as earlier, in proportionate response to enemy acts but at will. The distinction between nuclear and non-nuclear weapons was blurred. A National Security Council report of January 1955 on basic policy envisaged the approach of a condition of mutual deterrence in which:

> a total war involving the use by both sides of available weapons would bring about such extensive destruction as to threaten the survival of both Western civilization and the Soviet system.

But war would remain possible: the United States must be prepared to fight it and, while retaining the support of appropriate major allies and avoiding provocation, be prepared to use nuclear weapons in local situations. Uncertainty as to the precise nature of an American response combined with certainty of its existence should help to deter communist aggression.

> So long as the Soviets are uncertain of their ability to neutralize the United States nuclear-air retaliatory power, there is little reason to expect them to initiate general war or actions which they believe would . . . endanger the regime or the security of the USSR.[80]

While defence spending remained static, and even declined as a proportion of GNP and the total budget, American involvement in Asia and the Middle East continued to grow. Despite reluctance to be drawn into south-east Asia, as displayed in the ANZUS negotiations in 1951, the first step there had been taken with a decision in May 1950 to give economic and military aid to the French-sponsored semi-independent governments of Indochina. The commitment was not substantial until after the Geneva conference of 1954. This, and the outcome in the division of Vietnam, represented a success for British influence as against Dulles's efforts to get others to help the French defeat the communist Vietminh. Within a year the French were pulling out, South Vietnam was taken under American protection, and American advisers, confident that unlike the French colonial administration and army they could provide effective disinterested expert help, were arriving in large numbers.[81]

In the Middle East the British position became weaker. The process can be illustrated by two cases: the Persian oil crisis of

1951 and the negotiations over the Suez base. The Anglo-
Iranian Oil Company had come to personify exploitative British
imperialism, and contributed to its own downfall by business
secretiveness and slowness to adapt. It was ready to negotiate
about increasing the Iranian share of oil royalties, but once
the American company ARAMCO had agreed in December 1950
to share profits equally with the Saudi Arabian government,
no other Middle East state was likely to accept less. Iranian
ownership of the oil was not contested: the issue was the government's right to expropriate the company's property in Iran,
including the great refinery at Abadan. The British and
Americans were divided in their reaction to the nationalization
launched in May 1951 by the populist prime minister Mohammed
Musaddiq. The Americans did not want to risk losing Iran and
the refinery at a moment when Middle East oil supplies were
important for the Korean war. The British wanted to defend
their position and property; but there was no manpower for a
forcible intervention; it was not clear what a landing at Abadan
would achieve; and in the last resort the Cabinet reckoned that
it 'could not afford to break with the United States on an issue
of this kind'.[82] British staff withdrew from Abadan; the refinery
closed. Two years later the Americans lost patience with Musaddiq
and engineered his overthrow. American firms gained an equal
share with British Petroleum in a new oil settlement.

In Egypt, negotiations were renewed in 1950 but again failed
to produce agreement. In the existing world situation it seemed
too dangerous to promise early withdrawal from the Suez base,
and the British were unable to convince the Egyptians or the
Arabs in general that they were part of the 'free world' that
the West claimed to be defending. In 1952 the situation changed.
On the one hand the Egyptian monarchy was overthrown and
the new radical military rulers had both stronger popular
foundations and different priorities. On the other side the end
of the Korean war and a new balance-of-payments crisis
contributed to new British thinking on strategy. In the changed
circumstances an agreement was at last reached in 1954 that
provided for evacuation of the Suez base within 20 months,
and the possibility (but not a guarantee) of re-entry in case of
war. Despite the outrage of a group of Conservative backbench
MPs, who talked of 'the grave of British greatness', 'the nadir

of our imperial fortunes',[83] the agreement was generally accepted although without much enthusiasm.

In all this the American government agreed on the vital importance of the Suez base and still agreed that Britain was primarily responsible for the defence of the Middle East. But it was taking on more responsibilities in the area and was doing so in a piecemeal fashion, without developing a coherent regional policy of its own or working out what value it attached to the British partnership and how far British interests should be supported. In August 1952, for example, the Secretary of Defence, Robert Lovett, argued that the United States would have, if necessary, to displace British influence in Iran even at the cost of damaging Anglo-American relations. In June 1954 Dulles complained to James Reston, the diplomatic correspondent of the *New York Times*, that association with Britain and France was preventing him from following 'American' policies in the colonial field and from demolishing Soviet accusations of imperialism.[84] The Americans did not support a British project in 1954–5 for a settlement between Egypt and Jordan and Israel. Nor would the United States give more than lukewarm approval to the Baghdad Pact of 1955 by which Britain attempted to substitute a regional defence organization for her bilateral treaties with various Arab states. The Baghdad Pact suffered from dangerous weaknesses. It alienated both Israel and Egypt, and left Jordan torn between conflicting priorities. Even in her heyday, the intensity of Arab anti-western feelings and the rivalries of the Arab states would have been beyond Britain's control. Now it seemed that all attempts to manage them from the outside made matters worse.

At the end of September 1955 it was announced that Egypt had concluded a large arms deal with Czechoslovakia. This did not instantly alter British or American policy, but after the dismissal by King Hussein of Jordan of the British commander of his armed forces, Sir John Glubb, the British decided to cease conciliating Colonel Nasser, the Egyptian leader, and instead to work against his aim of leading the Arab states; and the Americans decided to withdraw their offer of a grant to help build a high dam at Aswan. This step was announced on 19 July 1956: a week later, in a deliberate challenge to the West, Nasser nationalized the Suez Canal.

There is no need to recount the development of the crisis from that point until the opening of hostilities between Britain and France and Egypt on 30 October.[85] What needs discussion is the intentions of the British, French and American governments, and the relations between them. As far as the British were concerned it is clear that from July the government was prepared to use force, if necessary alone, to restore effective international control over the Suez canal, and that for Eden at any rate the preferred outcome was the overthrow of Nasser. There were doubts in the Cabinet, there was concern about parliamentary and public opinion; and if the negotiations of the summer first for a Suez Canal Users' Association and then for Egyptian management under international supervision had contained guarantees, the government would probably have accepted. But the issues felt to be at stake were the dependence of the British economy on Middle East oil and Britain's influence as a world power, so when provision for effective sanctions against Egyptian default was not forthcoming, the balance tipped in favour of force. What was to come afterwards was not considered: most of the Foreign Office, and missions in the Middle East, were kept in the dark, so the element of political planning was notably absent. It took an embarrassingly long time to assemble the necessary forces in the Mediterranean; once they were in place it was difficult to keep them waiting. On 22–4 October collusion with Israel, rejected in August, was accepted as providing the best chance of wrecking Nasser's position. In all this the Commonwealth was not a source of strength: indeed it was obviously divided. Menzies, the Australian Prime Minister, was the only supporter of British policy; the Indian government was frankly pro-Egyptian; the Canadians pinned their faith on the United Nations but helped to pick up the pieces afterwards.

The French were equally anxious to overthrow Nasser, because Egypt was supporting the nationalist campaign against France in Algeria; but French policy in the Middle East was at odds with Britain's, France was if anything more unpopular in the region than Britain, and the alliance was purely tactical and short lived. Afterwards the French, more than ever disillusioned with Britain, turned more to Europe and friendship with west Germany; the British abandoned France and bent every effort to mend relations with the United States.

The position of the American government was quite different. American interest in the Suez canal was marginal; no consider-ations of vital communications or prestige were involved. Dulles wanted safeguards for canal users, but since he made it plain that the Users' Association he proposed would have no teeth and the Aswan dam grant had been withdrawn, he had no leverage with Egypt either before or after the event: his promise in November, for example, to secure Israeli rights of passage through the canal was not fulfilled. Dulles wished to restrain Britain and France from using force: the considerable leverage he should have had in their need (especially Britain's – the French had larger reserves) for economic support did not work until after the event.

Why this was so remains a puzzle. How could the Cabinet have so miscalculated the American reaction? The charge that they were misled is not substantiated. Eisenhower made his opposition to the use of force plain to Eden from the end of July; in September the embassy in Washington warned that the United States would not support military action, and that without such support action could lead to disaster. Dulles, it is true, was equivocal and several times appeared to go back on his word: Eden in particular disliked and distrusted him. But Dulles and Eisenhower were of one mind: Eisenhower's position never changed. The Americans were angered by what they saw as British deception of the President (on the eve of the presidential election to boot) and reacted accordingly, withholding help to sterling for four crucial weeks after the ceasefire until unconditional withdrawal was promised. It seems that British ministers – especially Macmillan, the Chancellor of the Exchequer, who was aware of the potentially disastrous effects on sterling and was an old friend and colleague of Eisenhower from the war – believed that the United States would not be able to avoid acquiescing in British action and would rate unity of the western bloc more highly than relations with the Arab world. Instead leading Americans from Eisenhower downwards reacted with anger at not being deferred to, and with instinctive and passionate anti-imperialism,[86] venting on Britain their frustration and guilt at not being able, after all their words about liberation, to help the Hungarian rising taking place at the same time. They were willing to protect Britain against Soviet threats, but no more. A combination of factors caused the British government to accept the United Nations call for a ceasefire on 6 November – the threat of sanctions, the Soviet threat, dismay in public opinion, division in the Conservative Party, and the American attitude. A speedy military victory would no doubt have secured party loyalty, but the invasion force had not yet even reached Egypt. All the other factors were predictable. The American attitude and its financial consequences were decisive.

Suez did not finish off Britain's role in the Middle East; but after 1956 the British knew that they could not act outside the Commonwealth without American consent, and that consent could not be counted upon. In that summer the government had embarked on a review of national policy, prompted by the realization that ever since 1945 Britain had been trying to do too much. She was no longer a first-class power in material terms: she did not have the great untapped sources of wealth of the United States, Russia, or Canada, India or China; she could not hope, on the basis of material strength alone, to play a major or dominant role in world affairs. To keep up an effective role, expand the resources she did have, and escape from the strain and danger of economic crisis that had persisted ever since 1945, would require great internal effort and the reduction of military commitments, especially in the Middle East and south-east Asia.[87] Significantly, apart from NATO, policy on Europe did not feature in this review: it was being discussed under a separate, commercial head. For the United States, a decade of power such as Britain had never enjoyed even in her heyday had brought much anxiety but not yet disillusion. The goal of global containment had led to intervention, first economic aid, then military aid, then commitments all round the world. Dulles relished the new opportunities in the Middle East, saying: 'We must fill the vacuum of power which the British filled for a century – not merely the ability to act in an emergency but day in day out presence there.'[88] But the Eisenhower doctrine of 1957, promising help to any Middle East nation threatened by aggression from a communist-controlled country, did not enhance regional security. American military power was handled with greater prudence than contemporaries or immediate successors would often allow, but the objectives were too vast ever to be wholly achieved.

List of Abbreviations

BD	*British Documents on the Origins of the War 1898–1914*
BDEE	*British Documents on the End of Empire*
BL	British Library
DBFP	*Documents on British Foreign Policy 1919–1939*
DBPO	*Documents on British Policy Overseas*
FRUS	*Papers Relating to the Foreign Relations of the United States*
HCDeb.	*The Parliamentary Debates*, 5th ser., House of Commons
HLDeb.	*The Parliamentary Debates*, 5th ser., House of Lords
NA	National Archives, Washington, DC
Parl. Deb.	*The Parliamentary Debates*, 3rd and 4th ser.
PRO	Public Record Office, Kew
PWW	*The Papers of Woodrow Wilson*

Notes

Introduction

1. Donald Cameron Watt, *Succeeding John Bull. America in Britain's Place* (Cambridge, 1984) is an excellent study in a short compass.
2. Comparative figures from P. Bairoch, 'International Industrialization Levels from 1750 to 1980', *Journal of European Economic History*, XI (1982) pp. 269–333. Other figures from B.R. Mitchell, *European Historical Statistics 1750–1970* (London, 1975); B.R. Mitchell, *International Historical Statistics. The Americas and Australasia* (London, 1983).
3. Memorandum by Sanderson, 21 Feb. 1907, *British Documents on the Origins of the War 1898–1914*, ed. G.P. Gooch and Harold Temperley (London, 1926–38), henceforth cited as *BD*, III, Appendix B.
4. A recent overview for the period before 1914, with references to other literature, is Avner Offner, 'The British Empire 1870–1914: A Waste of Money?', *Economic History Review*, XLVI (1993), pp. 215–38.
5. Imperial Conference 1926, proceedings, quoted in Anne Orde, *Great Britain and International Security 1920–1926* (London, 1977) p. 164. Comparative figures for 1907–10 can be found in the article cited in note 4.
6. Figures from Mitchell, *International Historical Statistics*.
7. Royal Institute of International Affairs, *The World in March 1939*, Survey of International Affairs 1939–1946 (London, 1952), p. 454; Peter Flora, *State, Economy and Society in Western Europe 1815–1975*, I (Frankfurt, 1983), p. 248.
8. See in particular papers by Lord Beloff and Wm Roger Louis in *The Special Relationship. Anglo-American Relations since 1945*, ed. Wm Roger Louis and Hedley Bull (Oxford, 1986), pp. 249–83.
9. *The Parliamentary Debates, House of Commons*, henceforth cited as *HCDeb.*, 5th ser., vol. 415, cols. 1295, 1299; Churchill to Bevin, 13 Nov. 1945, *Documents on British Policy Overseas*, ed. R.D'O. Butler and M. Pelly, and others, henceforth cited as *DBPO*, ser. 1, III, no. 102. For a discussion of the myth see Max Beloff, 'The Special Relationship; An Anglo-American Myth', in *A Century of Conflict 1850–1950. Essays for A.J.P. Taylor*, ed. Martin Gilbert (London, 1966).

10. Christopher Grayling and Christopher Langdon, *Just Another Star? Anglo-American Relations since 1945* (London, 1988).
11. See papers by Admiral Sir James Eberle and by Ernest R. May and Gregory F. Treveton in *The Special Relationship*, ed. Louis and Bull, pp. 151–82; and John Baylis, *Anglo-American Defense Relations 1945–1984: The Special Relationship* (New York, 1981).
12. Bruce M. Russett, *Community and Contention. Britain and America in the Twentieth Century* (Cambridge, MA, 1963) puts forward a theory of responsiveness and attempts to measure certain variables.

Chapter 1

1. For British external policy see Aaron L. Friedberg, *The Weary Titan. Britain and the Experience of Relative Decline 1895–1905* (Princeton, 1988); J.A.S. Grenville, *Lord Salisbury and Foreign Policy: The Close of the Nineteenth Century* (London, 1964); George Monger, *The End of Isolation. British Foreign Policy 1900–1907* (London, 1963); Paul Kennedy, *The Realities behind Diplomacy: Background Influences on British External Policy, 1865–1980* (London, 1981), Part 1. For United States foreign policy see Charles S. Campbell, *The Transformation of American Foreign Relations 1865–1900* (New York, 1976). For American attitudes to participation in world politics see Robert Endicott Osgood, *Ideals and Self-Interest in American Foreign Relations* (Chicago, 1953). For Anglo-American relations see Charles S. Campbell, *Anglo-American Understanding 1898–1903* (Baltimore, 1957); A.E. Campbell, *Great Britain and the United States 1895–1903* (London, 1960); Bradford Perkins, *The Great Rapprochement. England and the United States 1895–1914* (New York, 1968).
2. The note is printed in United States, Department of State, *Papers Relating to the Foreign Relations of the United States* (Washington, 1862 ff.), henceforth cited as *FRUS* (with year or special volume title), *1895*, pp. 545–76. For the earlier history of the boundary problem see R.A. Humphreys, *Tradition and Revolt in Latin America, and other essays* (London, 1969) pp. 186–202. For the crisis see, in addition to works cited in note 1, J.A.S. Grenville and G.B. Young, *Politics, Strategy and American Diplomacy. Studies in Foreign Policy 1873–1917* (New Haven and London, 1966).
3. *FRUS, 1895*, pp. 542–5.
4. Scruggs's propaganda campaign and his book *British Aggression in Venezuela, The Monroe Doctrine on Trial* (Atlanta, 1895), aroused much public attention.
5. Chamberlain to Selborne, 20 Dec. 1895; Chamberlain diary, 9 Jan. 1896; Chamberlain to Salisbury, 1 Feb., University of Birmingham, Chamberlain Papers, JC 7/5/1B/4; JC 7/5/1B/14; JC 5/67/45; J.L. Garvin, *The Life of Joseph Chamberlain*, III (London, 1934), p. 160.
6. Blanche Dugdale, *Arthur James Balfour* (London, 1936), pp. 225–6.

7. *Economist,* 26 Jan. 1896; William Watson, *The Purple East* (London, 1896), pp. 25–6. This book was a collection of poems about Armenia, first published in the *Westminster Gazette.* In the one quoted above, Watson suggested that if the United States found peace too tame she should join Britain in smiting Turkey and succouring the Armenians.

8. *Nineteenth Century,* Jan. 1896, pp. 7–15.

9. For example in *The Times,* 19 Dec. 1895; *Spectator,* 11 Jan. 1896.

10. Bryce to Roosevelt, 1 Jan. 1896; Bryce to Villard, 4 Jan., H.A.L. Fisher, *James Bryce, Viscount Bryce of Dechmont, O.M.* (London and New York, 1927), pp. 318–20. For Bryce's early visits to the United States see Edmund Ions, *James Bryce and American Democracy 1870–1922* (London, 1968).

11. *The Times,* 20 Dec. 1895–2 Jan. 1896; *National Review,* Jan. 1896. The 'Anglo-Saxon kinship' concept is discussed on pp. 28–30.

12. Franklin Eastman, *Atlantic Monthly,* Dec. 1894.

13. Godkin to Bryce, 9 Jan. 1896, *The Gilded Age. Letters of E.L. Godkin,* ed. William M. Armstrong (Albany, 1974), pp. 477–9.

14. George Burton Adams, *Why Americans Dislike England* (Philadelphia, 1896), pp. 17–20.

15. John A. Garraty, *Henry Cabot Lodge* (New York, 1953), pp. 152–3; William C. Widenor, *Henry Cabot Lodge and the Search for an American Foreign Policy* (Berkeley and Los Angeles, 1979), p. 90; Lodge, *Speeches and Addresses, 1884–1909* (Boston, 1909), pp. 181–94; Lodge, *Forum,* Mar. 1895; Lodge, *North American Review,* Jun.

16. Theodore S. Woolsey, *Forum,* Feb. 1896.

17. *New York Evening Post,* 20 Jan. 1896; *New York Nation,* 23 Jan.

18. A.T. Mahan in *Harper's New Monthly Magazine,* Oct. 1895, reprinted in Mahan, *The Interest of America in Sea Power, Present and Future* (Boston, 1897), pp. 168–70; Mahan to James Thursfield, 10 Jan. 1896; Mahan to Bouverie Clark, 17 Jan., *Letters and Papers of Alfred Thayer Mahan,* ed. Robert Seager and Doris D. Maguire (Annapolis, 1975), II, pp. 441–4.

19. Sidney Low, *Nineteenth Century,* Dec. 1896.

20. Accounts of the whole episode in J.A.S. Grenville, 'Great Britain and the Isthmian Canal, 1898–1901', *American Historical Review,* LXI (1955) pp. 48–69; A. Campbell, *Great Britain and the United States;* Grenville, *Lord Salisbury;* C. Campbell, *Anglo-American Understanding.* For the development of American power in the Caribbean see David Healy, *Drive to Hegemony. The United States in the Caribbean 1898–1917* (Madison, 1988).

21. Memorandum by Ardagh, 9 Dec. 1898; Board of Trade to Foreign Office, 2 Feb. 1899, Public Record Office, FO 55/392 (documents in the Public Record Office are cited as PRO, with class, group and document number).

22. Benjamin Taylor, *Nineteenth Century,* Mar. 1900.

23. Roosevelt to Hay, 18 Feb. 1900, *Letters of Theodore Roosevelt,* ed. E.E. Morison (Cambridge, MA, 1951–4), II, p. 1192.

24. Garraty, *Lodge*, pp. 215–17.
25. Memorandum by Lansdowne, 13 Dec. 1900, PRO, FO 55/399; Admiralty memorandum for the Cabinet, 5 Jan. 1901, CAB 37/56.2, printed in C. Campbell, *Anglo-American Understanding*, pp. 357–60.
26. *Economist*, 23 Nov. 1901; A. Maurice Low, *National Review*, Nov.; *Review of Reviews*, Dec.
27. *Parl. Deb.*, 4th ser., vol. 101, col. 87, 16 Jan. 1902. Until 1908 the Parliamentary Debates are cited as *Parl. Deb.* From 1909 they are cited as *HCDeb.* and *HLDeb.* for House of Commons and House of Lords respectively.
28. *Economist*, 23 Nov. 1901. There had been some correspondence in the *Spectator* in the early summer of 1897 on the question 'Does America hate England?'
29. Samuel E. Moffat, *Nineteenth Century*, Aug. 1901.
30. Lee to Roosevelt, 2 Apr. 1901; Roosevelt to Lee, 18 Mar., D.H. Burton, *Theodore Roosevelt and his English Correspondents* (Philadelphia, 1973), pp. 11, 43–4; Roosevelt, *Letters*, III, pp. 19–21.
31. For the whole question see Norman Penlington, *The Alaska Boundary Dispute, a critical reappraisal* (Toronto, 1972); *The Alaska Boundary Dispute*, ed. John A. Munro (Ottawa, 1970); C.P. Stacey, *Canada and the Age of Conflict*, I (Toronto, 1977); C. Campbell, *Anglo-American Understanding*.
32. *The Times*, 21 Oct. 1903; also *Spectator*, 24 Oct.
33. Donald F. Warner, *The Idea of Continental Union. Agitation for the Annexation of Canada to the United States 1849–1893* (Lexington, 1960); Albert K. Weinberg, *Manifest Destiny* (Baltimore, 1935). Goldwin Smith, a figure in English university and other reform, lived in Canada from 1871 and wrote prolifically in newspapers and journals. He disliked Canadian loyalism and 'came to the conviction that the separation of the two great bodies of English-speaking people on the American continent would not last forever, and that union, free and equal, was . . . the decree of destiny'. Goldwin Smith, *Reminiscences* (New York, 1910), p. 439. See his *Canada and the Canadian Question* (London, New York and Toronto, 1891); Elisabeth Wallace, *Goldwin Smith: Victorian Liberal* (Toronto, 1957).
34. Salisbury to Hicks Beach, 2 Jan. 1896, quoted by Grenville, 'Great Britain and the Isthmian Canal', p. 51.
35. Dufferin to the Queen, 1 Jan. 1896, quoted by Kenneth Bourne, *Britain and the Balance of Power in North America, 1815–1908* (London, 1967), pp. 339–40. The two-power standard had been effectively laid down in 1889, and reaffirmed in 1893. *Parl. Deb.*, 3rd ser., vol. 333, col. 1171; 4th ser., vol. 19, col. 1817.
36. Cabinet memorandum by Lansdowne, 8 Jan. 1897, PRO, CAB 37/44.2.
37. Memorandum by Ardagh, 12 Dec. 1897, PRO, WO 106/40, B1/5.
38. Godley to Curzon, 10 Nov. 1899, India Office Library, Curzon Papers, MSS Eur. F/lll/ 144.

39. Cabinet memorandum by Selborne, 17 Jan. 1901, PRO, CAB 37/
    56/8; Selborne to Curzon, 19 Apr., cited by Monger, *The End of
    Isolation*, pp. 11, 72 n. 1. The Committee of Imperial Defence on
    14 May 1908 decided in effect that the contingency of war with
    the United States was so remote that it need not be taken into
    account in framing the standards of defence: CID, 99th meeting,
    PRO, CAB 2/2.
40. Mahan, *Atlantic Monthly*, Dec. 1890, vol. 66, reprinted in *The Interest
    of America in Sea Power*; Sir G.S. Clarke, *Nineteenth Century*, Feb.
    1898.
41. Pauncefote to Salisbury, 26 May 1898, quoted by R.G. Neale, *Britain
    and American Imperialism, 1898–1900* (Brisbane, 1965), p. 113.
42. Roosevelt to Selous, 7 Feb. 1900, *Letters*, II, pp. 1175–7; Lodge to
    Roosevelt, 2 Feb., *Selections from the Letters of Theodore Roosevelt and
    Henry Cabot Lodge*, ed. H.C. Lodge (New York, 1925), I, p. 446;
    Samuel E. Moffat, *Nineteenth Century*, Aug. 1901. It is ironic that
    it appears to have been Lodge who, in his book *The War with
    Spain*, started the myth that the British ships, positioning themselves
    between the German squadron and Admiral Dewey's force
    bombarding Manila in April 1898, did so in order to prevent a
    German attack on the United States ships: Thomas A. Bailey, 'Dewey
    and the Germans at Manila Bay', *American Historical Review*, XLV
    (1939), pp. 59–81.
43. Mahan, *Forum*, Mar. 1893, reprinted in *The Interest of America in
    Sea Power*.
44. Salisbury to Satow (Tokyo), 27 Jul. 1898, PRO, FO 115/1077.
45. *Nineteenth Century*, Sep. 1898. Kipling's poem was published in
    The Times of 4 Feb. 1899 and in the *New York Sun* and *Tribune* on
    5 Feb. Kipling had sent it to Roosevelt in January. For American
    imperialist opinion see David Healy, *US Expansionism. The Imperial
    Urge in the 1890s* (Madison, 1970).
46. W.E. Gladstone, *North American Review*, Sep.–Oct. 1878. For the
    intellectual origins of the talk of Anglo-Saxon kinship see Hugh
    Tulloch, 'Changing British Attitudes towards the United States
    in the 1880s', *Historical Journal*, XX (1977), pp. 825–40; Hugh
    Tulloch, *James Bryce's American Commonwealth. The Anglo-American
    Background* (London, 1988).
47. Occasionally, as in *The Times* correspondence of December 1895,
    writers in the British press pointed to the fact. The *Spectator* in
    the summer of 1898 printed articles and letters on the question
    'Are the Americans Anglo-Saxons?' Most of the letter-writers thought
    they were: one Irish correspondent strongly disagreed.
48. W.T. Stead, *The Last Will and Testament of Cecil John Rhodes* (London, 1902). By a codicil Rhodes established scholarships for German students also, 'for a good understanding between England,
    Germany and the United States of America will secure the peace
    of the world and educational relations form the strongest tie'.
49. Thomas Archdeacon, *Becoming American. An Ethnic History* (New

York and London, 1983), pp. 25–6; United States, Department of Commerce, Bureau of the Census, *Historical Statistics of the United States. Colonial Times to 1970*, Bicentennial ed. (Washington, 1975), Part 1, pp. 8, 116–18.

50. Ralph Waldo Emerson, *English Traits* (London, 1856): *Works* (London, 1894 ed.) II, p. 122; Josiah Strong, *Our Country* (New York, 1885), pp. 200–18; George Burton Adams, *Atlantic Monthly*, Jul. 1896; Brooks Adams, *America's Economic Supremacy* (New York, 1900), *passim;* Francis A. Walker, *Forum*, 1891, 642.

51. Lodge, *Historical and Political Essays* (Boston, 1892), pp. 142–66.

52. F.P. Dunne, *Mr Dooley in Peace and in War* (Boston, 1899), pp. 53–7. For 'Mr Dooley' see Elmer Ellis, *Mr Dooley's America. A Life of Finley Peter Dunne* (New York, 1941). For Anglo-Saxonism and the restriction of immigration see Barbara Miller Solomon, *Ancestors and Immigrants. A Changing New England Tradition* (Cambridge, MA, 1956); John Higham, *Strangers in the Land. Patterns of American Nativism 1860–1925* (New York, 1955).

53. Arthur Silva White, *North American Review*, Apr. 1894.

54. Alfred Austin, 'A Voice from the West', *The Times*, 29 Mar. 1898. W.T. Stead, although approving of an alliance, nevertheless warned against excessive enthusiasm, and printed in the *Review of Reviews*, May 1898, a parody of Austin's poem sent to him by the novelist 'Ouida'.

55. A.V. Dicey, *Contemporary Review*, Apr. 1897.

56. Andrew Carnegie, *North American Review*, Jun. 1893, Jan. 1899; Carnegie, *The Reunion of Britain and America: A Look Ahead* (Edinburgh, 1898): he saw no problem over the British colonial empire or India, which would soon be put on the road to independence; and he included the Irish among Britons. Cf. Carnegie to Balfour, 23 Jul. 1903, Burton J. Hendrick, *Life of Andrew Carnegie* (Garden City, NY, 1932), II, pp. 190–3.

57. W.T. Stead, *The Americanization of the World* (London and New York, 1901), p. 151.

58. Garvin, *Chamberlain*, III, pp. 282–3, 301–2.

59. *Parl. Deb.*, 4th ser., vol. 58, cols 1436–8.

60. Garvin, *Chamberlain*, III, pp. 506–8.

61. *Spectator*, 21 May, 17 Dec. 1898; *National Review*, Jun.; 'Politicus', *Contemporary Review*, May; Bryce, A.V. Dicey, *Atlantic Monthly*, Jul., Oct.; Frederick Greenwood, G.S. Clarke, E. Dicey, *Nineteenth Century*, Jul., Aug., Sep.

62. Olney, *Atlantic Monthly*, May 1898; Tyler Dennett, *John Hay* (New York, 1934), p. 221.

63. *Nation*, 13 Jun. 1901.

64. Memorandum by Lansdowne, 11 Nov. 1901, *BD*, II, no. 92.

65. Mahan, *National Review*, Feb. 1903, reprinted in Mahan, *Naval Administration and Warfare* (Boston, 1908).

66. *The Times*, 14 Feb. 1903.

67. Cabinet report, 4 May 1904, PRO, CAB 41/29/14.

68. Roosevelt to Elihu Root, 20 May 1904, *Letters*, IV, p. 801, also pp. 821–2; Roosevelt's annual message for 1904, *FRUS, 1904*, pp. xli–xlii.
69. Archibald Hurd, *Nineteenth Century*, Mar. 1907; Ottley to Vaughan Nash, 26 May 1909, quoted by Arthur S. Marder, *From the Dreadnought to Scapa Flow. The Royal Navy in the Fisher Era 1904–1919*, I (London, 1961), pp. 184–5.
70. The United States was not included in Brassey's *Naval Annual* comparative tables of effective fighting ships built and building until 1900. The rise to third place is partly accounted for by Russian losses in the war with Japan.
71. *Nineteenth Century*, Dec. 1904.
72. Mahan, *Letters and Papers*, II, p. 589; III, pp. 291–2; Mahan, *North American Review*, Mar. 1911, reprinted in Mahan, *Armaments and Arbitration* (New York, 1912), pp. 181–5.
73. Capt. P.R. Hobson, *North American Review*, Oct. 1902.
74. George Harvey, *Nineteenth Century*, Apr. 1904; Roosevelt to Spring Rice, 11 Aug. 1899, *Letters*, II, pp. 1049–53.
75. Sir Christopher Furness, *The American Invasion* (London, 1902), pp. 29–30; B.H. Thwaite, *The American Invasion. Or England's Commercial Danger and the Triumphal Progress of the United States, with Remedies proposed to enable England to Preserve her Industrial Position* (London, 1902), p. 5; F.A. Mackenzie, *The American Invaders* (London, 1902), pp. 142–3; *Review of Reviews*, Oct. 1901, 'Wake Up! John Bull' supplement; J. Ellis Barker, *Drifting* (London, 1901). The *Review of Reviews* ran a series of supplements on the condition of Britain from September 1901 to the middle of 1904. See Richard Heathcote Heindel, *The American Impact on Great Britain 1898–1914* (Philadelphia, 1940).
76. Carden to Grey, 12 Sep. 1913, PRO, FO 371/1676. See D.C.M. Platt, *Latin America and British Trade 1806–1914* (London, 1972).
77. *Economist*, 29 Dec. 1900; 7 Mar. 1903. The *Economist* apparently did not think American competition warranted any articles in the years 1900–3.
78. Vivian Vale, *The American Peril. Challenge to Britain on the North Atlantic* (Manchester, 1984) is a thorough account of the whole episode.
79. John Bassett Moore, address to the Society of the University of Virginia, 1899, *Collected Papers of John Bassett Moore*, ed. Edwin Borchard (New Haven, 1944), II, p. 202. See also Archibald R. Colquhoun, *Greater America* (London and New York, 1904); Archibald Cary Coolidge, *The United States as a World Power* (New York, 1908).
80. Herbert Croly, *The Promise of American Life* (New York, 1909), ch. 10 (in 1914 Croly became founding editor of the *New Republic);* Lewis Einstein, *American Foreign Policy* (Boston, 1909), pp. 183–92.
81. Roosevelt to Whitelaw Reid, 28 Apr. 27 Jun. 1906, *Letters*, V, pp. 230–51, 318–20; Hermann Freiherr von Eckardstein, *Die Isolierung*

Deutschlands (Leipzig, 1921), p. 175; Howard K. Beale, *Theodore Roosevelt and the Rise of America to World Power* (Baltimore, 1956), chs 5–6.

82. Roosevelt to Dunne, 23 Nov. 1904; Roosevelt to Lee, 6 Jun. 1905, *Letters*, IV, pp. 1042, 1207. For the Panama canal tolls see Warren G. Kneer, *Great Britain and the Caribbean 1901–1913: A Study in Anglo-American Relations* (East Lansing, 1975). For Mexico see Peter Calvert, *The Mexican Revolution 1910–1914. The Diplomacy of Anglo-American Conflict* (Cambridge, 1968).

83. Mahan to Roosevelt, 24 Aug. 1906, quoted by Richard D. Challener, *Admirals, Generals, and American Foreign Policy 1898–1914* (Princeton, 1973), pp. 26–8. None of the papers presented to the Naval War College's summer conference of 1913 included the possibility of war with Britain as a serious factor in American strategic calculations: William Reynolds Braisted, *The United States Navy in the Pacific 1909–1922* (Austin and London, 1971), p. 142.

84. *BD*, VIII, pp. 503–604. See Ian Nish, *Alliance in Decline. A Study in Anglo-Japanese Relations 1908–23* (London, 1972).

85. *The Times*, 17 May 1909; *Spectator*, 22 May; A. Maurice Low, *National Review*, Jun. and Jul.; Sidney Brooks, *Fortnightly Review*, Jun.

86. Kenneth Young, *Arthur James Balfour* (London, 1963), pp. 277–83. Balfour sent a copy of the paper to Roosevelt.

87. Roland Usher, *Atlantic Monthly*, Apr. 1912; *Review of Reviews*, May; A. Maurice Low, *National Review*, Aug.; 'Washington', *National Review*, Jan. 1913.

88. *The Times*, 3 and 5 Dec. 1910; *Contemporary Review*, Jan. 1911; *Review of Reviews*, Jan.; Elting E. Morison, *Admiral Sims and the Modern American Navy* (Boston, 1942), pp. 276–85. 'Woodman, spare that tree', by George Pope Morris, an American poet and journalist, was written about 1837 and set to music by Henry Russell. The ballad, and instrumental versions, were reissued many times in the next 40 years. The title was still well enough known to be reused in the 1940s.

Chapter 2

1. Military history of the war is not discussed in this chapter. A useful account of the political side is David Stevenson, *The First World War and International Politics* (Oxford, 1988). For American neutrality, Ernest R. May, *The World War and American Isolation 1914–1917* (Cambridge, MA, 1959); Patrick Devlin, *Too Proud to Fight. Woodrow Wilson's Neutrality* (London, 1974). For American belligerency: David F. Trask, *The United States in the Supreme War Council. American War Aims and Inter-Allied Strategy 1917–1918* (Middletown, CT, 1961); E.B. Parsons, *Wilsonian Diplomacy. Allied-American Rivalries in War and Peace* (St Louis, 1978); David R. Woodward, *Trial by Friendship. Anglo-American Relations 1917–1918*

(Lexington, 1993); Arthur Walworth, *America's Moment 1918. American Diplomacy at the End of World War I* (New York, 1977). For the peace conference, see note 56.

2. For example James F. Muirhead, *Nation*, 15 Oct. 1914; *Spectator*, 29 Aug., 12 Sep., 31 Oct.

3. *Literary Digest*, 14 Nov. 1914. Of 367 editors of papers all over the United States who replied to the questions, 105 reported themselves as pro-Allied, 20 pro-German, and 242 neutral.

4. See for example A. Maurice Low, *National Review*, May 1915; Lindsay Rogers, *Contemporary Review*, May; Eustace Percy (Foreign Office) to A. Willert (*The Times* correspondent in Washington), 12 Feb., Yale University, Willert Papers, box 4.

5. Armin Rappaport, *The British Press and Wilsonian Neutrality* (Stanford and London, 1951) charts the ups and downs of British press reactions to American events and policy.

6. For an analysis of American opinion see Arthur S. Link, *Wilson* (Princeton, 1960–5), III, pp. 6–31; John Milton Cooper, jr., *The Vanity of Power. American Isolationism and the First World War 1914–1917* (Westport, CT, 1969).

7. Mary R. Kihl, 'A Failure of Ambassadorial Diplomacy', *Journal of American History*, LVII (1970–1) pp. 636–53.

8. For House and his relationship with Wilson see especially Link, *Wilson*, III–V. The text of House's diary and correspondence printed in *The Papers of Woodrow Wilson*, ed. Arthur S. Link *et al.* (Princeton, 1978 ff., hereafter cited as *PWW*), is to be preferred to that in Charles Seymour, *The Intimate Papers of Colonel House* (Boston, 1926–8).

9. Grey to Spring Rice, 22 Dec. 1914; Spring Rice to Grey, 24 Dec., Grey to Spring Rice, 2 Jan. 1915, *PWW*, XXXI, pp. 517–20, 522–3. For the whole subject see George W. Egerton, *Great Britain and the Creation of the League of Nations* (London, 1979).

10. Grey to House, 22 Sep. 1915, *PWW*, XXXV, pp. 71–2, n. 3.

11. House to Wilson, 10 Nov. 1915; Wilson to House, 24 Dec.; House to Wilson, 11 Jan. 1916, *PWW*, XXXV, pp. 186–7, 387–8, 465–6.

12. *PWW*, XXXVI, p. 180.

13. See J.M. Cooper Jr, 'The British Response to the House–Grey Memorandum. New Evidence and New Questions', *Journal of American History*, LIX (1973) pp. 958–71.

14. *PWW*, XXXVII, pp. 113–16. For press reaction see for example *Spectator*, 3 Jan. 1916.

15. See for example Grey to House, 28 Jun., 28 Aug. 1916, *PWW*, XXXVII, pp. 412–13; XXXVIII, 38, pp. 89–90; Spring Rice to Grey, 19 May, 14 and 31 Jul. 1916, *The Letters and Friendships of Sir Cecil Spring Rice*, ed. Stephen Gwynn (London, 1929), II, pp. 331–3, 339, 342–3.

16. See for example Norman Angell, *North American Review*, May 1915; *American Review of Reviews*, Dec.

17. See Link, *Wilson*, IV, pp. 48, 50; *PWW*, XXXVI, pp. 114–21, 173–5: the version of the speech published by Ray Stannard Baker and

William E. Dodd, *The Public Papers of Woodrow Wilson* (New York, 1925–7), IV, pp. 106–15 says 'incomparably the most adequate navy in the world'; *Literary Digest*, 19 Feb., 11 Mar. 1916; Archibald Hurd, *Fortnightly Review*, 1 Jun.

18. See Anne Orde, *British Policy and European Reconstruction after the First World War* (Cambridge, 1990), pp. 9–11, 13; Carl P. Parrini, *Heir to Empire. United States Economic Diplomacy 1916–1923* (Pittsburgh, 1969), pp. 15–21, 31–7; Burton K. Kaufman, *Efficiency and Expansion. Foreign Trade Organization in the Wilson Administration 1913–1921* (Westport, CT, 1974), pp. 166–70, 172–5.

19. House diary, 24 Sep. 1916, Yale University, House Papers, cited by Link, *Wilson*, IV, p. 337; see also Wilson to House, 23 Jul., *PWW*, XXXVII, pp. 466–7.

20. See *Literary Digest*, 16 Sep. 1916; Redfield to Lansing, 23 Oct., *FRUS, 1916, Supplement, The World War*, pp. 466–77.

21. Memorandum by Keynes, 10 Oct. 1916, J.M. Keynes, *Collected Writings*, ed. Elizabeth Johnson (London, 1971–83), XVI, pp. 197–8. For the whole story of Anglo-American financial relations see Kathleen Burk, *Britain, America and the Sinews of War 1914–1918* (Boston and London, 1985).

22. Memorandum by McKenna, 24 Oct. 1916, Keynes, *Collected Writings*, XVI, pp. 198–200.

23. Memorandum by Grey, 20 Oct. 1916, PRO, CAB 37/158/3; minute by Percy, 8 Sep., 182388/63430, FO 371/2795; memorandum by Percy, 21 Oct., CAB 37/158/3.

24. House diary, 15 Nov., 14 Dec. 1916; Wilson to House, 24 Nov., *PWW*, XXXVIII, pp. 656–61; XL, pp. 62–3, 237–41.

25. See Stanley J. Kernek, 'The British Government's Reaction to President Wilson's "Peace" Note of December 1916', *Historical Journal*, XIII (1970) pp. 721–66. Lloyd George's speech in the House of Commons in reply to the German note, also aimed partly at American opinion with an evocation of Abraham Lincoln, in *HCDeb.*, 5th ser., vol. 88, cols 1333–8.

26. *FRUS, 1917, Supplement, The World War*, I, pp. 6–9, 17–21.

27. See for example *Spectator*, 27 Jan. 1917; *New Statesman*, 27 Jan.

28. War Cabinet 54, 5 Feb. 1917, PRO, CAB 23/1; *FRUS, 1917, Supplement*, I, pp. 41–4, 119.

29. Wiseman to Spring Rice, 6 Mar. 1917, printed in *PWW*, XLI, pp. 346–8.

30. A useful general account is David Kennedy, *Over Here. The First World War and American Society* (New York, 1980). See also John A. Thompson, *Reformers and War. American Progressive Publicists and the First World War* (Cambridge, 1987).

31. See Trask, *The United States in the Supreme War Council*; Woodward, *Trial by Friendship*. For Russia see R.H. Ullman, *Anglo-Soviet Relations 1917–1921*, I, *Intervention and War* (Princeton, 1961).

32. Imperial War Cabinet 7, 3 Apr. 1917, PRO, CAB 23/40.

33. *FRUS, 1917, Supplement 2*, I, pp. 543–5.

34. Bonar Law to Page, 20 Jul. 1917, PRO, FO 371/3120, 144764/ 29503. Emphasis in original.
35. Bonar Law to Reading, 8 May 1918, PRO, T 172/445; Keynes, *Collected Writings*, XVI, pp. 287–8.
36. Wilson to House, 21 Jul. 1917, *PWW*, XLII, pp. 237–8.
37. For the episode see David F. Trask, *Captains and Cabinets. Anglo-American naval relations, 1917–1918* (Columbia, MO, 1972). For American shipping and trade see Jeffrey J. Safford, *Wilsonian Maritime Diplomacy 1913–1921* (New Brunswick, NJ, 1978); Kaufman, *Efficiency and Expansion.*
38. War Cabinet 142, 22 May 1917, PRO, CAB 23/2; Cecil to Balfour, 19 May, 4 Jun., PRO, FO 371/3119, 110785, 110787/97867; memorandum by Balfour, 25 May, *PWW*, XLII, pp. 296, 354, 396–401, 450–1; memorandum by Balfour, 22 Jun., GT 1138, CAB 24/17. For Anglo-Japanese relations, and these discussions in that context, see Nish, *Alliance in Decline*, chs 10–12.
39. Balfour to Bayley, New York, 5 Jul. 1917, PRO, FO 800/209; *PWW*, XLIII, pp. 125–6.
40. Bayley to Balfour, 13 Jul. 1917, PRO, FO 800/209. Wiseman's memorandum of his conversation with Wilson is printed in *PWW*, XLIII, pp. 172–5; Wilton Bonham Fowler, *British–American Relations 1917–1918. The Role of Sir William Wiseman* (Princeton, 1969), pp. 243–6.
41. For this see Trask, *Captains and Cabinets.*
42. Memorandum by Wiseman, Aug. 1917, Fowler, *British–American Relations*, pp. 246–54; Cecil to Balfour, 25 Aug. 1917, circulated to the War Cabinet as GT 2074, 18 Sep., PRO, CAB 24/26.
43. *PWW*, XLV, pp. 272–4.
44. Wiseman to Reading, 20 Aug. 1918, PRO, FO 800/225; Wilson to Lansing, 29 Aug.; Wilson to Hurley, 29 Aug., *PWW*, XLIX, pp. 100–1, 373–4.
45. Wilson to Hurley, 29 Aug. 1918, *PWW*, XLIX, p. 374.
46. Hurley to Baruch, 21 May 1918, quoted by Safford, *Wilsonian Maritime Diplomacy*, pp. 145–7; Kaufman, *Efficiency and Expansion*, pp. 187–8.
47. Reading to Wiseman, 28 Aug. 1918; Wiseman to Reading, 5 Sep., PRO, FO 800/233, 225; Fowler, *British–American Relations*, pp. 214–15.
48. Conference of ministers, 13 Oct. 1918, GT 5967, PRO, CAB 24/ 66; memorandum by Wemyss, 17 Oct., GT 6018, CAB 24/67.
49. Geddes to Lloyd George, 13 Oct. 1918; memorandum by Wiseman, 16 Oct., *PWW*, LI, pp. 314–17, 325–6, 347–52; Fowler, *British–American Relations*, pp. 283–90.
50. Accounts of the episode in Trask, *Captains and Cabinets;* V.H. Rothwell, *British War Aims and Peace Diplomacy 1914–1918* (Oxford, 1971); Stevenson, *First World War and International Politics*; correspondence in *PWW*, LI.
51. Memorandum by Wiseman, 'The attitude of the United States

and of President Wilson towards the peace conference', c. 20 Oct. 1918, Fowler, *British–American Relations*, pp. 290–6.

52. Memorandum by Smuts, 24 Oct. 1918, GT 6091, PRO, CAB 24/67; War Cabinet 491B, 26 Oct., CAB 23/14.

53. See accounts of the Cabinet meeting of 22 Oct. 1918 by Daniels and Lane, printed in *PWW*, LI, pp. 412–15.

54. Derby to Balfour, 20 and 22 Dec. 1918, *PWW*, LIII, pp. 456–7.

55. Imperial War Cabinet, 47, 48, 30 and 31 Dec. 1918, PRO, CAB 23/42. On the colonial settlement see Wm. Roger Louis, *Great Britain and Germany's Lost Colonies 1914–1919* (Oxford, 1967). Members of the War Cabinet were willing to encourage American involvement in German colonial territory or Ottoman territory, in areas where Britain did not have paramount interests.

56. A useful overview of the problems and the outcome of the peace conference is given by Stevenson, *First World War and International Politics*, ch. 6. For British preparations see Erik Goldstein, *Winning the Peace. British Diplomatic Strategy, Peace Planning, and the Paris Peace Conference* (Oxford, 1991). For Anglo-American relations see Seth P. Tillman, *Anglo-American Relations at the Paris Peace Conference of 1919* (Princeton, 1961).

57. See Inga Floto, *Colonel House in Paris*, 2nd edn (Princeton, 1981); Arthur Walworth, *Wilson and his Peacemakers. American Diplomacy at the Paris Peace Conference* (New York, 1986).

58. See *PWW*, LIII, pp. 337–40, 350–6, 389–91, 394–6, 525–6, 531–3, 574–7; Fowler, *British–American Relations*, pp. 234–5.

59. See for example *Westminster Gazette*, 4 Jan. 1919; *Spectator*, 8 Feb.; Archibald Hurd, *Fortnightly Review*, Feb.; *Daily Telegraph*, 2 May; Long to Lloyd George, 7 Mar., House of Lords Record Office, Lloyd George Papers, F/33/2/22.

60. Hankey diary, 24 Nov. 1918, Stephen Roskill, *Hankey, Man of Secrets*, II (London, 1972), p. 25; minute by Drummond, 27 Nov.; C.F.Dormer to Drummond, 28 Nov., PRO, FO 800/329.

61. Minute by Drummond, 27 Nov. 1918; Dormer to Drummond, 28 Nov., PRO, FO 800/329; Geddes to Lloyd George, 18 Jan. 1919, Lloyd George Papers, F/18/3/3; memorandum by Long, 14 Mar., ADM 116/1773; figures of fleet strengths in GT 7229, 7 May, CAB 24/79. For statement by Admiral Badger see *New York Times*, 13 Dec. 1918.

62. Planning Section memorandum, 4 Nov. 1918, in Trask, *Captains and Cabinets*, pp. 350–2; *PWW*, LVIII, pp. 458–9; Naval Advisory Staff memorandum, 13 Mar. 1919, *PWW*, LV, pp. 515–24; Benson to Wilson, 9 Apr., LVII, pp. 180–8; Benson to Wilson, 5 May, LVIII, pp. 456–7.

63. Cmd 1614 of 1922, *Memorandum circulated by the Prime Minister on March 25th, 1919. Some Considerations for the Peace Conference before they finally draft their terms (The Fontainebleau Memorandum); PWW*, LVI, pp. 259–70.

64. Accounts of the whole episode, dubbed by Daniels the 'sea battle

of Paris', in Egerton, *League of Nations*; Braisted, *United States Navy in the Pacific;* Tillman, *Anglo-American Relations at the Paris Peace Conference*; Marder, *From the Dreadnought to Scapa Flow*, V.

65. Correspondence printed in *PWW*, LVII, pp. 143–4, 178–80, 215–17.
66. Hoover to Wilson, 24 Oct. 1918; Hoover to Cotton, 7 Nov., *PWW*, LI, pp. 437–8, 634–6. See papers by Murray N. Rothbard and Robert H. Van Meter jr. in *Herbert Hoover. The Great War and its Aftermath 1914–23*, ed. Laurence E. Gelfand (Iowa City, 1979).
67. For French policy see Marc Trachtenberg, *Reparation in World Politics. France and European Economic Diplomacy 1916–1923* (New York, 1980), chs 1–2. For American policy see Parrini, *Heir to Empire*, chs 1–3. See also Orde, *European Reconstruction*, ch. 2.
68. Keynes, *Collected Writings*, XVI, pp. 429–36.
69. W.M. Hughes to Lloyd George, 18 Dec. 1918, Lloyd George Papers, F/28/2/18. For the origins of British reparation policy see Robert E. Bunselmeyer, *The Cost of the War 1914–1919. British Economic War Aims and the Origins of Reparation* (Hamden, CT, 1975). Bruce Kent, *The Spoils of War. The Politics, Economics and Diplomacy of Reparations 1918–1932* (Oxford, 1989), pp. 28–40 is a useful short account of the discussions at the peace conference.
70. Wilson to House, 21 Jul. 1917, *PWW*, XLIII, pp. 237–8.

Chapter 3

1. For imperial relations see Royal Institute of International Affairs, *Survey of British Commonwealth Affairs*, I, *Problems of Nationality 1918–1936* (London, 1937); Max Beloff, *Imperial Sunset*. II, *Dream of Commonwealth 1921–42* (London, 1989); R.F. Holland, *Britain and the Commonwealth Alliance 1918–1939* (London, 1981). For Canada, the least disposed to accept joint responsibility, see P.C. Wigley, *Canada and the Transition to Commonwealth. British–Canadian Relations 1917–1926* (Cambridge, 1977); essays by Max Beloff and Norman Hillmer in *Britain and Canada. Survey of a Changing Relationship*, ed. Peter Lyon (London, 1976).
2. See the essays in *Anglo-American Relations in the 1920s. The Struggle for Supremacy*, ed. B.K.C. McKercher (London, 1991), especially those by John R. Ferris and the editor.
3. D.C. Watt, *Personalities and Politics* (London, 1965), p. 211. For a contemporary statement of the connection between Britain's interests and peace see *Documents on British Foreign Policy 1919–1939*, ed. E.L. Woodward and R.D'O. Butler, and others (London, 1947–84), henceforth cited as *DBFP*, ser. 1A, I, appendix.
4. For Atlanticism in the early postwar years see M.G. Fry, *Illusions of Security. North Atlantic Diplomacy 1918–22* (Toronto, 1972).
5. Accounts of the rejection of the League include T.A. Bailey, *Woodrow Wilson and the Great Betrayal* (New York, 1945); Ralph Allen Stone,

The Irreconcilables. The Fight Against the League of Nations (Lexington, 1970); Lloyd C. Ambrosius, *Woodrow Wilson and the American Diplomatic Tradition* (Cambridge, 1987). General accounts of American foreign policy in the 1920s include L.E. Ellis, *Republican Foreign Policy 1921–1933* (New Brunswick, 1968); Selig Adler, *The Uncertain Giant 1921–1941. American Foreign Policy between the Wars* (New York, 1965).

6. *DBFP*, ser. 1, v, no. 360.

7. See *DBFP*, ser. 1, v, nos 373–97, 399, 414; *HCDeb.*, 5th ser., vol. 123, cols 769–72.

8. *DBFP* ser. 1, v, no. 428; *The Times*, 31 Jan. 1920. For the whole episode see the article by George W. Egerton in McKercher, *Anglo-American Relations*, the same author's 'Britain and the "Great Betrayal": Anglo-American relations and the struggle for United States ratification of the Treaty of Versailles', *Historical Journal*, XXI (1976) pp. 885–911, and his *Great Britain and the Creation of the League of Nations*.

9. See Orde, *Great Britain and International Security 1919–1926*.

10. For example James M. Burk, *Fortnightly Review*, Jan. 1920; Holford Knight, *Fortnightly Review*, Mar.; Walford D. Green, *Nineteenth Century*, Apr.; *Spectator*, 27 Nov., 4 Dec. The *Spectator* went on discussing amending the Covenant in order to satisfy the United States well into 1921.

11. For example Professor George McLean Harper, *Yale Review*, Apr. 1920; Walford D. Green, *Nineteenth Century*, Apr.; A.G. Gardiner, *Contemporary Review*, Nov.; *Review of Reviews*, Nov.; Lord Charnwood, *Contemporary Review*, Feb. 1921; H.H. Powers, *The American Era* (New York, 1920), pp. 1–11.

12. Dr Frank Crane, 'What a War Between Great Britain and the USA Means', reprinted in *The Times*, 10 Feb. 1921; *Nation*, Apr–Jun.; David F. Calahan, *Forum*, Mar.; William McClellan, *North American Review*, Sep.

13. Memoranda by Grey, 29 Jul. 1919, Lloyd George Papers, F/12/1/30, and 5 Aug., India Office Library, Curzon Papers, MSS Eur. F 112/211; House to Wilson, 30 Jul., 8 Aug., *FRUS, The Paris Peace Conference*, XI, pp. 620–3, 630–1.

14. Memorandum by Hankey, 17 Jul. 1919, PRO, CAB 29/159. See J. Kenneth McDonald, 'Lloyd George and the Search for a Postwar Naval Policy', in *Lloyd George. Twelve Essays*, ed. A.J.P. Taylor (London, 1971).

15. Cabinet Finance Committee, 11 Aug. 1919, PRO, CAB 27/71; Cabinet, 15 Aug., WC 616A, CAB 23/15.

16. Conference of ministers, 25 Feb. 1920, C 13(20), appendix, PRO, CAB 23/20; *HCDeb*, 5th ser., vol. 126, cols 2296–2319.

17. Memorandum by Beatty, 7 Jan. 1920, PRO, ADM 167/61. For the whole question see John Robert Ferris, *The Evolution of British Strategic Policy 1919–26* (London, 1989); and Ferris's article in McKercher, *Anglo-American Relations*.

18. See Stephen Roskill, *Naval Policy between the Wars*, I (London, 1968). Press articles include a series in *The Times*, 29 Nov–17 Dec. 1920; A.G. Gardiner, *Contemporary Review*, Nov.; Archibald Hurd, *Fortnightly Review*, Dec.; *New Statesman*, 18 Dec.; *Spectator*, 11 Dec. and 1 Jan. 1921; Vice-Adm. Mark Kerr, *Review of Reviews*, Jan.

19. See Christopher Hall, *Britain, America and Arms Control 1921–37* (London, 1987); Roskill, *Naval Policy*, I; Roger Dingman, *Power in the Pacific. The Origins of Naval Arms Limitation 1914–1922* (Chicago, 1976). Examples of American naval opinion: Rear-Adm. Caspar F. Goodrich, *North American Review*, Jan. 1921; speech by Adm. H. McL. P. Huse. reported in *The Times*, 24 Feb. Other speeches quoted by Hector C. Bywater, *Navies and Nations. A Review of Naval Developments since the Great War* (London, 1927), pp. 109–11. On Harding, memorandum by Willert, May 1921, Yale, Willert papers, ser. 1, box 4.

20. Good accounts include Braisted, *The United States Navy in the Pacific*; Nish, *Alliance in Decline*; Roskill, *Naval Policy*, I.

21. For the problem see Nish, *Alliance in Decline*; Wm Roger Louis, *British Strategy in the Far East 1919–1939* (Oxford, 1971).

22. See for example Archibald Hurd, *Fortnightly Review*, Nov. 1921; *Spectator*, 10 Dec.; *Nation and Athenaeum*, 17 Dec.; Wemyss, *Nineteenth Century*, Mar. 1922.

23. See for example *DBFP*, ser. 1, XIV, no. 547; *Round Table*, Jan. 1922; *American Review of Reviews*, Jan., May; Bywater, *Navies and Nations*.

24. See Orde, *British Policy and European Reconstruction*.

25. Accounts of American policy in Werner Link, *Die Amerikanische Stabilisierungspolitik in Deutschland 1921–1932* (Düsseldorf, 1970); Melvyn P. Leffler, *The Elusive Quest. America's Pursuit of European Stability and French Security, 1919–1933* (Chapel Hill, 1979).

26. A full modern study is Stephen A. Schuker, *The End of French Predominance in Europe* (Chapel Hill, 1976).

27. See Orde, *Great Britain and International Security*.

28. For a full discussion see William C. McNeil, *American Money and the Weimar Republic. Economics and Politics on the Eve of the Great Depression* (New York, 1986).

29. Details in Harold G. Moulton and Leo Pasvolsky, *War Debts and World Prosperity* (Washington, 1932).

30. For the negotiations to 1923 see Orde, *British Policy and European Reconstruction*.

31. For press comment see for example Walter Layton, *Nineteenth Century*, Mar. 1923. The *National Review*, Feb., thought that the settlement should help to 'eliminate that spurious sentimentalism in which the Pilgrims' Society and the English-Speaking Union with the weekly encouragement of the *Spectator* seek to envelop Anglo-American affairs.'

32. See for example A. Wyatt Tilley, *Nineteenth Century*, Sep. 1926; Philip Snowden, *Atlantic Monthly*, Sep.; A.G. Gardiner, *Foreign Affairs*, Oct.; statement by professors of Columbia University, *The Times*,

20 Dec.; Frank H. Simonds, *American Review of Reviews*, Feb. 1927.
33. See for example George Harvey, *North American Review*, Dec. 1925; J.M. Kenworthy and newspaper comments, *North American Review*, Mar. 1926; articles by Tilley and Gardiner cited in note 32 above; W.R. Inge, *England* (London, 1926), pp. 275–90; *Nation*, 30 Mar. 1927; *DBFP*, ser. 1A, I, no. 1.
34. Frederick Bausman, *Facing Europe* (New York, 1926), pp. 6–7, 13–14, 25–8, 30, 306–7, 320–2.
35. Accounts of the conference in Roskill, *Naval Policy*, I; B.J.C. McKercher, *The Second Baldwin Government and the United States 1924–1929* (Cambridge, 1984); Hall, *Britain, America and Arms Control*; David Carlton, 'Great Britain and the Coolidge Naval Conference of 1927', *Political Science Quarterly*, LXXXIII (1968) pp. 573–98.
36. Memorandum by Churchill, 20 Jul. 1927, Martin Gilbert, *Winston S. Churchill*, V (London, 1976), Companion vol. I, pp. 1030–5. For the argument about the cruiser programme see Roskill, *Naval Policy*, I.
37. Hankey to Balfour, 29 Jun. 1927, Balfour Papers, BL Add. MS 49704.
38. Cecil to Salisbury, 18 Jul., Cecil Papers, BL Add. MS 51086.
39. General Board report No. 438, 3 Jun. 1925; memorandum by Rear-Adm. Phelps, 15 Jul., quoted by Raymond G. O'Connor, *Perilous Equilibrium. The United States and the London Naval Conference of 1930* (Lawrence, KS, 1962), pp. 13–14.
40. General Board report, 25 Apr. 1927, quoted by O'Connor, *Perilous Equilibrium*, p. 16; General Board study 3(h), 22 Apr., quoted by Gerald E. Wheeler, *Prelude to Pearl Harbor: the United States and the Far East 1921–1931* (Columbia, 1963), p. 62. The dropping by the Labour government in 1924 of the construction of the Singapore base was not generally welcomed by American writers. The Vice-President of the American Navy League regarded the construction of the base as in American interests: *Fortnightly Review*, Nov. 1924; see also Howard to FO, 5 Mar. 1925, F958/9/61, PRO, FO 371/10958; Chilston to FO, 16 Aug. 1928, A 6034/1/45, FO 371/12799.
41. See for example *DBFP*, ser. 1A, III, no. 360; *Literary Digest*, 20 Aug. 1927.
42. See for example *Round Table*, Sep. 1927; Hugh Spender, *Fortnightly Review*, Aug. and Sep.; *National Review*, Aug.; Rennie Smith, *Contemporary Review*, Sep.; Lt-Cdr. J.M. Kenworthy, *Review of Reviews*, Jul.–Aug., Sep.–Oct.; *Spectator*, 26 Nov.; *New Statesman*, 17 Dec.
43. *New York World*, 24 Jun. 1927; Frank H. Simonds, *American Review of Reviews*, Sep. See also *Nation and Athenaeum*, 16 Jul., 1 Oct.; *Quarterly Review*, Jan. 1929.
44. *DBFP*, ser. 1A, III, nos. 480, 503. For Adm. Plunkett see *The Times*, 24 and 25 Jan. 1928.
45. Discussions of the problem in, for example, *DBFP*, ser. 1A, IV, no. 227; Wickham Steed, *Review of Reviews*, Dec. 1927; Frank H.

Simonds, *American Review of Reviews*, Mar. 1928; George Young, *Contemporary Review*, Mar.; *Round Table*, Mar.; 'Augur', *Fortnightly Review*, Apr.; Leonard Stein, *Nation and Athenaeum*, 26 May.

46. See McKercher, *Second Baldwin Government and the United States*.

47. Accounts of the affair in Hall, *Britain, America and Arms Control*; McKercher, *Second Baldwin Government;* David Carlton, 'The Anglo-French Compromise on Arms Limitation, 1928', *Journal of British Studies*, VIII (1969).

48. See R.H. Ferrell, *Peace in Their Time. The Origins of the Kellogg–Briand Pact* (New Haven, 1952); McKercher, *Second Baldwin Government*, The implications of the pact for American neutrality policy were much discussed in the early 1930s: see chapter 4.

49. See *New York World*, 25 Aug., 8 and 11 Sep. 1928; *Literary Digest*, 18 Aug., 13 Oct.; *Nation*, 10 Oct.; Leonard Stein, *Nation and Athenaeum*, 27 Oct.; *DBFP*, ser. 1A, V, no. 452.

50. *Spectator*, 29 Sep. 1928; *Observer*, 28 Oct.; *Nation and Athenaeum*, 29 Sep., 6 Oct.; *Economist*, 29 Sep., 6 Oct.; *Review of Reviews*, Oct., Nov. and Dec.; *HCDeb*, 5th ser., vol. 222, cols 721–834.

51. *DBFP*, ser. 1A, V, no. 490. Some American writers were suggesting that the Pacific Dominions would soon look to the United States rather than Britain, or urging them to do so: for example *Washington Post*, 27 Nov. 1924; Nicholas Roosevelt, *The Restless Pacific* (New York, 1928), p. 280; memorandum by Wellesley, 1 Jan. 1925; Howard to FO, 12 Nov., F 29, 5652/9/61, PRO, FO 371/10958. Sir Francis Fox argued, in *The Mastery of the Pacific. Can the British Empire and the United States Agree?* (London, 1928), that agreement on policy was possible if both peoples freed their minds of false ideas and hypocrisy.

52. *DBFP*, ser. 1A, V, no. 497, Gilbert, *Churchill*, V, companion vol. I, pp. 1340–3, 1348–9, 1380–2; memorandum by Amery, 26 Nov., CP 367(28), PRO, CAB 24/198.

53. Coolidge's address was printed in full in the American press and in *The Times* of 12 Nov. 1928. For comment see for example *Nation*, 28 Nov.; *National Review*, Nov.; *The Times*, 13 Nov.; *New Statesman*, 17 Nov.; *Spectator*, 17 Nov.

54. See for example George Young, *Contemporary Review*, Mar. 1928; *Spectator*, 21 Apr., 1 Sep., 1 Dec., 23 Feb, 1929; 'Augur', *Fortnightly Review*, Apr. 1928; J.M. Kenworthy, *Review of Reviews*, Jan. 1929; Philip Kerr, *Saturday Review of Literature*, 26 Jan., 2 Feb.; F.G. Stone, *Nineteenth Century*, Feb.; *Round Table*, Mar.; J.M. Kenworthy and George Young, *Freedom of the Seas* (London, 1928).

55. *Economist*, 1 Dec. 1928; *Spectator*, 2 Mar. 1929.

56. See for example *New York World*, 12 Nov. 1927; Frank H. Simonds, *American Review of Reviews*, Feb. 1928; Charles P. Howland, *Yale Review*, Jul.; *Nation*, 26 Dec., 2 Jan. 1929; Allen Dulles, *Foreign Affairs*, Jan.; *Literary Digest*, 9 Feb.; Simonds, *National Review*, Mar.; Simonds, *American Review of Reviews*, Apr.; John W. Davis, *Foreign Affairs*, Apr.

57. Murray to Levinson, 2 Dec. 1928, Oxford, Bodleian Library, MS Gilbert Murray 54, fols 214–28; *New York World*, 24 Jun. 1927.
58. Lippmann to Kerr, 4 Dec. 1928; Kerr to Lippmann, 20 Dec., Yale University, Lippmann Papers, ser. 1, box 16; *DBFP*, ser. lA, v, no. 517; Lippmann, *Saturday Review of Literature*, 9 Feb. 1929; Allen Dulles, *Foreign Affairs*, Jan.
59. See Robert Boyce, *British Capitalism at the Crossroads 1919–1932* (Cambridge, 1987); D.E. Moggridge, *British Monetary Policy 1924–1931. The Norman Conquest of $4.86* (Cambridge, 1972).
60. See Stephen V.O. Clarke, *Central Bank Cooperation 1924–31* (New York, 1967); Idem, *The Reconstruction of the International Monetary System. The Attempts of 1922 and 1933* (Princeton, 1973); Frank Costigliola, 'Anglo-American Financial Rivalry in the 1920s', *Journal of Economic History*, XXXVII (1972) pp. 911–34.
61. For this question see Orde, *British Policy and European Reconstruction*; Richard Meyer, *Bankers' Diplomacy. Monetary Stabilization in the Twenties* (New York, 1970); Lester V. Chandler, *Benjamin Strong, Central Banker* (Washington, 1958); Neal Pease, *Poland, the United States and the Stabilization of Europe, 1919–1933* (New York, 1986); Joan Hoff Wilson, *American Business and Foreign Policy 1920–1933* (Lexington, 1971).
62. The aggressive aspect is emphasized particularly by Parrini, *Heir to Empire*; Frank Costigliola, *Awkward Dominion. American Political, Economic and Cultural Relations with Europe, 1919–1933* (Ithaca, 1984). The cooperative aspect is emphasized by Michael J. Hogan, *Informal Entente. The Private Structure of Cooperation in Anglo-American Economic Diplomacy* (Columbia, 1977).
63. See Marion Kent, *Oil and Empire. British Policy and Mesopotamian Oil 1900–1920* (London, 1976).
64. See for example Edward G. Acheson, *Forum*, Nov. 1920; Daniels, *Cabinet Diaries*, pp. 370, 575 (21 Jan. 1919, 18 Dec. 1920); Benjamin H. Williams, *Economic Foreign Policy of the United States* (New York, 1929), p. 58.
65. E.M. Edgar quoted (from *Sperling's Journal*, Sep. 1919) by Edward G. Acheson, *Forum*, Nov.; *Nation*, 15 May 1920; E.H. Davenport and S.R. Cooke, *The Oil Trusts and Anglo-American Relations* (London, 1923), p. ix; *Sunday Times*, 18 Apr. 1920. See John A. De Novo, 'The Movement for an Aggressive American Oil Policy Abroad 1918–1920', *American Historical Review*, LXVI (1965–6) pp. 854–76.
66. See *DBFP*, ser. 1, XIII, nos 57, 247; *FRUS, 1920*, II, pp. 649–75; *FRUS, 1921*, II, pp. 80–105.
67. See Geoffrey Jones, *The State and the Emergence of the British Oil Industry* (London, 1981); Hogan, *Informal Entente*; Ludwell Denny, *We Fight for Oil* (New York and London, 1928), pp. 273–4.
68. For the Stevenson scheme see Sir Andrew McFadyean, *The History of Rubber Regulation 1934–1943* (London, 1944). Examples of American opinion are in George O. May, *Atlantic Monthly*, Jun. 1926; Jacob Viner, *Foreign Affairs*, Jul.

69. See Joseph B. Brandes in *Herbert Hoover as Secretary of Commerce*, ed. Ellis W. Hawley (Iowa City, 1981).
70. Denny, *We Fight for Oil*, pp. 13–14; John Carter, *Conquest. America's Painless Imperialism* (New York, 1928), pp. 4–5, 281–2. Two years later, Denny had even abandoned the idea of compromise and was confident of American victory: 'If Britain is foolish enough to fight us, she will go down more quickly, that is all': Denny, *America Conquers Britain. A Record of Economic War* (New York, 1930), p. 407.
71. David Marquand, *Ramsay MacDonald* (London, 1977); Hall, *Britain, America and Arms Control*; O'Connor, *Perilous Equilibrium*. Actual British cruiser strength was little affected, the controversial 70 of 1927 not having been reached. Favourable American press comment on MacDonald's visit, with occasional warnings against excessive optimism, in for example *Literary Digest*, 28 Sep., 14 Oct. 1929; *New York Times*, 13 Oct.; *Nation*, 9 Oct., 23 Oct.; Walter Lippmann, *Nation and Athenaeum*, 2 Nov. The press comment in Britain was generally one of relief, with some criticism of the lack of a *quid pro quo* for the acceptance of parity: for example Archibald Hurd, *Nineteenth Century*, Nov.; Sir Charles Mallet, *Contemporary Review*, Dec.
72. Accounts of the conference in O'Connor, *Perilous Equilibrium;* Hall, *Britain, America and Arms Control*; Roskill, *Naval Policy*, II; Marquand, *MacDonald*.

Chapter 4

1. For the depression in general see Charles P. Kindleberger, *The World in Depression 1929–1939* (London, 1973). For international aspects of the United States see H.A. Lary, *The United States in the World Economy* (Washington, 1943). For Britain see D.N. Aldcroft, *The Inter-war Economy* (London, 1970).
2. Useful summaries include William R. Rock, *British Appeasement in the 1930s* (London, 1977); Kennedy, *Realities behind Diplomacy*, pp. 223–312; R.A.C. Parker, *Chamberlain and Appeasement. British Policy and the Coming of the Second World War* (London and Basingstoke, 1993). Other works include William R. Rock, *Appeasement on Trial* (Hamden, CT, 1966); Neville Thompson, *The Anti-Appeasers* (Oxford, 1971); Maurice Cowling, *The Impact of Hitler* (London, 1975). For an analysis, Gustav Schmidt, *England in der Krise. Grundzüge und Grundlagen der Britischen Appeasement-Politik* (Opladen, 1981), Eng. trans. *The Politics and Economics of Appeasement* (Leamington Spa, 1986).
3. For an analysis of the ideas see Manfred Jonas, *Isolationism in America 1935–1941* (Ithaca, 1966); more generally Selig Adler, *The Isolationist Impulse* (New York, 1957).
4. For Hoover see Ellis, *Republican Foreign Policy*. For Stimson see

Richard N. Current, *Secretary Stimson. A Study in Statecraft* (New Brunswick, 1954); Henry L. Stimson and McGeorge Bundy, *On Active Service in Peace and War* (New York and London, 1948).

5. For Roosevelt see Robert Dallek, *Franklin D. Roosevelt and American Foreign Policy 1932–1945* (New York, 1979). For Hull see Julius W. Pratt, *Cordell Hull 1933–1944* (New York, 1964).

6. See for example Wickham Steed, *American Review of Reviews*, Jan. 1930; *Sunday Times*, 31 Aug. and 14 Sep.; F.L. Simonds, *American Review of Reviews*, Jan.; James Truslow Adams, *Forum*, Nov.; Nicholas Roosevelt, *America and England?* (New York and London, 1930); J.L. Garvin in *Problems of Peace*, 5th ser. (London, 1931); Norman Angell in Carl Russell Fish, Norman Angell, and Rear Adm. Charles L. Hussey, *American Policies Abroad. The United States and Great Britain* (Chicago, 1932).

7. Stimson diary, 7 Aug. 1931, Yale University, Stimson Papers; *DBFP*, ser. 2, III, no. 217; *FRUS, 1931*, I, pp. 514–17.

8. Stimson diary, 23 Oct. 1931.

9. Text of address in *FRUS, 1932*, III, pp. 575–83. Stimson diary, 24 Jul. 1934.

10. *Economist*, 13 Aug. 1932; Frank Darvall, *Contemporary Review*, Oct.; Raymond Buell, *Political Quarterly*, Oct.; Frank L. Simonds, *Can America Stay at Home?* (New York, 1932), p. 361.

11. *DBFP*, ser. 2, IV, nos 205, 210, 211.

12. *FRUS, 1933*, I, pp. 143–5, 154–9; *DBFP*, ser. 2, V, no. 146.

13. Christopher Thorne, *The Limits of Foreign Policy. The West, the League and the Far Eastern Crisis of 1931–1933* (London, 1972) supersedes all earlier accounts. Henry L. Stimson, *The Far Eastern Crisis* (New York, 1936) is a version written by a major participant soon after the events. Reginald Bassett, *Democracy and Foreign Policy. A Case History. The Sino-Japanese Dispute 1931–33* (London, 1952) has a polemical purpose but is useful for British press opinion. Ian Nish, *Japan's Struggle with Internationalism. Japan, China and the League of Nations 1931–3* (London and New York, 1993) uses Japanese sources.

14. *Manchester Guardian*, 25 Jan. 1932; *Economist*, 16 Jan., 6 Feb., 20 Feb.

15. Norman Angell, *The Defence of the Empire* (London, 1937), pp. 92–115.

16. *DBFP*, ser. 2, IX, nos. 153, 239, 665.

17. Report by Chiefs of Staff, 22 Feb. 1932, CP 104(32), PRO, CAB 24/229; *DBFP*, ser. 2, IX, no. 636 n.

18. For the whole subject see N.H. Gibbs, *Grand Strategy* (History of the Second World War, UK military series), I, *Rearmament Policy* (London, 1976); also G.C. Peden, *British Rearmament and the Treasury 1932–1939* (Edinburgh, 1979); Robert Paul Shay jr., *British Rearmament in the Thirties* (Princeton, 1977).

19. CP 64(34), PRO, CAB 24/247.

20. Full accounts in Ann Trotter, *Britain and East Asia 1933–1937*

(London, 1975); S.L. Endicott, *Diplomacy and Enterprise. British China Policy 1933–1937* (Manchester, 1975).

21. Memoranda by Fisher, 29 Jan., 17 Feb., 19 Apr. 1934, DRC 12, 19, PRO, CAB 16/109; NCM(35) 3, CAB 29/148; *DBFP*, ser. 2, XIII, Appendix 1.
22. See minute by Vansittart, 15 Dec. 1933, A 9235/252/45, PRO, FO 371/16612; Vansittart to Fisher, May 1934, A 4114/1938/45, FO 371/17597.
23. Minute by Hankey, 30 Jul. 1934, PRO, CAB 21/398; Cabinet, 31 Jul., C 31(34), CAB 23/79.
24. For the talks see *DBFP*, ser. 2, XIII; *FRUS, 1934*, I.
25. See Edgar B. Nixon (ed.), *Franklin D. Roosevelt and Foreign Affairs* (Cambridge, MA, 1969), II, pp. 250–4, 258–61, 263, 290–3, 315–19.
26. *New York Herald Tribune*, 11 Jan. 1935, reprinted in Walter Lippmann, *Interpretations, 1933–1935* (New York, 1936), pp. 355–6.
27. Memorandum by Lothian, *DBFP*, ser. 2, XIII, no. 18; *Round Table*, Sep. 1934; *Economist*, 4 Nov., 22 Dec.; Garvin and Lothian in *Observer*, 4 Nov., 18 Nov. See Watt, *Personalities and Politics*, pp. 94–9.
28. *British Commonwealth Relations. Proceedings of the First Unofficial Conference on British Commonwealth Relations, Held at Toronto from September 11–21, 1933*, ed. Arnold Toynbee (London, 1934); *Round Table*, Dec. 1933; Sir A. Zimmern, *Fortnightly Review*, Apr. 1934; and *International Affairs*, May.
29. A.R.M. Lower, *Nineteenth Century*, Sep. 1933. See in general Ritchie Ovendale, *'Appeasement' and the English-Speaking World* (Cardiff, 1975); Holland, *Britain and the Commonwealth Alliance*.
30. Articles by Lothian in *Round Table*, Dec. 1933, Mar., Jun. and Sep. 1934; and *International Affairs*, Sep.
31. Dafoe to Lothian, 10 Oct. 1934, Scottish Record Office, Edinburgh, Lothian Papers, GD 40/17/281.
32. See Michael Dunne, *The United States and the World Court 1920–1935* (London, 1988). On the neutrality legislation see Wayne S. Cole, *Roosevelt and the Isolationists 1932–1945* (Lincoln, NE, 1983); Robert A. Divine, *The Illusion of Neutrality* (Chicago, 1962). Also, for the intellectuals who argued that intervention in 1917 had been a crime or an error, Warren I. Cohen, *The American Revisionists. The Lessons of Intervention in World War I* (Chicago, 1967).
33. See for example Hamilton Butler, *North American Review*, Jun. 1934; Oswald Garrison Villard, *Nation*, 17 Jul. 1935.
34. *New York Herald Tribune*, 2 Feb. 1935, reprinted in Lippmann, *Interpretations, 1933–35*, pp. 347–50.
35. Samuel Flagg Bemis, *Yale Review*, Dec. 1935.
36. See for example Charles Warren, *Yale Review*, Mar. 1935; George Soule, *New Republic*, 21 Aug.; Frank Darvall, *New Statesman*, 5 Oct.; editorial in *New Republic*, 25 Dec.; *Nation*, 8 Jan., 29 Jan., 12 Feb. 1936; T.J. Wertenbaker, *Atlantic Monthly*, Jan.; Quincy Wright, *The United States and Neutrality* (Chicago, 1935); Edwin DeWitt Dickinson

in *Neutrality and Collective Security*, ed. Quincy Wright (Chicago, 1936); Phillips Bradley, *Can We Stay Out of War?* (New York, 1936); Allen Dulles and Hamilton Fish Armstrong, *Can We be Neutral?* (New York, 1936). An example of Anglophobic isolationism: Quincy Howe, *England Expects Every American to Do His Duty* (New York, 1937).

37. See for example *New Republic*, 9 Jan., 20 Mar. 1935; H.B. Monkland, *North American Review*, Feb.; *Nation*, 13 Mar.; Raymond Buell, *Political Quarterly*, Jul.; Walter Millis, *The Future of Sea Power in the Pacific* (New York, 1935); Eugene J. Young, *Powerful America. Our place in a rearming world* (New York, 1936). For a full discussion of American policy see Dorothy Borg, *The United States and the Far Eastern Crisis of 1933–1938* (Cambridge, MA, 1964).

38. *DBFP*, ser. 2, xx, nos 70, 76, 87.

39. *DBFP*, ser. 2, xx, nos 321, 390, 419.

40. Foreign Office memorandum, 16 May 1937, F 2638/599/61, PRO, FO 371/21024. See Trotter, *Britain and East Asia*; *DBFP*, ser. 2, xx, xxi. At the imperial conference the Australians proposed a Pacific non-aggression pact. The unlikelihood of the Americans undertaking any obligation was pointed out in London, and the worsening of the situation in China put an end to further discussion.

41. DRC 37, 21 Nov. 1935, annexed to CP 26(36), PRO CAB 24/259. See Gibbs, *Grand Strategy*, i, pp. 254–68.

42. See J.T. Emmerson, *The Rhineland Crisis, 7 March 1936* (London, 1977).

43. See Laurence R. Pratt, *East of Malta, West of Suez* (Cambridge, 1975).

44. See Cabinet, 6 Jul. 1936, *DBFP*, ser. 2, xvi, appendix 2.

45. See for example *The Times*, 25, 26, 27 Nov. 1935; 10 Feb., 30 Oct., 2 Nov. 1936; 25, 26, 27 Oct. 1937; B.H. Liddell Hart, *When Britain Goes to War* (London, 1935); *Europe in Arms* (London, 1937). On Liddell Hart and his influence see Brian Bond, *Liddell Hart, a Study of his Military Thought* (London, 1977); John J. Mearsheimer, *Liddell Hart and the Weight of History* (Ithaca, 1988).

46. See for example *Economist*, 25 Apr., 9 May, 27 Jun. 1936. The paper continued to demand a robust British lead and denounced spending on defence (29 Aug. 1936, 13 and 20 Feb. 1937).

47. *Spectator*, 24 Jul., 21 Aug. 1936; Bartlett, *World Review of Reviews*, May, vol. 1.

48. Sir Charles Mallett, *Contemporary Review*, Dec. 1936.

49. Lothian, *Round Table*, Sep. and Dec. 1936, Mar. 1937; *Contemporary Review*, Oct. See also J.R.M. Butler, *Lord Lothian* (London, 1960).

50. See Holland, *Britain and the Commonwealth Alliance*; Beloff, *Dream of Commonwealth*; James Eayrs, *In Defence of Canada. Appeasement and Rearmament* (Toronto, 1965), pp. 81–91; H. Blair Neatby, *William Lyon Mackenzie King*. ii, *The Prism of Unity 1932–1939* (Toronto, 1976).

51. CP 296(37), 12 Nov. 1937, PRO, CAB 24/273.
52. CP 316(37), 15 Dec. 1937, PRO, CAB 24/273; CP 24(38), 8 Feb. 1938, CAB 24/274.
53. *DBFP*, ser. 2, XIX, ch. 7; Earl of Avon, *The Eden Memoirs*, I, *Facing the Dictators* (London, 1962), pp. 586–606; Iain Macleod, *Neville Chamberlain* (London, 1961), pp. 211–17; A.R. Peters, *Anthony Eden at the Foreign Office 1931–1938* (Aldershot, 1986), pp. 321–57.
54. Lindsay to FO, 26 Jan. 1937, A 665/38/45, PRO, FO 371/20651; Runciman to Baldwin, 8 Feb., PREM 1/291.
55. *DBFP*, ser. 2, XVIII, nos 202, 250, 268, 285, 290, 357; J.M. Blum (ed.), *From the Morgenthau Diaries*, I, *Years of Crisis 1928–1938* (Boston, 1959), pp. 456–9, 463–7.
56. Lindsay to FO, 22 Mar. 1937, A 2378/38/45, PRO, FO 371/20651.
57. See Ian M. Drummond, *Imperial Economic Policy 1917–1939* (London, 1974); Ian M. Drummond and Norman Hillmer, *Negotiating Freer Trade* (Waterloo, Ontario, 1989).
58. See Benjamin M. Rowland (ed.), *Balance of Power or Hegemony. The Interwar Monetary System* (New York, 1976).
59. Accounts of the negotiations in Drummond and Hillmer, *Negotiating Freer Trade;* Richard N. Kottman, *Reciprocity and the North Atlantic Triangle 1932–1938* (Ithaca, 1968).
60. Correspondence, Jun.–Jul. 1937 in PRO, PREM 1/261; A 4370, 4412, 4527, 4881/228/45, FO 371/20660–1; *DBFP*, ser. 2, XIX, no. 25. See William R. Rock, *Chamberlain and Roosevelt* (Columbus, Ohio, 1988); C.A. MacDonald, *The United States, Britain and Appeasement 1936–1939* (London, 1981).
61. Text of the 'Quarantine' speech in *FRUS, Japan 1931–1941*, I, pp. 379–83; *The Public Papers and Addresses of Franklin D. Roosevelt*, ed. Samuel I. Rosenman (New York, 1938–50), VI, pp. 406–11. For the Sino-Japanese war and British and American policy see Borg, *Far Eastern Crisis*; Bradford A. Lee, *Britain and the Sino-Japanese War 1937–1939* (Stanford, 1973); Peter Lowe, *Great Britain and the Origins of the Pacific War* (Oxford, 1977).
62. See for example *The Times*, 6 Oct. 1937; *Economist*, 9 Oct.; *New Statesman*, 9 Oct.; *New Republic*, 13 Oct.; *Nation*, 16 Oct.; Sir A. Salter, *Political Quarterly*, Oct.; *DBFP*, ser. 2, XXI, no. 300. Further press quotations in John Dizikes, *Britain, Roosevelt and the New Deal* (New York, 1979), pp. 293–5.
63. Chamberlain to Hilda Chamberlain, 9 Oct., Chamberlain Papers, NC 18/1/1023.
64. *DBFP*, ser. 2, XXI, no. 328. For the December proposals see, in addition to the works cited in note 61 above, Laurence Pratt, 'The Anglo-American Naval Conversations on the Far East of January 1938', *International Affairs*, XLVII (1971). It was on this occasion that Chamberlain wrote to his sister: 'It is always best and safest to count on *nothing* from the Americans but words'; but he added: 'at the moment they are nearer to "doing something" than I have ever known them and I cannot altogether repress hopes.'

Chamberlain to Hilda, 17 Dec. 1937, Chamberlain Papers, NC 18/1/1032.

65. See for example *New York Times* editorial, 30 Nov. 1937; David L. Cohen, *Atlantic Monthly*, Nov.; Livingston Hartly, *Is America Afraid?* (New York, 1937).

66. See Sumner Welles, *The Time for Decision* (New York, 1944); Adolf A. Berle, *Navigating the Rapids* (New York, 1973), pp. 140–1, 143–5, 162–3; *FRUS, 1937*, I, pp. 667–8; Donald B. Schewe, *Franklin D. Roosevelt and Foreign Affairs 1937–1939* (New York and London, 1979), IV, no. 748.

67. *DBFP* ser. 2, XIX, nos 422–5, 427–63; MacDonald, *United States, Britain and Appeasement*; Rock, *Chamberlain and Roosevelt*.

68. See especially Keith Middlemas, *Diplomacy of Illusion. The British Government and Germany 1937–1939* (London, 1972).

69. Professor H.N. Fieldhouse, *International Affairs*, May–Jun. 1938; *Round Table*, Mar. See Ovendale, '*Appeasement' and the English-speaking World*.

70. See for example Livingston Hartley and Quincy Howe, *North American Review*, spring and summer 1938; W.Y. Elliott, *Political Quarterly*, Apr.; *Nation*, 17 and 24 Sep.

71. Harold L. Ickes, *The Secret Diary of Harold L. Ickes* (New York, 1954), II, pp. 476–81, 497–8.

72. For the Anglo-German talks see *Documents on German Foreign Policy 1918–1945*, ser. D, IV, nos 257, 262, 267, 273; Berndt Jürgen Wendt, '*Economic Appeasement'. Handel und Finanz in der Britischen Deutschlandpolitik* (Düsseldorf, 1971), p. 256.

73. See for example *Economist*, 19 and 26 Nov. 1938; *Spectator*, 25 Nov.; *New Statesman*, 26 Nov.

74. Minute by Sir R. Hopkins, 29 Oct. 1938, PRO, PREM 1/236; minute by B. Gilbert, 17 Jan. 1939, T 161/904/S.34610/39; Cabinet, 2 and 22 Feb., C 5(39), C 8(39), PRO, CAB 23/97.

75. Notes by R. Byron, Jan. 1939, A 1143/1143/45, PRO, FO 371/22827; Bertrand Russell, *Nation*, 11 Feb. 1939.

76. Hankey to Lothian, 7 Dec. 1938; Lothian to Lindsay, 31 Mar. 1939, Lothian Papers, GD 40/17/372, 383; Roosevelt to R. Merriman, 15 Feb., Schewe, *Roosevelt and Foreign Affairs*, VIII, no. 1594; G.M. Trevelyan to Halifax, 25 Feb., PRO, FO 794/18. See Rock, *Chamberlain and Roosevelt*, pp. 143–5.

77. Notes by A. Murray, Oct–Nov. 1938, PRO, PREM 1/367; Murray to Roosevelt, 15 Nov., Schewe, *Roosevelt and Foreign Affairs*, VIII, no. 1481; Lothian in *Observer*, 19 and 26 Feb. 1939; memorandum by Sir A. Willert, 25–26 Mar., A 2907/1292/45, FO 371/22829.

78. Berle, *Navigating the Rapids*, pp. 206–10, 230.

79. See Divine, *Illusion of Neutrality*; Cole, *Roosevelt and the Isolationists*; minute by R.A. Butler, 3 Jul. 1939, A 4583/98/45, PRO, FO 371/22814; *The Times*, 3, 7, 13, 15, 17 Jul. 1939; *Economist*, 1, 15, 22 Jul.

80. *DBFP*, ser. 3, VIII, nos 308, 433.
81. See *DBFP*, ser. 3, VIII, appendix I.
82. Strategic Appreciation Committee, PRO, CAB 16/209; memoranda and minutes, 1–15 Mar. 1939, W 3784, 4831/108/50, FO 371/23981; PREM 1/309; CAB 29/93; *Documents on Australian Foreign Policy 1937–1949*, II, ed. R.G. Neale, nos 42, 46, 60, 70, 111–13, 118. See Gibbs, *Grand Strategy*, I, pp. 421–6. For the whole history of the Singapore base see W. David McIntyre, *The Rise and Fall of the Singapore Naval Base* (London, 1979).
83. Berle, *Navigating the Rapids*, p. 243.
84. Tweedsmuir to Runciman, 1 Mar. 1937, University of Newcastle upon Tyne, Runciman Papers, WR 285. Examples of continuing belief in neutrality and a hemispheric policy: George Fielding Eliot, *The Ramparts We Watch* (New York, 1939); Charles A. Beard, *A Foreign Policy for America* (New York, 1940); Edwin M. Borchard and William Peter Lage, *Neutrality for the United States* (New Haven, 1940).

Chapter 5

1. The principal authority for this period and later is H. Duncan Hall, *North American Supply* (London, 1955).
2. Correspondence in *FRUS, 1939*, II; *FRUS, 1940*, II–III. For relations to 1941 see David Reynolds, *The Creation of the Anglo-American Alliance 1937–1941* (London, 1981). The most authoritative account of American policy to the summer of 1940 is still William L. Langer and S. Everett Gleason, *The Challenge to Isolation 1937–1940* (New York, 1952). See also Sir Llewellyn Woodward, *British Foreign Policy in the Second World War*, I (London, 1970).
3. Mark Skinner Watson, *The War Department. Chief of Staff, Prewar Plans and Preparations* (Washington, 1950), p. 312. See also M. Matloff and E.M. Snell, *Strategic Planning for Coalition Warfare 1941–42* (Washington, 1953).
4. WP(40) 168, 25 May 1940; WP(40) 209, Jun., PRO, CAB 66/7, 8. For British strategy to the summer of 1940 see J.R.M. Butler, *Grand Strategy*, II (London, 1957),
5. Chamberlain to Ida, 27 Jan. 1940, Chamberlain Papers, NC 18/1/1140.
6. See for example his minute to Halifax, 4 Oct. 1940, Winston S. Churchill, *The Second World War*, II (London, 1949), pp. 599–600.
7. Churchill to Roosevelt, 15 May 1940; Roosevelt to Churchill, 16 May, Warren F. Kimball (ed.), *Churchill and Roosevelt. The Complete Correspondence* (Princeton, 1984), pp. 37–9. This edition is more complete than, and supersedes, *Roosevelt and Churchill, Their Secret Wartime Correspondence*, ed. Francis Lowenheim, Harold D. Langley, and Manfred Jonas (New York, 1975).
8. WP(40) 276, 18 Jul. 1940, PRO, CAB 66/10.

9. Full accounts in Woodward, *British Foreign Policy*, I; Langer and Gleason, *Challenge to Isolation*; James R. Leutze, *Bargaining for Supremacy. Anglo-American Naval Collaboration 1937–1941* (Chapel Hill, 1977).

10. *HCDeb.*, 5th ser., vol. 364, col. 1171; *Economist*, 7 Sep. 1940.

11. For these negotiations see R.S. Sayers, *Financial Policy 1939–1945* (London, 1956); W.L. Langer and S.E. Gleason, *The Undeclared War 1940–1941* (New York, 1953); Warren F. Kimball, *The Most Unsordid Act. Lend-Lease 1939–1941* (Baltimore, 1969).

12. Churchill to Roosevelt, 8 Dec. 1940, Kimball, *Churchill and Roosevelt*, I, pp. 89–109; Woodward, *British Foreign Policy*, I, pp. 388–95; Rosenman, *Public Papers and Addresses*, IX, pp. 604–15, 633–44.

13. For example *The Times*, 9 and 13 Jan. 1941; *Economist*, 4 and 11 Jan.

14. In addition to Sayers, *Financial Policy*, and Hall, *North American Supply*, see Warren F. Kimball, 'Beggar thy Neighbour: America and the British interim financial crisis 1940–1941', *Journal of Economic History*, XXIX (1969).

15. Plan D, 11 Nov. 1940, Roosevelt Library, PSF, box 4: italics in original. See Leutze, *Bargaining for Supremacy*; Matloff and Snell, *Strategic Planning 1941–2*. For overall American policy in 1941 see Waldo Heinrichs, *Threshold of War. Franklin Roosevelt and American Entry into World War II* (New York, 1988).

16. For the talks see Leutze, *Bargaining for Supremacy*; Matloff and Snell, *Strategic Planning 1941–2*.

17. See for example Josiah Wedgwood, *Contemporary Review*, Feb. 1941; *Economist*, 31 May; George W. Keeton, *Political Quarterly*, Oct.; Clarence Streit, *Union Now with Britain* (New York and London, 1941): Streit had in 1939 advocated a federation of all the democracies of the northern Atlantic; George Catlin, *One Anglo-American Nation. The Foundation of Anglo-Saxony as Basis of World Federation* (London, 1941).

18. Keynes, *Collected Writings*, XXIII, pp. 103–13.

19. See Butler, *Grand Strategy*, II, pp. 547–51; III (London, 1964), pp. 125–30.

20. See Langer and Gleason, *Undeclared War*, pp. 738–41; Matloff and Snell, *Strategic Planning 1941–2*, pp. 58–62; Watson, *Chief of Staff*, pp. 338–58.

21. Useful accounts of the Lend-Lease negotiations and American policy are Alan P. Dobson, *US Wartime Aid to Britain 1940–1946* (London, 1986); Randall Bennett Woods, *A Changing of the Guard. Anglo–American Relations, 1941–1946* (Chapel Hill, 1990).

22. Churchill, *Second World War*, III, pp. 539–40.

23. See for example *New York Times*, 12 Dec. 1941: the United States is 'the natural leader of the democratic forces'; *Chicago Tribune*, 10 Jan. 1942: 'If there is to be a partnership between the United States and Britain, we are, by every right, the controlling partner.' Henry Luce claimed that only the United States could make sense

of the war, and would inherit much of Britain's responsibility for world order: *Life*, 16 Feb. 1942; also Luce, *The American Century* (New York, 1941).

24. Accounts of the Washington conference in Gwyer and Butler, *Grand Strategy*, III, pp. 349–99 and appendix 1; Matloff and Snell, *Strategic Planning 1941–2*, pp. 97–119.

25. These questions are discussed in Alex Danchev, *Very Special Relationship. Field-Marshal Sir John Dill and the Anglo-American Alliance 1941–44* (London, 1986); papers by John Gooch and Danchev in *War, Strategy and Politics, Essays in honour of Sir Michael Howard*, ed. Lawrence Freedman, Paul Hayes, and Robert O'Neill (Oxford, 1992). Expressions of American distrust are to be found in many published diaries.

26. Full accounts in Gwyer and Butler, *Grand Strategy*, III; Matloff and Snell, *Strategic Planning 1941–2*. A very useful summary is in Michael Howard, *Grand Strategy*, IV (London, 1972), pp. xv–xxv.

27. For the whole subject of Anglo-American and Commonwealth relations see Christopher Thorne, *Allies of a Kind. The United States, Britain and the War against Japan 1941–1945* (London, 1978).

28. *New York Times*, 30 Mar. 1942.

29. *Washington Post*, 21 Feb. 1942; also *New York Herald Tribune*, 7 Apr. and 3 Oct.; Lippmann to Keynes, 2 and 18 Apr., printed in John Morton Blum (ed.), *Public Philosopher. Selected Letters of Walter Lippmann* (New York, 1985), pp. 417–21.

30. *Life*, 12 Oct. 1942.

31. Quoted in Wm Roger Louis, *Imperialism at Bay 1941–1945. The United States and the Decolonization of the British Empire* (Oxford, 1977), p. 199. Willkie, *One World* (New York, 1943), p. 185.

32. *Nation*, 17 and 31 Oct. 1942; see also *Christian Science Monitor*, 12 Dec.

33. For American opinion see for example Walter Lippmann, *U.S. War Aims* (Boston, 1944), pp. 19–22; *Fortune* editorial, Jan. 1944. For official opinion see for example OSS report, 2 Apr. 1945, quoted by Thorne, *Allies of a Kind*, p. 600; Berle, *Navigating the Rapids*, pp. 539–42. For Roosevelt see Louis, *Imperialism at Bay*, pp. 226–7.

34. See Louis, *Imperialism at Bay*, pp. 259–73, 327–36, 351–77; Thorne, *Allies of a Kind*, pp. 489–92, 595–6.

35. See *India. The Transfer of Power, 1942–7*, ed. Nicholas Mansergh, I (London, 1970); R.J. Moore, *Churchill, Cripps and India, 1939–1945* (Oxford, 1979).

36. See for example articles by Margery Perham in *The Times*, 20 and 21 Nov. 1942, and *Foreign Affairs*, Apr. 1944, reprinted in Margery Perham, *Colonial Sequence, 1930 to 1949*, London 1967. See also W.K. Hancock, *Argument of Empire* (Harmondsworth and New York, 1943.

37. See Ivison S. Macalan, *International Affairs*, Oct. 1944; Lyon, *Britain and Canada*, p. 46.

38. WP(42) 492, 21 Sep. 1942, PRO, CAB 66/30.
39. Roosevelt Library, Morgenthau diaries, 5 Aug. 1942; Blum, *From the Morgenthau Diaries*, III, *Years of War*, pp. 143–6.
40. See Howard, *Grand Strategy*, IV.
41. Accounts of the conference in Howard, *Grand Strategy*, IV; M. Matloff, *Strategic Planning for Coalition Warfare 1943–1944* (Washington, 1959).
42. Matloff, *Strategic Planning 1943–4*, pp. 106–7; memorandum by Gens. S.D. Embick and M.S. Fairchild, 4 Jan. 1943, quoted by Mark A. Stoler, *The Politics of the Second Front. American Military Planning and Diplomacy in Coalition Warfare 1941–1943* (Westport, CT, 1977), pp. 72–3.
43. Eisenhower to Gen. T.T. Handy, 28 Jan. 1943, *The Papers of Dwight D. Eisenhower, The War Years*, ed. Alfred D. Chandler, Stephen D. Ambrose, and others (Baltimore, 1970), II, pp. 927–9.
44. Marshall to Stilwell, 1 Jul. 1943, quoted by Matloff, *Strategic Planning 1943–4*, p. 204.
45. Stoler, *Politics of the Second Front*, pp. 82–3; Stimson diary, 23 and 27 Jul. 1942; Stimson to Roosevelt, 10 Aug. 1943, Stimson and Bundy, *On Active Service in Peace and War*, pp. 228–30.
46. For the discussions of the summer and the Quebec conference see Howard, *Grand Strategy*, IV; Matloff, *Strategic Planning 1943–4*.
47. As told by Sir John Colville in J.W. Wheeler-Bennett, *Action This Day. Working with Churchill* (London, 1968), p. 96.
48. Gardiner to Grew, 12 Mar. 1943, quoted by Thorne, *Allies of a Kind*, p. 293.
49. A full account of the argument in Howard Ehrman, *Grand Strategy*, V (London, 1956), pp. 421–504.
50. Ehrman, *Grand Strategy*, V, pp. 517–24 includes minutes of the meeting of the Combined Chiefs of Staff on 14 September.
51. Woodward, *British Foreign Policy*, V, pp. 14–18. This volume contains an account of British official thinking and policy.
52. See for example Charles A. Beard, *The Republic* (New York, 1943); Carl Becker, *How New will the Better World Be?* (New York, 1944); Ely Culbertson, *Total Peace* (New York, 1943); Walter Lippmann, *U.S. Foreign Policy* (Boston, 1943); Emery A. Reves, *A Democratic Manifesto* (New York, 1942); John MacCormac, *America and World Mastery* (New York, 1942). For the discussion, and the internationalist organizations, see Robert A. Divine, *Second Chance. The Triumph of Internationalism in America during World War II* (New York, 1967). For the State Department see Harley Notter, *Postwar Foreign Policy Preparation 1939–1945* (Washington, 1949).
53. George H. Gallup, *The Gallup Poll and Public Opinion 1935–1971*, I (New York, 1972), pp. 340, 377. In the winter of 1943, 30 per cent of respondents to a survey by the Office of Public Opinion Research believed that the United States had been a member of the League of Nations, and 26 per cent did not know one way or the other. For fears of a return to isolationism see for example memoranda by J.J. McCloy, Assistant Secretary for War, 8 and 25

Nov. 1943, Hopkins Papers, box 331; Stimson diary, 29 Oct.

54. For the whole subject see Aaron David Miller, *Search for Security. Saudi Arabian Oil and American Foreign Policy 1939–1949* (Chapel Hill, 1980); Michael B. Stoff, *Oil, War and Security. The Search for a National Policy on Foreign Oil 1941–1949* (New Haven, 1980); Irvine H. Anderson, *ARAMCO, the United States and Saudi Arabia. A Study of the Dynamics of Foreign Oil Policy* (Princeton, 1981).

55. Churchill–Roosevelt messages, 20 Feb.–7 Mar. 1944, Kimball, *Churchill and Roosevelt*, II, pp. 734, 744–5, 754–5; III, pp. 14, 17–18, 27.

56. For the whole subject see Armand van Dormael, *Bretton Woods. Birth of a Monetary System* (London, 1978); Richard N. Gardner, *Sterling–Dollar Diplomacy* (Oxford, 1956); Roy Harrod, *The Life of John Maynard Keynes* (London, 1951); L.S. Pressnell, *External Economic Policy Since the War*, I, *The Post-War Financial Settlement* (London, 1986); Keynes's papers in *Collected Writings*, XXV.

57. Memoranda by Beaverbrook, WP(44) 95, 148, PRO, CAB 66/46, 47; memorandum by Amery, WP(44) 129, CAB 66/47.

58. *HLDeb.*, 5th ser., vol. 131, cols 838–49. For the debate in Britain see Gardner, *Sterling–Dollar Diplomacy*, pp. 121–9.

59. Accounts of the conference in van Dormael, *Bretton Woods*; Gardner, *Sterling–Dollar Diplomacy*; Harrod, *Life of Keynes*.

60. See for example *Economist*, 29 Jul. 1944; *The Times*, 21, 22, 23 Aug.; van Dormael, *Bretton Woods*, pp. 224–30.

61. *Economist*, 21 Jul. 1945.

62. W.K. Hancock and M.M. Gowing, *British War Economy* (London, 1949), pp. 500, 518–24; Sayers, *Financial Policy*, pp. 439, 465–8, 503, 524.

63. Blum, *Morgenthau Diaries*, III, pp. 308–09.

64. For the talks see Dobson, *US Wartime Aid*; Woods, *Changing of the Guard*; Sayers, *Financial Policy*; Keynes, *Collected Writings*, XXIV. For Morgenthau's views see for example Diaries, 25 Aug., 6 Oct. 1944.

65. Keynes, *Collected Writings*, XXIV, pp. 192–223 (and see pp. 185–92).

66. See Alan P. Dobson, *Peaceful Air Warfare. The United States, Britain, and the Politics of International Aviation* (Oxford, 1991).

67. For the last stages see Sayers, *Financial Policy*; Pressnell, *External Economic Policy*; Woods, *Changing of the Guard* (which emphasises the confusion in American policy).

68. Churchill to Halifax, 3 Jan. 1945, PRO, PREM 4/7/10. Hull had retired after the 1944 elections. For the whole episode see Robert M. Hathaway, *Ambiguous Partnership. Britain and America 1944–1947* (New York, 1981), pp. 89–111.

69. *New Statesman*, 23 Dec. 1944; *Economist*, 23 and 30 Dec.; *The Times*, 3 Jan. 1945.

70. *New York Times Magazine*, 14 Jan. 1945; *Life* editorial, 29 Jan.; Reinhold Niebuhr in *Nation*, 13 Jan.; in *Spectator*, 16 Feb.

71. Berle, *Navigating the Rapids*, pp. 456–7.

72. For the whole wartime story see Margaret Gowing, *Britain and Atomic Energy 1939–1945* (London, 1964); Richard Hewlett and Oscar Anderson, *A History of the United States Atomic Energy Commission*, I (Philadelphia, 1962).
73. *Documents on British Policy Overseas*, eds R. D'O. Butler and M. Pelly (London,1984 ff.), hereafter cited as *DBPO*, ser. 1, III, no. 3.
74. FO memorandum, 21 Mar. 1944, AN 1538/16/45, PRO, FO 371/38523.
75. Churchill, *Second World War*, II, pp. 21–2.
76. The impact upon all concerned of the presence in Britain of large numbers of American servicemen is examined by David Reynolds, *Rich Relations. The American Occupation of Britain 1942–1945* (London and New York, 1995). For Churchill and Roosevelt see Warren F. Kimball, 'Wheel Within a Wheel: Churchill, Roosevelt, and the Special Relationship,' in *Churchill*, ed. Robert Blake and Wm Roger Louis (Oxford and New York, 1993), pp. 291–307.

Chapter 6

1. The literature on all aspects of postwar American foreign and security policy is much larger than that for any earlier period. Many of the works published in the 1950s and 60s are now of greater interest for the light they cast on the politics and perceptions of those decades than for the history of the 1940s. Useful later works on the American origins of the cold war include: John Lewis Gaddis, *The United States and the Origins of the Cold War 1941–1947* (New York, 1972); Daniel Yergin, *Shattered Peace. The Origins of the Cold War and the National Security State* (Boston, 1977); John Lewis Gaddis, *The Long Peace. Inquiries into the History of the Cold War* (New York, 1987), pp. 20–47. Michael J. Lacey (ed.), *The Truman Presidency* (Cambridge, 1989) contains essays on a variety of aspects of policy. Melvyn P. Leffler, *A Preponderance of Power. National Security, the Truman Administration and the Cold War* (Stanford, 1992) is an exhaustive study for the whole period down to 1952, and contains a full bibliography. Works on the British origins of the cold war include Victor Rothwell, *Britain and the Cold War 1941–1947* (London, 1982); Alan Bullock, *Ernest Bevin, Foreign Secretary* (Oxford, 1983); John Kent, *British Imperial Strategy and the Origins of the Cold War 1944–49* (Leicester, 1992).
2. Memorandum by Sargent, 11 Jul. 1945, *DBPO*, ser. 1, I, no. 102.
3. Ibid.; memorandum by Bevin, 8 Nov., no. 99.
4. Bevin conversation with Molotov, 23 Sep. 1945, *DBPO*, ser. 1, II, no. 108.
5. Memorandum by Bevin, 8 Nov. 1945; Churchill to Bevin, 13 Nov., *DBPO*, ser. 1, III, nos 99, 102.
6. For left-wing intellectuals see for example articles by Richard

Crossman and Aylmer Valance, *Political Quarterly*, Jan. 1946. For reactions to Churchill's speech see for example *The Times*, 6 Mar.; *Economist*, 9 Mar.

7. John Fischer, *Harper's Magazine*, Aug. 1945. For deferring to American insistence see W. Averell Harriman and Elie Abel, *Special Envoy to Churchill and Stalin, 1941–1946* (New York, 1975), p. 531.

8. Accounts of the negotiations in Pressnell, *External Economic Policy since the War*, I; Gardner, *Sterling–Dollar Diplomacy*; documents in *DBPO*, ser. 1, III; Keynes, *Collected Writings*, XXIV.

9. *Economist*, 15 Dec. 1945; *HCDeb*, 5th ser., vol. 417, cols 652–3; *The Times*, 11 Dec. (letter from Sir J. Wardlaw-Milne).

10. Gallup, *The Gallup Poll*, I, pp. 529–30.

11. PHP(45) 29(0) (Final), 29 Jun. 1945, PRO, CAB 81/46; WP(45) 256, 13 Apr., CAB 66/65; CP(45)55, CAB 66/67. For the whole subject see Julian Lewis, *Changing Direction. British Military Planning for Postwar Strategic Defence 1942–1947* (London, 1988).

12. See minutes, 8–12 Mar. 1946, U 2749/106/70, PRO, FO 371/57173; memorandum by Bevin, 13 Mar., *British Documents on the End of Empire*, henceforth cited as *BDEE*, ser. A, II, *The Labour Government and the End of Empire 1945–1951*, ed. Ronald Hyam (London, 1992), pt. 3, no. 277; DO(46), 22nd meeting, CAB 131/1; memorandum, 'The strategic aspect of British foreign policy', 15 Oct., COS(46) 239(O), CAB 80/102, part printed in Lewis, *Changing Direction*, appendix 6.

13. See G.M. Alexander, *The Prelude to the Truman Doctrine. British Policy in Greece 1944–47* (Oxford, 1982).

14. Memorandum by Attlee, 1 Sep. 1945, *DBPO*, ser. 1, II, no. 18; memorandum by Attlee, 2 Mar. 1946; Attlee to Bevin, 1 Dec., memorandum by Attlee, 5 Jan. 1947; Bevin to Attlee, 9 Jan., *BDEE*, II, pt. 3, nos. 276, 279, 282.

15. See Leffler, *Preponderance of Power*. A useful shorter account is John Lewis Gaddis, *Strategies of Containment. A Critical Appraisal of Postwar American National Security Policy* (New York, 1982).

16. George F. Kennan, *Memoirs, 1925–1950* (Boston, 1967), pp. 583–98; *FRUS, 1946*, VI, pp. 696–709.

17. 'X', 'The sources of Soviet conduct', *Foreign Affairs*, Jul. 1947, pp. 576–82. On Kennan see Walter L. Hixson, *George F. Kennan, Cold War Iconoclast* (New York, 1989); David Allan Mayers, *George Kennan and the Dilemmas of US Foreign Policy* (New York, 1989).

18. Clifford–Elsey report, 24 Sep. 1946, printed in Arthur Krock, *Memoirs. Sixty Years in the Firing Line* (New York, 1968), pp. 422–82; conclusions in Thomas H. Etzold and John L. Gaddis (eds), *Containment. Documents on American Policy and Strategy 1945–1950* (New York, 1978), pp. 64–71. Earlier defence planning is discussed by Michael Sherry, *Preparing for the Next War. American Plans for Postwar Defense 1941–45* (New Haven, 1977).

19. Walter Lippmann, *The Cold War* (New York, 1947): the collected articles were an explicit critique of Kennan. A contrasting example

is James Burnham, *The Struggle for the World* (New York, 1947).

20. See Bruce R. Kuniholm, *The Origins of the Cold War in the Near East. Great Power Conflict and Diplomacy in Iran, Turkey and Greece* (Princeton, 1980). Joseph M. Jones, *The Fifteen Weeks* (New York, 1955) is useful for the domestic aspect. Truman's message to Congress is printed in *Public Papers of the Presidents of the United States, Harry S. Truman*, 1947 vol. (Washington, 1963), no. 56.

21. Report by Chiefs of Staff, 'Future defence policy', May 1947, printed in Lewis, *Changing Direction*, appendix 7.

22. Wm Roger Louis, *The British Empire in the Middle East 1945–51* (Oxford, 1984) is important for the whole area. For defence policy see David R. Devereux, *The Formulation of British Defence Policy towards the Middle East 1948–56* (London, 1990).

23. See *FRUS, 1947*, V, pp. 485–626.

24. Memorandum by Kennan, 24 Feb. 1948, *FRUS, 1948*, I, pp. 509–29. Italics in original.

25. NSC 7, 30 Mar. 1948, *FRUS, 1948*, I, pp. 545–50.

26. NSC 20/1, 18 Aug. 1948; NSC 20/4, 23 Nov., *FRUS, 1948*, I, pp. 609–11, 662–9.

27. Useful books include Michael J. Cohen, *Palestine and the Great Powers 1945–1948* (Princeton, 1982); Martin Jones, *Failure in Palestine. British and United States Policy after the Second World War* (London, 1985); Kenneth Roy Bain, *The March to Zion. United States Policy and the Founding of Israel* (College Station, 1979).

28. Memorandum by Bevin, 14 Jan. 1947, CP(47)30, PRO, CAB 129/16.

29. Memorandum by Henderson, 24 Nov. 1947, *FRUS, 1947*, V, pp. 1281–2.

30. See R.J. Moore, *Escape from Empire. The Attlee Government and the Indian Problem* (Oxford, 1983). Documents in Nicholas Mansergh (ed.), *India. The Transfer of Power*.

31. *HLDeb.*, 5th ser., vol. 145, cols 928–92, 996–1070; *HCDeb.*, 5th ser., vol. 434, cols 494–603, 663–72.

32. *BDEE*, II, pt. 1, no. 66.

33. See for example minute by Sir N. Brook, the Cabinet Secretary, *op. cit.*, pt. 2, no. 121. For the whole subject of colonial development see D.J. Morgan, *The Official History of Colonial Development*, 5 vols (London, 1980) (III for the East Africa groundnuts scheme); *BDEE*, II, pt 3. Expectations of colonial independence, see Colonial Policy Committee, 6 Sep. 1957, CPC(57) 30, Revise, PRO, CAB 134/1556. In general see John Darwin, *Britain and Decolonisation. The Retreat from Empire in the Postwar World* (London, 1988).

34. For the whole subject see John W. Young, *Britain, France and the Unity of Europe* (Leicester, 1984); John W. Young, *Britain and European Unity 1945–1992* (London, 1993).

35. See Alan Milward, *The Reconstruction of Western Europe 1945–51* (London, 1984), chs 1–3; John Gimbel, *The Origins of the Marshall Plan* (Stanford, 1976); Michael Hogan, *The Marshall Plan. America,*

Britain and the Reconstruction of Western Europe 1947–1952 (Cambridge and New York, 1987), despite its title, uses little British material.

36. Memorandum by Bevin, 'The first aim of British foreign policy', 4 Jan. 1948, *BDEE*, II, pt 2, no. 142; also memorandum by Bevin and Cripps, 6 Mar., CP(48) 75, PRO, CAB 129/25.
37. See *HCDeb.*, 5th ser., vol. 446, cols 387–409; *The Times*, 23 Jan. 1948; *Economist*, 31 Jan.
38. Memorandum by Bevin and Cripps, 25 Jan. 1949, EPC(49) 6, PRO, CAB 134/221.
39. Foreign Office memorandum, 'A third world power or western consolidation?', 23 Mar. 1949, W 3114/3/50, PRO, FO 371/76384; *DBPO*, ser. 1, II, no. 20; *BDEE*, II, pt. 3, no. 152.
40. See Nicholas Henderson, *The Birth of NATO* (London, 1982); Richard A. Best, *'Cooperation with Like-minded Peoples.' British influence on American security policy 1945–1949* (Westport, CT, 1986).
41. NSC 68, 'United States Objectives and Programs for National Security', 14 Apr. 1950, *FRUS, 1950*, I, pp. 234–92 and related correspondence.
42. Memorandum by Kennan, 7 Jul. 1949, PPS 55, Department of State, *The State Department Policy Planning Staff Papers* (New York, 1983), pp. 82–100. See also Kennan's memorandum of 24 Feb. 1948, *FRUS, 1948*, I, pp. 509–29.
43. For example Ray Crowley in *Wall Street Journal*, 16 Aug. 1949; Walter Lippmann in *New York Herald Tribune*, 26 Sep.
44. Acheson to Perkins, Paris, 19 Oct. 1949; Bevin to Acheson, 25 Oct.; Acheson to Bevin, 28 Oct., *FRUS, 1949*, IV, pp. 347–9, 469–72. For Acheson see his memoirs, *Present at the Creation* (New York, 1969); David S. McLellan, *Dean Acheson. The State Department Years* (New York, 1976).
45. Memoranda by Bevin and Cripps, 24 and 25 Oct. 1949, CP(49) 203, 204, PRO, CAB 129/37; Cabinet, 27 Oct., *BDEE*, II, pt. 3, nos. 153–4.
46. Minute by McNeil, 30 Sep. 1949, W 5460/2/50, PRO, FO 371/76383.
47. FO memoranda, 22, 24, 27 Apr. 1950, *DBPO*, ser. 2, II, nos 27, 30, 43.
48. Shuckburgh to Gore-Booth, Washington, 21 Jun. 1950, *DBPO*, ser. 2, II, no. 117; see also minute by Shuckburgh, 20 Apr., no. 24, n. 9. Records of April talks, *op. cit.*, nos 29, 34. See *FRUS, 1950*, III, pp. 63–5, 617–22.
49. For the background of the Schuman Plan see Milward, *Reconstruction of Western Europe*, ch. 12. British documents in *DBPO*, ser. 2, I.
50. *DBPO*, ser. 2, I, no. 24; *Economist*, 20 May 1950; *The Times*, 22 May (letters).
51. Labour Party, *European Unity* (London, 1950). The statement was drafted by Denis Healey. See also for example *Spectator*, 9 Jun. 1950; *New Statesman*, 8 Jul.

52. See Edward Fursdon, *The European Defence Community* (London, 1980); Saki Dockrill, *British Policy for West German Rearmament 1950–5* (London, 1991).
53. PUSC(51) 12 (Final), 12 Dec. 1951, *DBPO*, ser. 2, I, no. 414. See also CP(55) 55, 28 Jun. 1955, PRO, CAB 129/76.
54. Cabinet, 30 Jun. 1955, CM(55) 19th, PRO, CAB 128/29.
55. Discussions in Mutual Aid Committee and Economic Steering Committee (officials) and Economic Policy Committee (ministers) in PRO, CAB 134/889, 1026–30, 1226–8.
56. See Cabinet memoranda and minutes, Jul.–Nov. 1956, *BDEE*, III, pt 3, nos 387, 389–92. Miriam Camps, *Britain and the European Economic Community 1955–1963* (London, 1964) is still a useful account of the negotiations.
57. Political and Economic Planning, *Growth in the British Economy* (London, 1960), pp. 30, 32, 150.
58. For all this see Susan Strange, *Sterling and British Policy* (London, 1971).
59. NSC 68/1, 21 Sep. 1950, NA, RG 273; introduction printed in *FRUS, 1950*, I, pp. 404–06.
60. Memorandum by Chiefs of Staff, 11 Jun. 1951, MDM(51) 2, PRO, CAB 21/1787.
61. Memorandum by Eden, 18 Jun. 1952; memorandum by Chiefs of Staff, 31 Oct., *BDEE*, III, pt 1, nos 3, 10. For the problem of defence spending and resources see Michael Chalmers, *Paying for Defence. Military spending and British decline* (London, 1985).
62. For the whole subject see Margaret Gowing, *Independence and Deterrence. Britain and Atomic Energy 1945–1952* (London, 1974); Andrew J. Pierre, *Nuclear Politics* (London, 1972); Timothy J. Botti, *The Long Wait. The Forging of the Anglo-American Nuclear Alliance* (New York, 1987); Ian Clark and Nicholas J. Wheeler, *The British Origins of Nuclear Strategy* (Oxford, 1989).
63. Note by Chiefs of Staff, 23 Dec. 1951, PRO, AIR 8/1808.
64. COS(54), 54th meeting, 12 May 1954, PRO, DEFE 4/70; Cabinet, 7–8 Jul., CC(54) 47th and 48th, CAB 128/27; *HCDeb.*, 5th ser., vol. 537, col. 2182.
65. *HCDeb.*, 5th ser., vol. 549, cols 1091–2, 1277–8, 1285, 28 Feb. 1956.
66. For the whole subject see Dorothy Borg and Waldo Heinrichs (eds), *Uncertain Years. Chinese–American Relations 1947–1950* (New York, 1980); William Whitney Stueck, jr., *The Road to Confrontation. American Policy towards China and Korea 1947–1950* (Chapel Hill, 1981); Nancy B. Tucker, *Patterns in the Dust. Chinese–American Relations and the Recognition Controversy 1949–1950* (New York, 1983).
67. British documents for the second half of 1950 in *DBPO*, ser. 2, IV. See Callum Macdonald, *Korea. The War before Vietnam* (Basingstoke, 1986).
68. Cabinet, 29 Nov. 1950, *DBPO*, ser. 2, IV, no. 79; press view for example *Economist*, 2 Dec.

69. *DBPO,* ser. 2, IV, nos 88, 89, 90, 93, 111; *FRUS, 1950,* III, pp. 1706–88.
70. *DBPO,* ser. 2, IV, nos 101 (iib), 114, 115, 118, 121.
71. Memorandum by John H. Ferguson, 8 Feb. 1951, *FRUS, 1951,* I, pp. 44–8.
72. See *DBPO,* ser. 2, IV, nos 127, 127 i, 131, 131 i; *BDEE,* II, pt. 3, nos 341–3; PRO, FO 371/920712, 920713; CC(52) 81st, 26 Sep. 1952, CAB 128/25; C(52) 395, CAB 129/56; *FRUS, 1951,* VI; *FRUS, 1952–4,* XII; *The Times,* 20 Apr. 1951.
73. See NSC 114/2, 12 Oct. 1951, *FRUS, 1951,* I, pp. 182–92, and related drafts and comments; Hans J. Morgenthau, *In Defense of the National Interest. A Critical Examination of American Foreign Policy* (New York, 1951), pp. 49–52; Acheson on 4 Aug. 1952; PPS papers and NSC discussion, Jul.–Sep. *FRUS, 1952–4,* II, pp. 11–156; XVIII, pp. 182–3. The possibility that the Americans might come to prefer a showdown to indefinite prolongation of the cold war was noted by the British Chiefs of Staff: COS(52) 361, 15 Jul., PRO, DEFE 5/40.
74. Dulles, 'A Policy of Boldness', *Life,* 19 May 1952. Italics in original. In his book *War or Peace* (New York, 1950) Dulles called for an American moral offensive to roll back the tide of despotism.
75. Dulles's testimony before the Senate Foreign Relations Committee, printed in Norman Graebner, *Cold War Diplomacy* (2nd edn, New York, 1977); Dulles speech to Council on Foreign Relations, New York, 12 Jan. 1953; Hamilton Fish Armstrong, *Foreign Affairs,* Jan. On Dulles see Michael Guhin, *John Foster Dulles* (New York, 1972); Townsend Hoopes, *The Devil and John Foster Dulles* (Boston, 1973); Frederick W. Marks, *Power and Peace. The Diplomacy of John Foster Dulles* (Westport, CT, 1993).
76. *Economist,* 30 Aug. 1952.
77. Dulles at NATO Council, 14 Dec. 1953, *FRUS, 1952–4,* V, p. 463.
78. James Shepley, 'How Dulles Averted War', *Life,* 15 Jan. 1956.
79. Gaddis, *Strategies of Containment,* p. 162.
80. NSC 5501, 7 Jan. 1955, 'Basic National Security Policy', *FRUS, 1955–7,* XIX, pp. 24–38. See also Gaddis, *The Long Peace,* pp. 104–46.
81. See Andrew J. Rotter, *The Path to Vietnam. Origins of the American Commitment to South-East Asia* (Ithaca, 1987); James Cable, *The Geneva Conference of 1954 on Indochina* (London, 1986).
82. Cabinet, 27 Sep. 1951, *BDEE,* II, pt. 2, no. 162.
83. *HCDeb.,* 5th ser., vol. 531, cols 745 (Capt. Waterhouse), 801 (Viscount Hinchingbroke), 31 Jul. 1954.
84. Lovett to Bruce, 16 Aug. 1952, quoted by Leffler, *Preponderance of Power,* p. 483; Reston to Lippmann, 18 Jan. 1954, Lippmann Papers, Yale University, ser. 3, box 98. See also *FRUS, 1952–4,* V, pp. 1715–18; J.C. Hurewitz, *Middle East Dilemmas* (New York, 1953), p. 253.
85. A large-scale account is Keith Kyle, *Suez* (London, 1991); also W.

Scott Lucas, *Divided We Stand. Britain, the United States and the Suez Crisis* (London, 1991). For analysis and discussion see especially Wm Roger Louis and Roger Owen (eds), *Suez 1956. The Crisis and its Consequences* (Oxford, 1989); Selwyn Ilan Troen and Moshe Sheresh (eds), *The Suez–Sinai Crisis of 1956. Retrospective and Reappraisal* (London, 1990); Diane B. Kunz, *The Economic Diplomacy of the Suez Crisis* (Chapel Hill, 1991). For the Commonwealth see James Eayrs, *The Commonwealth and Suez. A Documentary Survey* (London, 1964).

86. An outburst by Dulles at the National Security Council meeting on 1 November is quoted by Wm Roger Louis in Richard H. Immerman (ed.), *John Foster Dulles and the Diplomacy of the Cold War* (Princeton, 1990), p. 153.

87. PR(56) 3, 1 Jun. 1956, *BDEE*, III, pt 1, no. 21.

88. Kunz, *Economic Diplomacy of the Suez Crisis*, p. 159. Between 1948 and 1954 Congress authorized some $6 billion annually in aid under the Mutual Security acts. The proportion devoted to military assistance grew from the early 1950s: William Adams Brown jr and Redvers Opie, *American Foreign Assistance* (Washington, 1953), p. 535; John D. Montgomery, *The Politics of Foreign Aid* (New York, 1962), p. 211.

Bibliography

I Unpublished Sources

1 Official Archives

GREAT BRITAIN

Public Record Office, Kew
  Admiralty (ADM 1, 116, 167)
  Air Ministry (AIR 8)
  Cabinet Office (CAB 2, 4, 5, 16, 21, 23, 24, 27, 29, 37, 41, 42, 53,
    63, 65, 66, 80, 81, 84, 96, 128, 129, 131, 134)
  Ministry of Defence (DEFE 4, 5, 6)
  Foreign Office (FO 55, 80, 115, 371, 382, 395, 414, 608, 794, 800)
  Prime Minister's Private Office (PREM 1, 3, 4, 8, 309)
  Treasury (T 1, 160, 161, 170, 172, 236, 247)
  War Office (WO 106)

UNITED STATES

National Archives, Washington, DC
  General Records of the Department of State (RG 59)
  Navy Department, General Board of the Navy (RG 80)
  Combined Chiefs of Staff (RG 218)
  National Security Council (RG 273)
Franklin D. Roosevelt Library, Hyde Park, NY
  Map Room Files
  President's Secretary's Files

2 Personal Papers

GREAT BRITAIN

Baldwin Papers, University Library, Cambridge
Balfour Papers, British Library, London
Bryce Papers, Bodleian Library, Oxford
Cecil of Chelwood Papers, British Library, London
Austen Chamberlain Papers, University Library, Birmingham

230

Joseph Chamberlain Papers, University Library, Birmingham
Neville Chamberlain Papers, University Library, Birmingham
Curzon Papers, British Library, London (India Office)
Dalton Papers, British Library of Political Science, London
Elibank Papers, National Library of Scotland, Edinburgh
P.J. Grigg Papers, Churchill College, Cambridge
Hankey Papers, Churchill College, Cambridge
Oliver Harvey Papers, British Library, London
Inskip Papers, Churchill College, Cambridge
Lloyd George Papers, House of Lords Record Office, London
Lothian Papers, Scottish Record Office, Edinburgh
McKenna Papers, Churchill College, Cambridge
Gilbert Murray Papers, Bodleian Library, Oxford
Phipps Papers, Churchill College, Cambridge
Runciman Papers, University Library, Newcastle-upon-Tyne
Salisbury Papers, Hatfield House, Hatfield
Simon Papers, Bodleian Library, Oxford
Spring Rice Papers, Churchill College, Cambridge
Vansittart Papers, Churchill College, Cambridge

UNITED STATES

Adolf Berle Diary, Roosevelt Library, Hyde Park, NY
Norman Davis Papers, Library of Congress, Washington
John Foster Dulles Papers, Princeton University, Princeton
Harry L. Hopkins Papers, Roosevelt Library, Hyde Park, NY
Edward M. House Papers, Yale University, New Haven
Walter Lippmann Papers, Yale University, New Haven
Pierrepont Moffat Papers, Harvard University, Cambridge, MA
Henry J. Morgenthau Papers, Roosevelt Library, Hyde Park, NY
William L. Phillips Papers, Harvard University, Cambridge, MA
Henry L. Stimson Papers, Yale University, New Haven
Arthur Willert Papers, Yale University, New Haven
William Wiseman Papers, Yale University, New Haven

II Printed Sources

1 Offical Publications

British Documents on the End of Empire, general editors D.J. Murray
and S.R. Ashton. II, *The Labour Government and the End of Empire
1945–1951*, ed. Ronald Hyam, 4 parts; III, *The Conservative Government
and the End of Empire 1951–1957*, ed. David Goldsworthy, 3 parts.
London: HMSO, 1992, 1994.
British Documents on the Origins of the War 1898–1914, ed. G.P. Gooch
and Harold Temperley, 11 vols. London: HMSO, 1926–8.
Documents on Australian Foreign Policy 1937–1949, ed. R.G. Neale, and
others. Canberra: Australian Government Publishing Service, 1975 ff.

Documents on British Foreign Policy 1919–1939 eds, E.L. Woodward, Rohan Butler and others. Series 1, 1A, 2, 3. London: HMSO, 1947–84.

Documents on British Policy Overseas, eds, R.D'O. Butler, M. Pelly and others. Series 1, 2. London: HMSO, 1984 ff.

Documents on German Foreign Policy 1918–1945, series D, eds, Raymond Sontag, J.W. Wheeler-Bennett, Maurice Baumont and others. London: HMSO, 1949 ff.

India. The Transfer of Power, ed. Nicholas Mansergh, 10 vols. London: HMSO, 1970.

The Parliamentary Debates. Official Report. 3rd and 4th series. London: HMSO.

The Parliamentary Debates. Official Report. 5th series. *House of Commons.* London: HMSO.

The Parliamentary Debates. Official Report. 5th series. *House of Lords.* London: HMSO.

Parliamentary Papers. *Memorandum circulated by the Prime Minister on March 25th, 1919, Some Considerations for the Peace Conference before they finally draft the terms (The Fontainebleau Memorandum).* Cmd 1614. London: HMSO, 1922.

Public Papers of the Presidents of the United States. Harry S. Truman. 8 vols. Washington: Government Printing Office, 1963.

United States, Department of Commerce, Bureau of the Census. *Historical Statistics of the United States, Colonial Times to 1970.* Bicentennial edn. Washington: Government Printing Office 1975.

United States, Department of State. *Papers Relating to the Foreign Relations of the United States.* Washington: Government Printing Office 1862 ff.

— *The State Department Policy Planning Staff Papers.* New York: Garland, 1983.

2   Collections of Papers

Baker, Ray Stannard and Dodd, William (eds) *The Public Papers of Woodrow Wilson,* 6 vols. New York: Harper & Bros, 1925.

Chandler, Alfred D., Ambrose, Stephen E. and others (eds) *The Papers of Dwight David Eisenhower. The War Years,* 5 vols. Baltimore: Johns Hopkins University Press, 1970.

Keynes, J.M. *Collected Writings,* ed. Elizabeth Johnson, 30 vols. London: Macmillan, 1971–89.

Kimball, Warren F. (ed.) *Churchill and Roosevelt. The Complete Correspondence,* 3 vols. Princeton: Princeton University Press, 1984.

Link, Arthur and others (eds) *The Papers of Woodrow Wilson,* 69 vols. Princeton: Princeton University Press, 1978–94.

Loewenheim, Francis, Langley, Harold D. and Jonas, Manfred (eds) *Roosevelt and Churchill. Their Secret Wartime Correspondence.* New York: Dutton, 1975.

Morison, Elting E. (ed.) *Letters of Theodore Roosevelt,* 8 vols. Cambridge, MA: Harvard University Press, 1951–4.

Nixon, Edgar B. (ed.) *Franklin Roosevelt and Foreign Affairs*, 3 vols. Cambridge, MA: Harvard University Press, 1969.

Rosenman. Samuel I. (ed.) *The Public Papers and Addresses of Franklin D. Roosevelt*, 13 vols. New York: Random House, 1938–50.

Schewe, Donald B. (ed.) *Franklin D. Roosevelt and Foreign Affairs January 1937–August 1939*, 11 vols. New York and London: Garland, 1979.

III Newspapers and Periodicals

GREAT BRITAIN

Brassey's Naval Annual
Contemporary Review
Daily Telegraph
Economist
Fortnightly Review
International Affairs
Manchester Guardian
Nation and Athenaeum
National Review
New Statesman
Nineteenth Century
Observer
Political Quarterly
Quarterly Review
Review of Reviews
Round Table
Spectator
Sunday Times
Time and Tide
The Times
Westminster Gazette
World Affairs

UNITED STATES

American Review of Reviews
Atlantic Monthly
Chicago Tribune
Christian Science Monitor
Current History
Foreign Affairs
Fortune
Forum
Harper's Magazine
Life
Literary Digest
Nation

New Republic
New York Evening Post
New York Herald Tribune
New York Times
New York World
North American Review
Saturday Evening Post
Saturday Review of Literature
Wall Street Journal
Washington Post
Yale Review

IV   Contemporary Books

Adams, Brooks. *America's Economic Supremacy.* New York: Macmillan, 1900.
Adams, George Burton. *Why Americans Dislike England.* Philadelphia: H. Altemus, 1896.
Angell, Sir Norman. *The Defence of the Empire.* London: Hamish Hamilton, 1937.
Barker, J. Ellis. *Drifting.* London: Grant Richards, 1901.
Bausman, Frederick. *Facing Europe.* New York: Century Books, 1926.
Beard, Charles A. *A Foreign Policy for America.* New York: Alfred A. Knopf, 1940.
— *The Republic.* New York: Viking Press, 1943.
Becker, Carl. *How New Will The Better World Be?* New York: Alfred A. Knopf, 1944.
Borchard, Edwin M., Chamberlain, Joseph P. and Duggan, Stephen (eds). *The Collected Papers of John Bassett Moore,* 7 vols. New Haven: Yale University Press, 1944.
Borchard, Edwin M. and Lage, William Potter. *Neutrality for the United States.* New Haven: Yale University Press, 1940.
Bradley, Phillips. *Can We Stay Out of War?* New York: W.W. Norton, 1936.
British Commonwealth Relations Conference. *British Commonwealth Relations. Proceedings of the First Unofficial Conference on British Commonwealth Relations, held at Toronto from September 11–21, 1933,* ed., Arnold Toynbee. London: Oxford University Press, 1934.
— *The British Commonwealth and the Future. Proceedings of the Second Unofficial Conference, Sydney 1938,* ed., H.V. Hodson. London: Oxford University Press, 1939.
Bryce, James. *The American Commonwealth.* London: Macmillan, 1888.
Burnham, James. *The Struggle for the World.* New York: John Day; London: Jonathan Cape, 1947.
Bywater, Hector C. *Navies and Nations. A Review of Naval Developments since the Great War.* London: Constable, 1927.
Carnegie, Andrew. *The Reunion of Britain and America: A Look Ahead.* Edinburgh: Andrew Elliot, 1898.

Carter, John. *Conquest. America's Painless Imperialism.* New York: Harcourt Brace, 1928.

Catlin, George. *One Anglo-Saxon Nation. The Foundation of Anglo-Saxony as Basis of World Federation. A British Response to Streit.* London: Andrew Dakers, 1941.

Colquhoun, Archibald R. *Greater America.* London and New York: Harper & Bros, 1904.

Coolidge, Archibald Cary. *The United States as a World Power.* New York: Macmillan, 1908.

Croly, Herbert. *The Promise of American Life.* New York: Macmillan, 1909.

Culbertson, Ely. *Total Peace.* New York: Doubleday Doran, 1943.

Davenport, E.H. and Cooke, S.R. *The Oil Trusts and Anglo-American Relations.* London: Macmillan, 1923.

Denny, Ludwell. *America Conquers Britain. A Record of Economic War.* New York: Alfred A. Knopf, 1930.

— *We Fight for Oil.* New York and London: Alfred A. Knopf, 1928.

Dulles, Allen W. and Armstrong, Hamilton Fish. *Can We Be Neutral?* New York: Council on Foreign Relations, 1936.

Dulles, John Foster. *War or Peace.* New York: Macmillan, 1950.

Dunne, Finley P. *Mr Dooley in Peace and in War.* Boston: Smith Maynard, 1899.

Eckardstein, Hermann Freiherr von. *Lebenserrinerungen und Politische Denkwurdigkeiten.* III, *Die Isolierung Deutschlands.* Leipzig: P. List, 1921.

Einstein, Lewis. *American Foreign Policy.* Boston: Houghton Mifflin, 1909.

Eliot, George Fielding. *The Ramparts We Watch.* New York: Reynal & Hitchcock, 1939.

Emerson, Ralph Waldo. *English Traits.* Boston: Phillips, Sampson, 1856.

Fish, Carl Russell, Angell, Sir Norman and Hussey, Rear-Adm. Charles L. *American Policies Abroad. The United States and Great Britain.* Chicago: Council on Foreign Relations, 1932.

Fox, Sir Frank. *The Mastery of the Pacific. Can the British Empire and the United States agree?* London: John Lane, 1928.

Furness, Sir Christopher. *The American Invasion.* London: Simpkin, Marshall, 1902.

Garvin, J.L. 'The League of Nations and the English-speaking world', in *Problems of Peace,* 5th ser. *Lectures delivered at the Geneva Institute of International Relations, August 1930.* London: Institute of International Relations, 1931.

Hancock, W.K. *Argument of Empire.* Harmondsworth: Penguin Books, 1943.

Hartley, Livingston. *Is America Afraid?* New York: Prentice Hall, 1937.

Howe, Quincy. *England Expects Every American to Do His Duty.* New York: Simon and Schuster, 1937.

Inge, W.R. *England.* London: Ernest Benn, 1926.

Kenworthy, J.M. and Young, George. *Freedom of the Seas.* London: Hutchinson, 1928.

Kipling, Rudyard. *Verse.* Inclusive ed., 1885–1918, 3 vols. London. Hodder & Stoughton, 1919.

Labour Party. *European Unity.* London: Labour Party, 1950.
Liddell Hart, B.H. *When Britain Goes to War.* London: Faber & Faber, 1935.
— *Europe in Arms.* London: Faber & Faber, 1937.
Lippmann, Walter. *The Cold War.* New York: Harper & Bros, 1947.
— *Interpretations, 1933–35.* New York: Macmillan, 1936.
— *U.S. Foreign Policy.* Boston: Little Brown, 1943.
— *U.S. War Aims.* Boston: Little Brown, 1944.
Lodge, Henry Cabot. *Historical and Political Essays.* Boston: Houghton Mifflin, 1892.
— *Speeches and Addresses, 1884–1909.* Boston: Houghton Mifflin, 1909.
Luce, Henry. *The American Century.* New York: Time Inc., 1941.
MacCormac, John. *America and World Mastery. The Future of the United States, Canada and the British Empire.* New York: Duell, Sloan & Pearce, 1942.
Mackenzie, F.A. *The American Invaders.* London: Grant Richards, 1902.
Mahan, Alfred T. *Armaments and Arbitration.* New York: Harper & Bros, 1912.
— *The Interest of America in Sea Power, Present and Future.* Boston: Little, Brown, 1897.
— *Naval Administration and Warfare.* Boston: Little, Brown, 1908.
Millis, Walter. *The Future of Sea Power in the Pacific.* New York: Foreign Policy Association, 1935.
Morgenthau, Hans J. *In Defense of the National Interest. A Critical Examination of American Foreign Policy.* New York: Alfred A. Knopf, 1951.
Morris, George Pope, 'Woodman, Spare that Tree'. New York: c. 1846.
Moulton, Harold G. and Pasvolsky, Leo. *War Debts and World Prosperity.* Washington: Brookings Institution, 1932.
Powers, H.H. *The American Era.* New York: Macmillan, 1920.
Problems of Peace. London: Institute of International Relations, 1927 ff.
Reves, Emery A. *A Democratic Manifesto.* New York: Random House, 1942.
Roosevelt, Nicholas. *America and England?* New York and London: Jonathan Cape, 1930.
— *The Restless Pacific.* New York: G. Scribner's Sons, 1928.
Scruggs, William Lindsay. *British Aggression in Venezuela. The Monroe Doctrine on Trial.* Atlanta: Franklin Printing and Publishing Corp., 1895.
Simonds, Frank H. *Can America Stay at Home?* New York: Harper & Bros, 1932.
Smith, Goldwin. *Canada and the Canadian Question.* London, New York & Toronto: Macmillan, 1891.
— *Reminiscences.* New York: Macmillan, 1910.
Stead, W.T. *The Americanization of the World, or the Trend of the Twentieth Century.* London & New York: H. Marckley, 1901.
— *The Last Will and Testament of Cecil John Rhodes.* London: 'Review of Reviews' Office, 1902.
Streit, Clarence. *Union Now. A Proposal for a Federal Union of the De-*

mocracies of the North Atlantic. New York: Harper & Bros; London: Jonathan Cape, 1939.

— *Union Now with Britain.* New York: Harper & Bros; London: Jonathan Cape, 1941.

Strong, Josiah. *Our Country.* New York: American Home Missionary Society, 1885.

Thwaite, B.H. *The American Invasion. Or England's Commercial Danger and the Triumphal Progress of the United States, with Remedies Proposed to Enable England to Preserve her Industrial Position.* London: Swan Sonnenschein, 1902.

Watson, William. *The Purple East.* London: John Lane, 1896.

Weinberg, Albert K. *Manifest Destiny.* Baltimore: Johns Hopkins Press, 1935.

Willkie, Wendell. *One World.* New York: Simon & Schuster, 1943.

Wright, Quincy. *The United States and Neutrality.* Chicago: University of Chicago Press, 1935.

— (ed.) *Neutrality and Collective Security.* Chicago: University of Chicago Press, 1936.

Young, Eugene. *Powerful America. Our Place in a Rearming World.* New York: Frederick A. Stokes, 1936.

V Other Books and Articles Cited

Acheson, Dean. *Present at the Creation. My Years at the State Department.* New York: Norton, 1969.

Adler, Selig. *The Isolationist Impulse.* New York: Abelard-Schuman, 1957.

— *The Uncertain Giant 1921–1941. American Foreign Policy Between the Wars.* New York: Macmillan, 1965.

Aldcroft, Derek H. *The Inter-war Economy. Britain 1919–1939.* London: Batsford, 1970.

Alexander, G.M. *The Prelude to the Truman Doctrine. British Policy in Greece 1944–47.* Oxford: Clarendon Press, 1982.

Ambrosius, Lloyd C. *Woodrow Wilson and the American Diplomatic Tradition.* Cambridge: Cambridge University Press, 1987.

Anderson, Irvine H. *ARAMCO, the United States and Saudi Arabia. A Study of the Dynamics of Foreign Oil Policy.* Princeton: Princeton University Press, 1981.

Archdeacon, Thomas J. *Becoming American. An Ethnic History.* New York: Free Press, 1983.

Armstrong, William M. *The Gilded Age. Letters of E.L. Godkin.* Albany: State University of New York Press, 1974.

Avon, Earl of. *The Eden Memoirs,* 3 vols. London: Cassell, 1960–65.

Bailey, Thomas A. 'Dewey and the Germans at Manila Bay', *American Historical Review,* XLV, (1939) pp. 59–81.

— *Woodrow Wilson and the Great Betrayal.* New York: Macmillan, 1945.

Bain, Kenneth Roy. *The March to Zion. United States Policy and the Founding of Israel.* College Station: A. & M. University Press, 1979.

Bairoch, P. 'International Industrialization Levels from 1750 to 1980', *Journal of European Economic History*, XI, (1982) pp. 269–333.

Bassett, Reginald. *Democracy and Foreign Policy. A Case History. The Sino-Japanese Dispute, 1931–33*. London: Longmans, Green, 1952.

Baylis, John. *Anglo-American Defense Relations 1939–1984. The Special Relationship*. New York: Macmillan, 1981.

Beale, Howard K. *Theodore Roosevelt and the Rise of America to World Power*. Baltimore: Johns Hopkins University Press, 1956.

Beloff, Max. *Imperial Sunset*. I, *Britain's Liberal Empire 1897–1921*; II, *Dream of Commonwealth 1921–42*. London: Methuen, 1969, 1989.

— 'The Special Relationship: An Anglo-American Myth', in *A Century of Conflict. Essays for A.J.P. Taylor*, ed. Martin Gilbert. London: Hamish Hamilton, 1966 and Beloff, Max. *The Intellectual in Politics and other Essays*. London: Weidenfeld & Nicolson, 1970.

Berle, Adolf. *Navigating the Rapids, 1918–1971*, ed. Beatrice Bishop Berle and Travis Beal Jacobs. New York: Harcourt Brace Jovanovich, 1973.

Best, Richard A. *'Cooperation with Like-minded Peoples'. British Influences on American Security Policy 1945–1949*. Westport, CT: Greenwood Press, 1986.

Blake, Robert and Louis, Wm Roger (eds). *Churchill*. Oxford & New York: Oxford University Press, 1993.

Blum, John Morton (ed.). *From the Morgenthau Diaries*. I, *Years of Crisis 1928–1938*; II, *Years of Urgency 1939–1941*; III, *Years of War 1941–1945*. Boston: Houghton Mifflin, 1959–67.

— *Public Philosopher. Selected Letters of Walter Lippmann*. New York: Ticknor & Fields, 1985.

Bond, Brian. *Liddell Hart. A Study of his Military Thought*. London: Cassell, 1977.

Borg, Dorothy. *The United States and the Far Eastern Crisis of 1933–1938*. Cambridge, MA: Harvard University Press, 1964.

— and Heinrichs, Waldo. *Uncertain Years. Chinese–American Relations 1947–1950*. New York: Columbia University Press, 1980.

Botti, Timothy. *The Long Wait. The Forging of the Anglo-American Nuclear Alliance*. New York: Greenwood Press, 1987.

Bourne, Kenneth. *Britain and the Balance of Power in North America 1815–1908*. London: Longman, 1967.

Boyce, Robert W.D. *British Capitalism at the Crossroads 1919–1932*. Cambridge: Cambridge University Press, 1987.

Braisted, William Reynolds. *The United States Navy in the Pacific 1909–22*. Austin and London: University of Texas Press, 1971.

Brown, William Adams, jr and Opie, Redvers. *American Foreign Assistance*. Washington: Brookings Institution, 1953.

Bullock, Alan. *Ernest Bevin, Foreign Secretary*. Oxford: Oxford University Press, 1983.

Bunselmeyer, Robert E. *The Cost of the War 1914–1919. British War Aims and the Origins of Reparations*. Hamden, CT: Archon Books, 1975.

Burk, Kathleen. *Britain, America and the Sinews of War 1914–1918*. Boston and London: George Allen and Unwin, 1985.

Burton, D.H. *Theodore Roosevelt and his English Correspondents.* Philadelphia: American Philosophical Society, 1973.
Butler, J.R.M. *Grand Strategy,* II, History of the Second World War, UK Military Series. London: HMSO, 1957.
— *Lord Lothian. Philip Kerr 1882–1940.* London: Macmillan, 1960.
Cable, James. *The Geneva Conference of 1954 on Indochina.* Basingstoke: Macmillan, 1986.
Calvert, Peter. *The Mexican Revolution of 1910–1914. The Diplomacy of Anglo-American Conflict.* Cambridge: Cambridge University Press, 1968.
Campbell, A.E. *Great Britain and the United States 1895–1903.* London: Longman, 1960.
Campbell, Charles S. *Anglo-American Understanding 1898–1903.* Baltimore: Johns Hopkins University Press, 1957.
— *The Transformation of American Foreign Relations 1865–1900.* New York: Harper & Row, 1976.
Camps, Miriam. *Britain and the European Community 1955–1963.* London: Oxford University Press; Princeton: Princeton University Press, 1964.
Carlton, David. 'The Anglo-French Compromise on Arms Limitation 1928', *Journal of British Studies,* VIII, (1969) pp. 141–62.
— 'Great Britain and the Coolidge Naval Conference of 1927', *Political Science Quarterly,* LXXXIII, (1968) pp. 573–98.
Challener, Richard D. *Admirals, Generals, and American Foreign Policy 1898–1914.* Princeton: Princeton University Press, 1973.
Chalmers, Michael. *Paying for Defence. Military Spending and British Decline.* London: Pluto Press, 1985.
Chandler, Lester V. *Benjamin Strong, Central Banker.* Washington: Brookings Institution, 1958.
Churchill, Winston S. *The Second World War,* 6 vols. London: Cassell, 1948–54.
Clark, Ian and Wheeler, Nicholas J. *The British Origins of Nuclear Strategy 1945–1955.* Oxford: Clarendon Press, 1989.
Clarke, Stephen V.O. *Central Bank Cooperation 1924–1931.* New York: Federal Reserve Bank of New York, 1967.
— *The Reconstruction of the International Monetary System. The attempts of 1922 and 1933.* Princeton: Princeton University Press, 1973.
Cohen, Michael J. *Palestine and the Great Powers 1945–1948.* Princeton: Princeton University Press, 1982.
Cohen, Warren I. *The American Revisionists. The Lessons of Intervention in World War I.* Chicago: University of Chicago Press, 1967.
Cole, Wayne S. *Roosevelt and the Isolationists 1932–1945.* Lincoln: University of Nebraska Press, 1983.
Cooper, John Milton, jr. 'The British Response to the House–Grey Memorandum. New Evidence and New Questions', *Journal of American History,* LIX, (1973) pp. 958–71.
— *The Vanity of Power. American Isolationism and the First World War 1914–1917.* Westport, CT: Greenwood Press, 1969.
Costigliola, Frank. 'Anglo-American Financial Rivalry in the 1920s', *Journal of Economic History,* XXXVII, (1977) pp. 911–34.

— *Awkward Dominion. American Political, Economic and Cultural Relations with Europe, 1919–1933.* Ithaca: Cornell University Press, 1984.

Cowling, Maurice. *The Impact of Hitler. British Politics and British Policy 1933–1940.* London: Cambridge University Press, 1975.

Current, Richard N. *Secretary Stimson. A Study in Statecraft.* New Brunswick, NJ: Rutgers University Press, 1954.

Dallek, Robert. *Franklin D. Roosevelt and American Foreign Policy 1932–1945.* New York: Oxford University Press, 1979.

Danchev, Alex. '"Being Friends": The Combined Chiefs of Staff and the Making of Allied Strategy in the Second World War', in Lawrence Freedman, Paul Hayes and Robert O'Neill (eds), *War, Strategy and International Politics. Essays in honour of Sir Michael Howard.* Oxford: Oxford University Press, 1992.

— *Very Special Relationship. Field-Marshal Sir John Dill and the Anglo-American Alliance 1941–1944.* London: Brassey's Defence, 1986.

Daniels, Josephus. *The Cabinet Diaries of Josephus Daniels 1913–1921,* ed. E. David Cronon. Lincoln: University of Nebraska Press, 1963.

Darwin, John. *Britain and Decolonisation. The Retreat from Empire in the Postwar World.* London: Macmillan, 1988.

Dennett, Tyler. *John Hay.* New York: Dodd, Mead, 1934.

De Novo, John A. 'The Movement for an Aggressive American Oil Policy Abroad 1918–1920', *American Historical Review*, LXVI, (1955–6) pp. 854–76.

Devereux, David R. *The Formulation of British Defence Policy towards the Middle East 1948–56.* Basingstoke: Macmillan, 1990.

Devlin, Patrick. *Too Proud to Fight. Woodrow Wilson's Neutrality.* London: Macmillan, 1974.

Dingman, Roger. *Power in the Pacific. The Origins of Naval Arms Limitation 1914–1922.* Chicago: University of Chicago Press, 1976.

Divine, Robert A. *The Illusion of Neutrality.* Chicago: University of Chicago Press, 1962.

— *Second Chance. The Triumph of Internationalism in America during World War II.* New York: Athenaeum, 1967.

Dizikes, John. *Britain, Roosevelt and the New Deal 1932–1938.* New York: Garland, 1979.

Dobson, Alan P. *Peaceful Air Warfare. The United States, Britain and the Politics of International Aviation.* Oxford: Clarendon Press, 1991.

— *US Wartime Aid to Britain 1940–1946.* London: Croom Helm, 1986.

Dockrill, Saki. *Britain's Policy for West German Rearmament 1950–5.* London: Cambridge University Press, 1991.

Drummond, Ian M. *Imperial Economic Policy 1917–1939. Studies in Expansion and Protection.* London: Allen and Unwin, 1974.

— and Hillmer, Norman. *Negotiating Freer Trade. The United Kingdom, the United States, Canada and the Trade Agreements of 1938.* Waterloo, Ontario: Wilfred Laurier University Press, 1989.

Dugdale, Blanche. *Arthur James Balfour.* London: Hutchinson, 1936.

Dunne, Michael. *The United States and the World Court 1920–1935.* London: Macmillan, 1988.

Eayrs, James. *The Commonwealth and Suez. A Documentary Survey.* London: Oxford University Press, 1965.

— *In Defence of Canada.* II, *Appeasement and Rearmament.* Toronto: University of Toronto Press, 1965.

Egerton, George W. 'Britain and the "Great Betrayal": Anglo-American Relations and the Struggle for American Ratification of the Treaty of Versailles 1919–1920', *Historical Journal*, XXI, (1978) pp. 885–911.

— *Great Britain and the Creation of the League of Nations. Strategy, Politics and International Organisation 1914–19.* London: Scolar Press, 1979.

Ehrman, Howard. *Grand Strategy,* V and VI, History of the Second World War, UK Military Series. London: HMSO, 1965.

Ellis, Elmer. *Mr Dooley's America. A Life of Finley Peter Dunne.* New York: Alfred A. Knopf, 1941.

Ellis, L. Ethan. *Republican Foreign Policy 1921–1933.* New Brunswick, NJ: Rutgers University Press, 1968.

Emmerson, J.T. *The Rhineland Crisis, 7 March 1936.* London: Temple Smith, 1977.

Endicott, S.L. *Diplomacy and Enterprise. British China Policy 1933–1937.* Manchester: Manchester University Press, 1975.

Etzold, Thomas H. and Gaddis, John L. (ed.), *Containment. Documents on American Policy and Strategy 1945–1950.* New York: Columbia University Press, 1978.

Ferrell, Robert H. *Peace in Their Time. The Origins of the Kellogg–Briand Pact.* New Haven: Yale University Press, 1952.

Ferris, John Robert. *The Evolution of British Strategic Policy 1919–1926.* London: Macmillan, 1989.

— 'The Symbol and the Substance of Sea Power: Great Britain, the United States, and the One-power Standard', in B.J.C. McKercher (ed.), *Anglo-American Relations in the 1920s.* Basingstoke: Macmillan, 1991.

Fisher, H.A.L. *James Bryce, Viscount Bryce of Dechmont, O.M.* New York and London: Macmillan, 1927.

Flora, Peter. *State, Economy and Society in Western Europe 1815–1975,* 2 vols. Frankfurt: Campus Verlag; London: Macmillan; Chicago: St James Press, 1983, 1987.

Floto, Inga. *Colonel House in Paris,* 2nd edn. Princeton: Princeton University Press, 1981.

Fowler, Wilton Bonham. *British–American Relations 1917–1918. The Role of Sir William Wiseman.* Princeton: Princeton University Press, 1969.

Freedman, Lawrence, Hayes, Paul and O'Neill, Robert (ed.). *War, Strategy and International Politics. Essays in honour of Sir Michael Howard.* Oxford: Oxford University Press, 1992.

Friedberg, Aaron L. *The Weary Titan. Britain and the Experience of Relative Decline 1895–1905.* Princeton: Princeton University Press, 1988.

Fry, Michael G. *Illusions of Security. North Atlantic Diplomacy 1918–22.* Toronto: University of Toronto Press, 1972.

Fursdon, Edward. *The European Defence Community.* London: Macmillan, 1980.

Gaddis, John Lewis. *The Long Peace. Inquiries into the History of the Cold War.* New York: Oxford University Press, 1987.

— *Strategies of Containment. A Critical Appraisal of Postwar American National Security Policy.* New York: Oxford University Press, 1982.

— *The United States and the Origins of the Cold War 1941–1947.* New York: Columbia University Press, 1972.

Gallup, George H. *The Gallup Poll and Public Opinion 1935–1971,* I. New York: Random House, 1972.

Gardner, Richard N. *Sterling–Dollar Diplomacy. Anglo-American Collaboration in the Reconstruction of Multilateral Trade.* Oxford: Clarendon Press, 1956.

Garraty, John A. *Henry Cabot Lodge.* New York: Alfred A. Knopf, 1953.

Garvin, J.L. *The Life of Joseph Chamberlain,* 3 vols. London: Macmillan, 1932–4.

Gelfand, Laurence E. (ed.). *Herbert Hoover. The Great War and its Aftermath 1914–23.* Iowa City: University of Iowa Press, 1979.

Gibbs, N.H. *Grand Strategy,* I, History of the Second World War, UK Military Series London: HMSO, 1976.

Gilbert, Martin. *Winston S. Churchill,* III–VIII and Companion vols. London: Heinemann, 1971–88.

— (ed.), *A Century of Conflict 1850–1950. Essays for A.J.P. Taylor.* London: Hamish Hamilton, 1966.

Gimbel, John. *The Origins of the Marshall Plan.* Stanford: Stanford University Press, 1976.

Goldstein, Erik. *Winning the Peace. British Diplomatic Strategy, Peace Planning, and the Paris Peace Conference.* Oxford: Clarendon Press, 1991.

Gooch, John. '"Hidden in the Rock": American Military Perceptions of Great Britain, 1919–1940', in Lawrence Freedman, Paul Hayes and Robert O'Neill (eds), *War, Strategy and International Politics. Essays in honour of Sir Michael Howard.* Oxford: Oxford University Press, 1991.

Gowing, Margaret. *Britain and Atomic Energy 1939–1945.* London: HMSO, 1964.

— *Independence and Deterrence. Britain and Atomic Energy 1945–1952.* London: HMSO, 1974.

Graebner, Norman A. *Cold War Diplomacy. American Foreign Policy 1945–1975,* 2nd edn. New York: Van Nostrand Reinhold, 1977.

— (ed.), *The National Security: Its Theory and Practice 1945–1960.* New York: Oxford University Press, 1986.

Grayling, Christopher and Laydon, Christopher. *Just Another Star? Anglo-American Relations since 1945.* London: Harrap, 1988.

Grenville, J.A.S. *Lord Salisbury and Foreign Policy: The Close of the Nineteenth Century.* London: Athlone Press, 1964.

— 'Great Britain and the Isthmian Canal, 1898–1901', *American Historical Review,* LXI, (1955) pp. 48–69.

— and Young, George B. *Politics, Strategy and American Diplomacy. Studies in Foreign Policy 1873–1917.* New Haven and London: Yale University Press, 1966.

Guhin, Michael A. *John Foster Dulles. A Statesman and his Times.* New York: Columbia University Press, 1972.

Gwyer, J.M.A. and Butler, J.R.M. *Grand Strategy*, III, History of the Second World War, UK Military Series. London: HMSO, 1964.

Gwynn, Stephen (ed.). *Letters and Friendships of Sir Cecil Spring Rice*, 2 vols. London: Constable, 1929.

Hall, Christopher. *Britain, America and Arms Control 1921–1937.* London: Macmillan, 1986.

Hall, H. Duncan. *North American Supply*, History of the Second World War, UK Civil Series. London: HMSO, 1955.

Hancock, W.K., *Survey of British Commonwealth Affairs*: see Royal Institute of International Affairs.

— and Gowing, M.M. *British War Economy*, History of the Second World War, UK Civil Series. London: HMSO, 1949.

Harriman, W. Averell and Abel, Elie. *Special Envoy to Churchill and Stalin, 1941–1946.* New York: Random House, 1975.

Harrod, Roy. *The Life of John Maynard Keynes.* London: Macmillan, 1951.

Hathaway, Robert M. *Ambiguous Partnership. Britain and America 1944–1947.* New York: Columbia University Press, 1981.

Hawley, Ellis W. (ed.). *Herbert Hoover as Secretary of Commerce. Studies in New Era thought and practice.* Iowa City: University of Iowa Press, 1981.

Healy, David. *Drive to Hegemony. The United States in the Caribbean 1898–1917.* Madison: University of Wisconsin Press, 1988.

— *US Expansionism. The Imperialist Urge in the 1890s.* Madison: University of Wisconsin Press, 1970.

Heindel, Richard Heathcote. *The American Impact on Great Britain, 1898–1914.* Philadelphia: University of Pennsylvania Press, 1940.

Heinrichs, Waldo. *Threshold of War. Franklin Roosevelt and American entry into World War II.* New York: Oxford University Press, 1988.

Henderson, Nicholas. *The Birth of NATO.* London: Weidenfeld & Nicolson, 1982.

Hendrick, Burton J. *The Life of Andrew Carnegie.* Garden City: Doubleday Doran, 1932.

Hewlett, Richard and Anderson, Oscar. *A History of the United States Atomic Energy Commission*, 2 vols. Philadelphia: Pennsylvania State University Press, 1962–9.

Higham, John. *Strangers in the Land. Patterns of American Nativism 1860–1925.* New Brunswick: Rutgers University Press, 1955.

Hixson, Walter L. *George F. Kennan, Cold War Iconoclast.* New York: Columbia University Press, 1989.

Hogan, Michael J. *Informal Entente. The Private Structure of Cooperation in Anglo-American Economic Diplomacy 1918–1928.* Columbia: University of Missouri Press, 1977.

— *The Marshall Plan. America, Britain and the Reconstruction of Western*

Europe 1947–1952. Cambridge and New York: Cambridge University Press, 1987.

Holland, R.F. *Britain and the Commonwealth Alliance 1918–1939.* London: Macmillan, 1981.

Hoopes, Townsend. *The Devil and John Foster Dulles.* Boston: Little, Brown, 1973.

Howard, Michael. *Grand Strategy,* IV, History of the Second World War, UK Military Series. London: HMSO, 1972.

Humphreys, R.A. *Tradition and Revolt in Latin America and other essays.* London: Weidenfeld & Nicolson, 1969.

Hurewitz, J.C. *Middle East Dilemmas.* New York: Harper & Bros, 1953.

Ickes, Harold L. *The Secret Diary of Harold L. Ickes,* 3 vols. New York: Simon & Schuster, 1954.

Immerman, Richard H. (ed.). *John Foster Dulles and the Diplomacy of the Cold War.* Princeton: Princeton University Press, 1990.

Ions, Edmund. *James Bryce and American Democracy 1870–1922.* London: Macmillan, 1968.

Jonas, Manfred. *Isolationism in America 1935–1941.* Ithaca: Cornell University Press, 1966.

Jones, Geoffrey. *The State and the Emergence of the British Oil Industry.* London: Macmillan, 1981.

Jones, Joseph M. *The Fifteen Weeks.* New York: Viking Press, 1955.

Jones, Martin. *Failure in Palestine. British and United States Policy after the Second World War.* London and New York: Mansell, 1985.

Kaufman, Burton K. *Efficiency and Expansion. Foreign Trade Organization in the Wilson Administration 1913–1921.* Westport, CT: Greenwood Press, 1974.

Kennan, George F. *Memoirs 1925–1950.* Boston: Little Brown, 1967.

Kennedy, David M. *Over Here. The First World War and American Society.* New York: Oxford University Press, 1980.

Kennedy, Paul M. *The Realities behind Diplomacy. Background Influences on British External Policy 1865–1980.* London: Fontana, 1981.

Kent, Bruce. *The Spoils of War. The Politics, Economics and Diplomacy of Reparations, 1918–1932.* Oxford: Clarendon Press, 1987.

Kent, John. *British Imperial Strategy and the Origins of the Cold War 1944–49.* Leicester: Leicester University Press, 1993.

Kent, Marion. *Oil and Empire. British Policy and Mesopotamian Oil 1900–1920.* London: Macmillan, 1976.

Kernek, S.J. 'The British Government's Reaction to President Wilson's "Peace" Note of December 1916', *Historical Journal,* XIII, (1970) pp. 721–66.

Kihl, Mary R. 'A Failure of Ambassadorial Diplomacy', *Journal of American History,* LVII, (1970–1) pp. 636–53.

Kimball, Warren F. 'Beggar thy Neighbour. America and the British Interim Financial Crisis 1940–1941', *Journal of Economic History,* XXIX, (1969) pp. 758–72.

— *The Most Unsordid Act. Lend-Lease 1939–1941.* Baltimore: Johns Hopkins University Press, 1969.

— '"Wheel within a Wheel". Churchill, Roosevelt and the Special Relationship', in Robert Blake and Wm Roger Louis (eds), *Churchill*. Oxford and New York: Oxford University Press, 1993.

Kindleberger, Charles P. *The World in Depression 1929–1939*. London: Allen Lane, 1973.

Kneer, Warren G. *Great Britain and the Caribbean 1901–1913. A Study in Anglo-American Relations*. East Lansing: Michigan State University Press, 1975.

Kottman, Richard N. *Reciprocity and the North Atlantic Triangle 1932–1938*. Ithaca: Cornell University Press, 1968.

Krock, Arthur. *Memoirs. Sixty Years in the Firing Line*. New York: Funk & Wagnalls, 1968.

Kuniholm, Bruce Robellant. *The Origins of the Cold War in the Near East. Great Power Conflict and Diplomacy in Iran, Turkey and Greece*. Princeton: Princeton University Press, 1980.

Kunz, Diane B. *The Economic Diplomacy of the Suez Crisis*. Chapel Hill: University of North Carolina Press, 1991.

Kyle, Keith. *Suez*. London: Weidenfeld & Nicolson, 1991.

Lacey, Michael J. (ed.). *The Truman Presidency*. Cambridge: Cambridge University Press, 1989.

Langer, William L. and Gleason, S. Everett. *The Challenge to Isolation 1937–1940*. New York: Harper & Bros, 1952.

— *The Undeclared War 1940–1941*. New York: Harper & Bros, 1953.

Lary, H.B. and others. *The United States in the World Economy. The International Transactions of the United States during the Interwar Period*. Washington: Government Printing Office, 1943.

Lee, Bradford A. *Britain and the Sino-Japanese War 1937–1939*. Stanford: Stanford University Press, 1973.

Leffler, Melvyn P. *The Elusive Quest. America's Pursuit of European Stability and French Security 1919–1923*. Chapel Hill: University of North Carolina Press, 1979.

— *A Preponderance of Power. National Security, the Truman Administration and the Cold War*. Stanford: Stanford University Press, 1992.

Leutze, James R. *Bargaining for Supremacy. Anglo-American Naval Collaboration 1937–1941*. Chapel Hill: University of North Carolina Press, 1977.

Lewis, Julian. *Changing Direction. British Military Planning for Postwar Strategic Defence 1942–1947*. London: Sherwood Press, 1988.

Link, Arthur S. *Wilson*, 5 vols. Princeton: Princeton University Press, 1947–65.

Link, Werner. *Die Amerikanische Stabilisierungspolitik in Deutschland 1921–1932*. Düsseldorf: Droste Verlag, 1970.

Lodge, Henry Cabot (ed.). *Selections from the Correspondence of Theodore Roosevelt and Henry Cabot Lodge*. New York: C. Scribner's Sons, 1925.

Louis, Wm Roger. 'American Anti-colonialism and the Dissolution of the British Empire', *International Affairs*, LXI, (1984–5) pp. 395–420.

— *The British Empire in the Middle East 1945–51. Arab Nationalism, the United States, and Postwar Imperialism.* Oxford: Clarendon Press, 1984.

— *British Strategy in the Far East 1919–1939.* Oxford: Clarendon Press, 1971.

— *Great Britain and Germany's Lost Colonies 1914–1919.* Oxford: Clarendon Press, 1967.

— *Imperialism at Bay 1941–1945. The United States and the Decolonisation of the British Empire.* Oxford: Oxford University Press, 1977.

— and Bull, Hedley (eds). *The Special Relationship. Anglo-American Relations since 1945.* Oxford: Clarendon Press, 1986.

— and Owen, Roger (eds). *Suez 1956. The Crisis and its Consequences.* Oxford: Clarendon Press, 1989.

Lowe, Peter. *Great Britain and the Origins of the Pacific War.* Oxford: Clarendon Press, 1977.

Lucas, W. Scott. *Divided We Stand. Britain, the US and the Suez Crisis.* London: Hodder & Stoughton, 1991.

Lyon, Peter (ed.). *Britain and Canada. Survey of a Changing Relationship.* London: Frank Cass, 1976.

MacDonald, Callum A. *Korea. The War before Vietnam.* Basingstoke: Macmillan, 1986.

— *The United States, Britain and Appeasement 1936–1939.* London: Macmillan, 1981.

McDonald, J. Kenneth. 'Lloyd George and the Search for a Postwar Naval Policy, 1919', in A.J.P. Taylor (ed.), *Lloyd George. Twelve Essays.* London: Hamish Hamilton, 1971.

McFadyean, Andrew (ed.). *The History of Rubber Regulation 1934–1943.* London: George Allen & Unwin, 1944.

McIntyre, W. David. *The Rise and Fall of the Singapore Naval Base.* London: Macmillan, 1979.

McKercher, B.J.C. *The Second Baldwin Government and the United States.* Cambridge: Cambridge University Press, 1984.

— (ed.). *Anglo-American Relations in the 1920s. The Struggle for Supremacy.* Basingstoke: Macmillan, 1991.

McLellan, David S. *Dean Acheson. The State Department Years.* New York: Dodd, Mead, 1976.

Macleod, Iain. *Neville Chamberlain.* London: Frederick Muller, 1961.

McNeil, William C. *American Money and the Weimar Republic. Economics and Politics on the Eve of the Great Depression.* New York: Columbia University Press, 1986.

Mansergh, Nicholas. *Survey of British Commonwealth Affairs:* see Royal Institute of International Affairs.

Marder, Arthur J. *From the Dreadnought to Scapa Flow. The Royal Navy in the Fisher Era, 1904–1919,* 5 vols. London: Oxford University Press, 1961–70.

Marks, Frederick W. *Power and Peace. The Diplomacy of John Foster Dulles.* Westport, CT: Praeger, 1993.

Marquand, David. *Ramsay MacDonald.* London: Jonathan Cape, 1977.

Matloff, Maurice. *Strategic Planning for Coalition Warfare 1943–1944*, The US Army in World War II. Washington: Office of the Chief of Military History, 1959.

— and Snell, Edwin M. *Strategic Planning for Coalition Warfare 1941–1942*, The US Army in World War II. Washington: Office of the Chief of Military History, 1953.

May, Ernest R. *The World War and American Isolation 1914–1917*. Cambridge, MA: Harvard University Press, 1959.

Mayers, David Allan. *George Kennan and the Dilemmas of US Foreign Policy*. New York: Oxford University Press, 1989.

Mearsheimer, John J. *Liddell Hart and the Weight of History*. Ithaca: Cornell University Press, 1988.

Meyer, Richard. *Bankers' Diplomacy. Monetary Stabilization in the Twenties*. New York: Columbia University Press, 1970.

Middlemas, Keith. *Diplomacy of Illusion. The British Government and Germany 1937–1939*. London: Weidenfeld & Nicolson, 1972.

Miller, Aaron David. *Search for Security. Saudi Arabian Oil and American Foreign Policy 1939–1949*. Chapel Hill: University of North Carolina Press, 1980.

Milward, Alan. *The Reconstruction of Western Europe 1945–51*. London: Methuen, 1984.

Mitchell, B.R. *British Historical Statistics*. Cambridge: Cambridge University Press, 1988.

— *European Historical Statistics 1750–1970*. London: Macmillan, 1975.

— *International Historical Statistics. The Americas and Australasia*. London: Macmillan, 1983.

Moggridge, D.E. *British Monetary Policy 1924–1931. The Norman Conquest of $4.86*. Cambridge: Cambridge University Press, 1972.

Monger, George. *The End of Isolation. British Foreign Policy 1900–1907*. London: Thomas Nelson & Sons, 1963.

Montgomery, John D. *The Politics of Foreign Aid*. New York: Praeger, 1962.

Moore, R.J. *Churchill, Cripps and India 1939–1945*. Oxford: Clarendon Press, 1979.

— *Escape from Empire. The Attlee Government and the India Problem*. Oxford: Clarendon Press, 1983.

Morgan, D.S. *The Official History of Colonial Development*, 5 vols. London: Macmillan, 1980.

Morison, Elting E. *Admiral Sims and the Modern American Navy*. Boston: Houghton Mifflin, 1942.

Munro, John A. (ed.). *The Alaska Boundary Dispute*. Toronto: Copp Clark, 1970.

Neale, R.G. *Britain and American Imperialism 1898–1900*. Brisbane: University of Queensland Press, 1965.

Neatby, H. Blair. *William Lyon Mackenzie King*. III, *The Prism of Unity 1932–1939*. Toronto: University of Toronto Press, 1976.

Nish, Ian. *Alliance in Decline. A Study in Anglo-Japanese Relations 1908–23*. London: Athlone Press, 1972.

— *Japan's Struggle with Internationalism. Japan, China and the League of Nations 1931–33.* London and New York: Kegan Paul International, 1993.

Notter, Harley. *Postwar Foreign Policy Preparation 1939–1945.* Washington: Department of State, 1949.

O'Connor, R.G. *Perilous Equilibrium. The United States and the London Naval Conference of 1930.* Lawrence: University of Kansas Press, 1962.

Offner, Avron. 'The British Empire 1870–1914: A Waste of Money?', *Economic History Review,* XLVI, (1993) pp. 215–38.

Orde, Anne. *British Policy and European Reconstruction after the First World War.* Cambridge: Cambridge University Press, 1990.

— *Great Britain and International Security 1920–1926.* London: Royal Historical Society, 1978.

Osgood, Robert Endicott. *Ideals and Self-Interest in America's Foreign Relations.* Chicago: University of Chicago Press, 1953.

Ovendale, Ritchie. *'Appeasement' and the English-Speaking World. The United States, the Dominions, and the Policy of 'Appeasement' 1937–1939.* Cardiff: University of Wales Press, 1975.

Parker, R.A.C. *Chamberlain and Appeasement. British Policy and the Coming of the Second World War.* Basingstoke: Macmillan, 1993.

Parrini, Carl P. *Heir to Empire. US economic diplomacy 1916–1923.* Pittsburgh: University of Pittsburgh Press, 1969.

Parsons, E.B. *Wilsonian Diplomacy. Allied–American Rivalries in War and Peace.* St Louis: Forum Press, 1978.

Pease, Neal. *Poland, the United States and the Stabilization of Europe, 1919–1933.* New York: Oxford University Press, 1986.

Peden, George C. *British Rearmament and the Treasury 1932–1939.* Edinburgh: Scottish Academic Press, 1979.

Penlington, Norman. *The Alaska Boundary Dispute. A Critical Reappraisal.* Toronto: McGraw Hill-Ryerson, 1972.

Perham, Margery. *Colonial Sequence, 1930 to 1949.* London: Methuen, 1967.

Perkins, Bradford. *The Great Rapprochement. England and the United States 1895–1914.* New York: Athenaeum, 1968.

Peters, A.R. *Anthony Eden at the Foreign Office 1931–1938.* Aldershot: Gower, 1986.

Pierre, Andrew J. *Nuclear Politics.* London: Oxford University Press, 1972.

Platt, D.C.M. *Latin America and British Trade 1806–1914.* London: Adam & Charles Black, 1972.

Political and Economic Planning. *Growth in the British Economy.* London: Allen & Unwin, 1960.

Pratt, Julius W. *Cordell Hull 1933–1944.* New York: Cooper Square, 1964.

Pratt, Laurence R. 'The Anglo-American Naval Conversations on the Far East of January 1938', *International Affairs,* XLVII, (1971) pp. 745–63.

— *East of Malta, West of Suez. Britain's Mediterranean Crisis 1936–1939.* Cambridge: Cambridge University Press, 1975.

Pressnell, L.S. *External Economic Policy Since the War.* I, *The Post-war Financial Settlement.* London: HMSO, 1986.

Rappaport, Armin. *The British Press and Wilsonian Neutrality.* Stanford and London: Stanford University Press, 1951.

Reynolds, David. *The Creation of the Anglo-American Alliance 1937–1941.* London: Europa Publications, 1981.

— *Rich Relations. The American Occupation of Britain 1942–1945.* London and New York: Harper Collins, 1995.

Rock, William R. *Appeasement on Trial. British Foreign Policy and its Critics 1938–1939.* Hamden, CT: Archon Books, 1966.

— *British Appeasement in the 1930s.* London: Edward Arnold, 1977.

— *Chamberlain and Roosevelt. British Foreign Policy and the United States 1937–1940.* Columbus: Ohio State University Press, 1988.

Roskill, Stephen W. *Hankey. Man of Secrets,* 3 vols. London: Collins, 1970–4.

— *Naval Policy between the Wars,* 2 vols. London: Collins, 1968–76.

Rothwell, V.H. *Britain and the Cold War 1941–1947.* London: Jonathan Cape, 1982.

— *British War Aims and Peace Diplomacy 1914–1918.* Oxford: Clarendon Press, 1971.

Rotter, Andrew J. *The Path to Vietnam. Origins of the American Commitment to South-East Asia.* Ithaca: Cornell University Press, 1987.

Rowland, Benjamin M. (ed.). *Balance of Power or Hegemony: The Interwar Monetary System.* New York: New York University Press, 1976.

Royal Institute of International Affairs. *Survey of British Commonwealth Affairs.* I, *Problems of Nationality 1918–1936,* by W.K. Hancock. London: Oxford University Press, 1937; II, *Problems of Wartime Cooperationa and Postwar Change 1939–1952,* by Nicholas Mansergh. London: Oxford University Press, 1958.

— *The World in March 1939,* Survey of International Affairs 1939–46. London: Oxford University Press, 1952.

Russett, Bruce M. *Community and Contention. Britain and America in the Twentieth Century.* Cambridge, MA: MIT Press, 1963.

Safford, Jeffrey J. *Wilsonian Maritime Diplomacy 1913–1921.* New Brunswick, NJ: Rutgers University Press, 1978.

Sayers, R.S. *Financial Policy 1939–1945,* History of the Second World War, UK Civil Series. London: HMSO, 1956.

Schmidt, Gustav. *England in der Krise. Grundzüge and Grundlagen der Britischen Appeasement-Politik.* Opladen: Westdeutsch Verlag, 1981; English translation, *The Politics and Economics of Appeasement. British Foreign Policy in the 1930s.* Leamington Spa: Berg, 1986.

Schuker, Stephen A. *The End of French Predominance in Europe. The Financial Crisis of 1924 and the Adoption of the Dawes Plan.* Chapel Hill: University of North Carolina Press, 1976.

Seager, Robert and Maguire, Doris D. (eds). *Letters and Papers of Alfred Thayer Mahan,* 3 vols. Annapolis: Naval Institute Press, 1975.

Seymour, Charles. *The Intimate Papers of Colonel House,* 4 vols. Boston: Houghton Mifflin, 1926–38.

Shay, Robert P. *British Rearmament in the Thirties.* Princeton: Princeton University Press, 1977.

Sherry, Michael. *Preparing for the Next War. American Plans for Postwar Defense 1941–1945.* New Haven: Yale University Press, 1977.

Sherwood, Robert P. *Roosevelt and Hopkins, an Intimate History.* New York: Harper & Bros, 1948; English edition, *The White House Papers of Harry L. Hopkins,* 2 vols. London: Eyre & Spottiswoode, 1948.

Solomon, Barbara Miller. *Ancestors and Immigrants, A Changing New England Tradition.* Cambridge, MA: Harvard University Press, 1956.

Stacey, C.P. *Canada and the Age of Conflict,* 2 vols. Toronto: University of Toronto Press, 1977–81.

Stevenson, David. *The First World War and International Politics.* Oxford: Oxford University Press, 1988.

Stimson, Henry L. *The Far Eastern Crisis.* New York: Harper & Bros, 1936.

— and Bundy, McGeorge. *On Active Service in Peace and War.* New York: Harper & Bros; London: Hutchinson, 1948.

Stoff, Michael B. *Oil, War and American Security. The Search for a National Policy on Foreign Oil 1941–1949.* New Haven: Yale University Press, 1980.

Stoler, Mark A. *The Politics of the Second Front. American Military Planning and Diplomacy in Coalition Warfare 1941–1943.* Westport, CT: Greenwood Press, 1977.

Stone, Ralph Allen. *The Irreconcilables. The Fight Against the League of Nations.* Lexington: University Press of Kentucky, 1970.

Strange, Susan. *Sterling and British Policy. A Political Study of an International Currency in Decline.* London: Oxford University Press, 1971.

Stueck, William Whitney, jr. *The Road to Confrontation. American Policy towards China and Korea 1947–1950.* Chapel Hill: University of North Carolina Press, 1981.

Taylor, A.J.P. (ed.). *Lloyd George. Twelve Essays.* London: Hamish Hamilton, 1971.

Thompson, John A. *Reformers and War. American Progressive Publicists and the First World War.* Cambridge: Cambridge University Press, 1987.

Thompson, Neville. *The Anti-Appeasers. Conservative Opposition to Appeasement in the 1930s.* Oxford: Clarendon Press, 1971.

Thorne, Christopher. *Allies of a Kind. The United States, Britain and the War against Japan 1941–1945.* London: Hamish Hamilton, 1978.

— *The Limits of Foreign Policy. The West, the League and the Far Eastern Crisis of 1931–1933.* London: Hamish Hamilton, 1972.

Tillman, Seth P. *Anglo-American Relations at the Paris Peace Conference of 1919.* Princeton: Princeton University Press, 1961.

Trachtenberg, Marc. *Reparation in World Politics. France and European Economic Diplomacy 1916–1923.* New York: Columbia University Press, 1980.

Trask, David. *Captains and Cabinets: Anglo-American Naval Relations 1917–1918.* Columbia: University of Missouri Press, 1972.
— *The United States in the Supreme War Council. American War Aims and Inter-Allied Strategy 1917–1918.* Middletown, CT: Wesleyan University Press, 1961.
Troen, Selwyn Ilan and Sheresh, Moshe (eds). *The Suez–Sinai Crisis 1956. Retrospective and reappraisal.* London: Frank Cass, 1990.
Trotter, Ann. *Britain and East Asia 1933–1937.* London: Cambridge University Press, 1975.
Tucker, Nancy B. *Patterns in the Dust. Chinese–American Relations and the Recognition Controversy 1949–1950.* New York: Columbia University Press, 1983.
Tulloch, Hugh. 'Changing British Attitudes towards the United States in the 1880s', *Historical Journal,* XX, (1970) pp, 825–40.
— *James Bryce's American Commonwealth. The Anglo-American Background.* London: Boydell Press, 1988.
Ullman, R.H. *Anglo-Soviet Relations 1917–1921.* I, *Intervention and War.* Princeton: Princeton University Press, 1961.
Vale, Vivian. *The American Peril. Challenge to Britain on the North Atlantic 1901–04.* Manchester: Manchester University Press, 1984.
Van Dormael, Armand. *Bretton Woods. Birth of a Monetary System.* London: Macmillan, 1978.
Wallace, Elizabeth. *Goldwin Smith: Victorian Liberal.* Toronto: University of Toronto Press, 1957.
Walworth, Arthur. *America's Moment 1918. American Diplomacy and the End of World War I.* New York: Norton, 1977.
— *Wilson and his Peacemakers. American Diplomacy at the Paris Peace Conference 1919.* New York and London: Norton, 1986.
Warner, Donald F. *The Idea of Continental Union. Agitation for the Annexation of Canada to the United States 1849–1893.* Lexington: University Press of Kentucky, 1960.
Watson, Mark Skinner. *The War Department. Chief of Staff, Prewar Plans and Preparations,* The US Army in the Second World War. Washington: Department of the Army, Historical Division, 1950.
Watt, Donald Cameron. *Personalities and Politics.* London: Longmans, 1965.
— *Succeeding John Bull. America in Britain's Place 1900–1975.* Cambridge: Cambridge University Press, 1984.
Welles, Sumner. *The Time for Decision.* New York: Harper & Bros, 1944.
Wendt, Bernd Jürgen. *'Economic Appeasement.' Handel und Finanz in der Britischen Deutschlandpolitik 1933–1939.* Düsseldorf: Bertelsman Universitätsverlag, 1971.
Wheeler, Gerald E. *Prelude to Pearl Harbor. The United States and the Far East 1921–1931.* Columbia: University of Missouri Press, 1963.
Wheeler-Bennett, J.W. (ed.). *Action This Day. Working with Churchill.* London: Macmillan, 1968.
Widenor, William C. *Henry Cabot Lodge and the Search for an American Foreign Policy.* Berkeley: University of California Press, 1979.

Wigley, P.G. *Canada and the Transition to Commonwealth. British–Canadian Relations 1917–1926.* Cambridge: Cambridge University Press, 1977.

Williams, Benjamin H. *Economic Foreign Policy of the United States.* New York: McGraw Hill, 1929.

Wilson, Joan Hoff. *American Business and Foreign Policy 1920–1933.* Lexington: University Press of Kentucky, 1971.

Woods, Randall Bennett. *A Changing of the Guard. Anglo-American relations, 1941–1946.* Chapel Hill: University of North Carolina Press, 1990.

Woodward, David R. *Trial by Friendship. Anglo-American Relations 1917–1918.* Lexington: University Press of Kentucky, 1993.

Woodward, Sir Llewellyn. *British Foreign Policy in the Second World War,* 5 vols. London: HMSO, 1970–76.

Yergin, Daniel. *The Shattered Peace. The Origins of the Cold War and the National Security State.* Boston: Houghton Mifflin, 1977.

Young, John W. *Britain and European Unity 1945–1992.* Basingstoke: Macmillan, 1993.

— *Britain, France and the Unity of Europe 1945–51.* Leicester: Leicester University Press, 1984.

Young, Kenneth. *Arthur James Balfour.* London: G. Bell & Sons, 1963.

Index